THE THOUGHT OF WORK

THE THOUGHT
OF WORK

John W. Budd

ILR Press
AN IMPRINT OF
CORNELL UNIVERSITY PRESS
Ithaca and London

First published 2011 by Cornell University Press
First printing, Cornell Paperbacks, 2011

Printed in the United States of America

Library of Congress Cataloging-in-Publication Data

Budd, John W.
   The thought of work / John W. Budd.
     p. cm.
   Includes bibliographical references and index.
   ISBN 978-0-8014-4983-3 (cloth : alk. paper)
   ISBN 978-0-8014-7761-4 (pbk. : alk. paper)
   1. Work—Philosophy. 2. Labor—Philosophy.
I. Title.
   HD4904.B78 2011
   331.01—dc22   2011000855

Cornell University Press strives to use environmentally responsible suppliers and materials to the fullest extent possible in the publishing of its books. Such materials include vegetable-based, low-VOC inks and acid-free papers that are recycled, totally chlorine-free, or partly composed of nonwood fibers. For further information, visit our website at www.cornellpress.cornell.edu.

Cloth printing   10 9 8 7 6 5 4 3 2 1
Paperback printing   10 9 8 7 6 5 4 3 2 1

Ah, why
Should life all labour be?

—Alfred, Lord Tennyson (1809–92)

CONTENTS

PREFACE

Despite being such an important aspect of our daily lives, work is frequently taken for granted rather than questioned or thought about very deeply. It is just something that we have to do. At the same time, scholars from an impressive breadth of disciplines in the social sciences, behavioral sciences, philosophy, and theology study work. But their provocative ideas and knowledge about the world of work are often segmented by discipline and separated by disciplinary-specific concepts, jargon, methodologies, conferences, and journals. The idea for this book arose from the excitement of discovering such a breadth of research revealing work's complexities and its deep importance from so many perspectives, paired with the twin frustrations of a personal sense that the importance of work is overlooked in public discourse and that scholars fail to appreciate the richness of the research on work that is located outside their own disciplines.

Scholars across the social and behavioral sciences frequently have differing perspectives on the empirical realities of work, such as wages and working conditions, technological change and "de-skilling," contingent work, the nature of occupations and careers, job satisfaction and other attitudes, work-family conflict, leadership or motivation of employees, and labor unions and other work-related institutions. Such differences are ultimately rooted in alternative ways of thinking about what work is. This book therefore seeks to bring together diverse perspectives on work to promote a multidisciplinary understanding of this essential part of the human experience by focusing fundamentally on how work is conceptualized—how we think about the role of work in our everyday lives, and in society more generally. But the result is more than just a framework for an improved understanding of work—it is a statement on the deep importance of work, a window into what societies value, and a demonstration that how we think about work matters for how work is experienced in our daily lives.

There are many ways in which this book could have been written. Herbert Applebaum's *The Concept of Work: Ancient, Medieval, and Modern* (1992) is a comprehensive chronology of conceptualizations of work. David Spencer's

The Political Economy of Work (2009) is a focused critique of how work is conceptualized in a single discipline, while edited volumes such as Marek Korczynski, Randy Hodson, and Paul Edwards's *Social Theory at Work* (2006) take more of a discipline-by-discipline or paradigm-by-paradigm approach. In *The Thought of Work,* I seek to build on and complement these approaches by integrating concepts of work across time and discipline to reveal the key, fundamental conceptualizations of work. The objective is not a historical narrative on concepts of work or a review of how specific disciplines view work, though the book facilitates an understanding of both of these important issues. Rather, the primary goal is to understand the key conceptualizations of work and their implications, and this book is therefore structured around concepts rather than time or disciplines.

With what has grown into ten conceptualizations of work, mathematically there are over three million options for ordering the ten chapters. At times it felt as if I tried out nearly all these combinations as I confronted new ideas, received feedback, and reconsidered my logic. The rationale for the order of the chapters is described in the introduction; I hope this sequencing is illuminating, but I do not have any pretensions that it is the only approach possible. Some might prefer to order the chapters based on some judgment of importance or universality, but such judgments would undoubtedly vary across disciplines, if not individuals, and also yield a multiplicity of approaches.

The breadth of work on work is underscored by the fact that over 800 sources are cited in the chapters that follow. To keep the number of notes manageable, references are cited by paragraph rather than by sentence. Wherever necessary, the notes contain brief annotations linking one or more sources to the relevant sentence(s) or idea(s) in the text. Please note that the annotations do not necessarily capture a source's content; rather, they point to a subject or a phrase in the text in order to connect the text and the sources. The order of the citations in each note follows the order of the cited ideas in each paragraph.

Like many other forms of work, writing this book has been a cooperative endeavor. For invaluable comments on one or more chapters and/or helpful conversations, I extend my sincere thanks to Patty Anderson, Avner Ben-Ner, Devasheesh Bhave, Joyce Bono, Bob Bruno, Dan Forbes, Theresa Glomb, Lonnie Golden, Lisa Leslie, Jim Scoville, David Spencer, Andrew Timming, Connie Wanberg, Stefan Zagelmeyer, two anonymous reviewers, and conference and workshop participants at the European Congress of the International Industrial Relations Association (Copenhagen), the Labor and Employment Relations Association annual meeting (Atlanta), the London

School of Economics, the University of Minnesota, Warwick University, and the central London BUIRA. I am also grateful to Linda Clarke, Alex Koch, and Mingwei Liu for graciously pointing me to the relevant research literature for some issues, to Greg Budd and Gaolee Vang for their detailed help with the references and quotations, to Fran Benson at Cornell University Press for her support, and to Ange Romeo-Hall and others at Cornell University Press for their expert work in navigating the manuscript smoothly through the production process. *The Thought of Work* was also many years in the making. Its completion would not have been possible without a sabbatical from the University of Minnesota, and I am extremely grateful for that year of being able to work almost exclusively on this project.

The Thought of Work is dedicated to my three children, who will soon need to come to terms with the thought of work in their own ways.

Minneapolis, Minnesota
August 2010

THE THOUGHT OF WORK

Introduction

My labour will sustain me.

—John Milton (1608–74)

This book is about how to think about work. Deeply and fundamentally. What really is work? And why does it matter?

The word *work* is rooted in the ancient Indo-European word *werg* meaning "to do" and is therefore etymologically related to *energy* ("in or at work"), *lethargy* ("without work"), *allergy* ("oppositional work"), *synergy* ("working together"), *liturgy* ("public work"), and *organ* ("a tool" as in "working with something"). The *Oxford English Dictionary* further lists twenty-one definitions of *work* as a noun and forty as a verb. These linguistic features of *work* reflect the realities of human work—embedded in many elements of the human experience and occurring in many ways. So in thinking about what work is, a comprehensive approach is required.

One might reflexively equate work with paid employment and formal jobs, but there are other forms of work, too. Some families pay cleaning services, child care centers, and nursing homes to take care of their housework, parenting, and elder care responsibilities; it is also work when individuals undertake these same tasks within their own families without being paid. As paid agricultural labor is work, so, too, is subsistence farming, even if the harvest is consumed by the household rather than sold as a cash crop. In fact, packaging tasks together into paid jobs is a very recent phenomenon in human history.[1] A broad definition of work is therefore needed to reflect and respect the diverse forms of work found throughout society and history.

But work should not be defined too broadly. Work always involves doing something, but so do many leisure activities. A meaningful definition of work, therefore, needs to lie somewhere between the overly narrow focus on paid employment and the excessively broad inclusion of all human activity. As such, work is defined in this book as purposeful human activity involving physical or mental exertion that is not undertaken solely for pleasure and that has economic or symbolic value. To be clear, employment is included within the definition of work, but work and employment are not synonymous, because work is broader. Also, work is commonly seen as producing economic value, but it can also have symbolic value, as in cases where work serves to create a sense of identity. Lastly, some authors distinguish between work and labor.[2] To avoid the inevitable confusion over semantic differences, labor is used throughout this book as a synonym for work, and any potential differences between these two terms are presented as different conceptualizations of work.

Admittedly, cultural norms define what is valued as work or who is deemed a worker across time and space. In China, paid jobs are seen as work, but there are diverse views as to whether farming, household businesses, and other activities are work. Turkish women frequently knit or engage in other handicraft activities on a paid, piecework basis, but they do not see these activities as work.[3] In many modern societies, unpaid housewives are not seen as workers. It is beyond the scope of this book to explain why certain social constructions of work dominate in different cultures or eras. The broad definition of work used here is therefore not intended as culturally specific—it does not specify that work occurs when society recognizes its economic value; rather, work is purposeful human activity involving physical or mental exertion that is not undertaken solely for pleasure and that has value when viewed from a broadly inclusive perspective. A Chinese son working in a family business, a Turkish daughter knitting for extra income, and an American housewife or househusband taking care of a family are all seen as working in this definition.

Put differently, the definition of work used in this book is intended to foster a broad, inclusive approach to thinking about work, not to delimit exactly what work is and is not. As sociologist Miriam Glucksmann asserts, defining work should not be "an argument about words, but about how to conceptualize labour [equivalently, work] in a useful and coherent manner." To reinforce a broad approach to work, Table 1 shows that work can occur within or outside of family households, and can be paid or unpaid. This schema includes not only the paid jobs and occupational pursuits that constitute work for many individuals in modern, industrialized societies, but

Table 1 Types of Work

SPHERE OF ACTIVITY	REMUNERATION	
	PAID	UNPAID
Outside the home / household	Wage and salaried jobs Casual employment Self-employment	Volunteering Civic service Slavery
Within the home / household	Household-based farming Family-run businesses Home-based contract work (putting-out or sweating system)	Subsistence farming Housework Elder and child care Slavery

also unpaid caring for others, self-employment, subsistence farming, casual work in the informal sector, and other activities outside the standard Western boundaries of paid jobs and career aspirations. Volunteer activities are also work. Even if such activities lack monetary rewards, they often consist of the same tasks as paid jobs and can provide the same intrinsic satisfaction and social benefits as paid employment. In other words, work involves the production of something of value, even if the producer is not paid and has motivations that extend beyond making a living.[4]

Nevertheless, the borders between work and other life activities, especially leisure, are often nebulous. Individuals in unrewarding jobs might see the dividing line between work and leisure quite easily, but for caregivers or individuals with fulfilling careers the boundary can be quite blurry. A parent taking a child to a swimming pool might see this as work one day and as leisure another. Playing golf is leisure for most people but work for professionals earning a living from it. The boundaries between work and nonwork spheres are also blurred by smart phones and other technologies that tie employees to their work around the clock, and by employers that try to regulate the nonwork activities of their employees, such as firing them for smoking, drinking, committing adultery, or riding a motorcycle outside of work.[5] All of these ambiguities reinforce the need for an inclusive approach to thinking about work—including paid and unpaid work—even if the boundaries of work are not always crystal clear.

The sheer breadth of work's importance for the human experience and the need for an inclusive approach are further reflected in the range of academic disciplines and fields that study work, including anthropology, archaeology, economics, ethnic studies, geography, history, human resources, industrial relations, law, management, organizational behavior, philosophy, political science, psychology, sociology, theology, and women's studies. The academic division of labor into specialized disciplines, however, creates distinct perspectives on work within disciplines. And thus, while the wide-ranging nature of work is reflected by its diverse academic conceptualizations—such as a way to serve or care for others, a source of freedom, an economic commodity, a method of personal fulfillment, or a social relation shaped by class, gender, and power— these conceptualizations are rarely integrated across disciplines. In *The Thought of Work* I seek to simultaneously harness this breadth while bridging this academic division of labor to promote a deeper, multidisciplinary understanding of work by extracting, integrating, and synthesizing the rich intellectual conceptions of work found across the social and behavioral sciences and various philosophical traditions.

Work through the Ages

Work has always been a central feature of the human experience. Our prehistoric ancestors had to hunt, scavenge, and gather food to survive. Since that time, the evolution of work has not followed a linear and uniform progression, but some broad trends are instructive. As early as 2.5 million years ago, workers removed flakes from stones to make simple tools with chopping or scraping edges to open nuts and remove meat from animals. Additional tools and tasks gradually emerged. Specialized tools of stone, bone, antler, and shell were used forty thousand years ago, and pottery and weaving were added to the list of prehistoric work tasks twenty-five thousand years ago. After the most recent ice age ended ten thousand years ago, the archetypal human transitioned from a nomadic hunter-gatherer to a more sedentary, storing hunter-gatherer. This increased use of food storage significantly changed the nature of work by increasing the intensity of work during growing and hunting seasons and allowing for less intense work during seasons in which stored food was consumed. The further transition to an agricultural society with cultivated plants and domesticated animals four thousand to nine thousand years ago reinforced these seasonal patterns of work and perhaps also altered gender roles, as both males and females needed to be involved in agricultural activities. The creation and management of a household or village labor force adequate for clearing fields and planting and harvesting at critical times subsequently emerged as an important dimension of work.[6]

Except for specific gender roles, prehistoric workers were rarely specialized. Six thousand years ago, a household raised its crops, tended its animals, cared for its young, gathered its firewood and building materials, and made its tools and storage containers. The next major step in the evolution of work was the emergence of craft specialization—the manufacturing of specific goods by a relatively small number of individuals who traded these goods for food and other subsistence products. There is evidence of specialized pottery producers in Mesopotamia six thousand years ago, and one thousand years later a standard professions list etched on a clay tablet contained one hundred occupations from king and other high officials down to cook, baker, coppersmith, jeweler, and potter. Early craft specialists included both part-time and full-time specialists and were either independent or attached to a sponsoring elite. Independent craft specialists likely produced tools and other utilitarian goods for trade, whereas attached specialists likely focused on making luxury items. The productivity gains from specialization are quite intuitive—as recognized by Plato in *The Republic* in the fourth century before the Common Era (BCE)—and craft specialization was a major milestone in the evolution of work.[7]

These changes in work accompanied the transition to hierarchical societies with ruling elites and social differentiation (what archaeologists and anthropologists label "complex societies"), such as Bronze Age chiefdoms, ancient Greek city-states, and today's modern nations. Agricultural innovations by early farming households allowed some households to produce more than they consumed. The resulting accumulation of surplus food not only created social differentiation but also paved the way for craft specialization, as metal craftsmen, for example, could now trade for food rather than have to grow it themselves. Craft specialization, in turn, helped provide the impetus for increasingly complex societies as raw materials such as copper ore needed to be mined, smelted, and transported—tasks unlikely to be accomplished by individual craftsmen or households.[8]

The next steps in the evolution of work were therefore an increased sophistication in the organization of work and a greater social differentiation between occupations. The building of the Egyptian pyramids more than four thousand years ago required the coordination of thousands of skilled and unskilled workers in mining, hauling, and cutting stone; making and carrying bricks; transporting sand; surveying and engineering the building of walls, passageways, and tombs; building roads and canals; brewing beer; baking bread; drying fish; making pottery bowls; and crafting furniture, jewelry, and sculptures. The exact working conditions are unknown—though the expected heavy exertion of manual laborers is confirmed in the arthritis found in the skeletons of both men and women—but most experts believe the pyramids were built by a combination of year-round skilled workers and rotating gangs of unskilled peasants conscripted from agricultural villages a few months at a time. In Mesopotamia around 2000 BCE, thousands of workers were employed by the government, the temples, and private parties and were paid primarily with barley and wool; there even appears to have been a minimum wage of thirty liters of barley per month. Three thousand years later, work in the Tang dynasty in China and in the Inca Empire in South America was similar. A range of hierarchical occupations spanned farmers, servants, specialized craftsmen, priests, and government officials. In the Tang dynasty, rural farmers could be conscripted for three years to work for the emperor. In the Inca Empire, each household, when called, had to provide a worker to serve the empire as a soldier, transporter of raw materials or finished products, builder, or craftsperson. Most work, though, was agricultural.[9]

Like the trajectory of societies more generally, the sophistication of work oscillates through history. The Indus civilization in south-central Asia around 2200 BCE had large cities, public architecture, extensive trading networks, refined craft products, and a diverse set of administrative workers and skilled and unskilled laborers to support such a civilization. But with the decline of this civilization after 2000 BCE, work again was largely limited to agriculture and small-scale crafts in pre-urban villages. A similar reversion occurred in Britain with the withdrawal of the Roman Empire in 410 CE. But then with the Viking era in Britain four hundred years later, increased trading of agricultural and craft products between growing towns spurred diverse craft work, such as in pottery, glass, iron, leather, and textiles. In some areas, a few craftsmen might have shared a workshop, but craft production was typically household-based.[10]

European medieval society is typically seen as having been composed of three classes: *oratores* (clergy—those who pray), *bellatores* (warriors—those who fight), and, most numerous, *laboratores* (workers—those who work). But this was not a static system. Craft work continued to expand, and master craftsmen formed guilds to control the standards of their craft and the training and entry of new workers through apprenticeship programs. As trade increased, merchants became a fourth class, and "fifteenth-century Europe became a blend of rural and city society, with a place for the merchant, the craftsman, the noble, the priest, and the peasant." These changes continued as feudalism was replaced by early capitalism in the Elizabethan era. Domestic service occupations such as servants and cooks emerged on a significant scale at this time. While the bulk of the population remained engaged in agricultural work, supplementary small-scale household production—the origin of the term "cottage industry"—became increasingly important.[11]

Some household production was undertaken by independent artisans; other household production consisted of a putting-out system, also referred to as an outwork or sweated system. In the putting-out system, a capitalist entrepreneur buys raw materials and "puts them out" to individual households who cut, sew, weave, or otherwise work on the materials in their homes or tenements. The work products are then returned to the merchant in exchange for a piece-rate payment, and the merchant sells the finished goods. Except in the aristocracy, women worked hard caring for others, doing domestic and agricultural chores and engaging in some agricultural and putting-out textile work for pay. Until the eighteenth century, full-time specialized occupations were the exception rather than the norm; generally, all members of typical nonaristocratic households would engage in a variety of domestic, farming, and paid tasks to survive and try to improve their living standards. In addition to Native Americans working the land as agriculturists and hunters, work in seventeenth- and eighteenth-century colonial America among European settlers similarly consisted of skilled artisans, apprentices, shopkeepers, merchants, and female domestic servants, and a mixture of free, indentured, and enslaved agricultural laborers growing both food and cash crops such as tobacco.[12]

The nature of work from 8000 BCE to 1750 CE therefore largely reflected the Neolithic Revolution's agricultural settlements and (later) cities. Most work revolved around crop cultivation and animal herding, though part-time and full-time craft specialists, administrative workers, unskilled laborers, and servants also existed at various times. A sexual division of labor with well-defined social norms about "women's work" and "men's work" also defined most work. Until 1750, slavery, serfdom, and other forms of coercive labor were widely acceptable and found in many societies in many eras.[13]

Precursors to the modern factory system also existed—complex business organizations and trading systems existed by the fourteenth century, brewers exported nearly one hundred million liters of beer from Holland in the late fifteenth century, silver mines in Saxony employed several thousand wage laborers in the early sixteenth century, and the putting-out system in Britain was quite extensive in the early eighteenth century—but it is the Industrial Revolution's transformation of a protoindustrial, household-based workforce into a full-time industrial workforce, supported by unpaid women in the home, that marks the broad-scale emergence of modern forms of work and today's employment relationship.[14]

The Industrial Revolution is popularly associated with technological advances in thread spinning, cotton weaving, and steam power generation in the second half of the 1700s that fostered the rise of British cotton mills in the first decades of the 1800s. The Industrial Revolution, however, was as much organizational as technical. The shift from the household-based putting-out system to the factory system was not simply to take advantage of new power-based machinery, but was also to increase the employer's control over the speed, quality, regularity, and security of the production process through direct supervision and monitoring of the workforce. The rise of the factory system also marked the end of merchant capitalism (a focus on *trading* household- or plantation-produced goods) and its replacement with industrial capitalism (a focus on *producing* goods and services for profit). These technological and organizational innovations then spurred the widespread growth of railroads and manufacturing industries in the remainder of the 1800s in Britain, the United States, Germany, and France.[15]

The Industrial Revolution and the rise of industrial capitalism revolutionized work in these countries as employment in factories and other non-household workplaces exploded, as wage labor increasingly became the sole source of subsistence and income rather than a source of supplementary income, and as labor markets emerged to determine workers' wages and working conditions. On a largely unprecedented scale, industrialists displaced households as the controllers of the production process, so individuals lost the autonomy and discretion to decide when and how to work. Before the Industrial Revolution, freely chosen work schedules among farmers, artisans, and home-based putting-out workers frequently alternated between periods of idleness and intense activity. But factory work forced individuals to conform to factory work schedules. It was at this time, then, that individuals went from "doing jobs"—working on "shifting clusters of tasks, in a variety of locations, on a schedule set by the sun, the weather, and the needs of the day"—to "having jobs," working exclusively for someone else. Women's unpaid caring work in the household was rendered invisible as new norms equated valuable work to paid employment. In the new factory workplaces, monitoring and motivating workers became critical issues, and new supervisory occupations arose to manage workers. Other managerial occupations emerged to administer finance, marketing, and other aspects of increasingly complex business organizations. The Industrial Revolution further affected work in other countries as colonization policies pushed farming households in Africa, South America, and elsewhere away from subsistence crops and toward cash crops and natural resources to supply the emerging industrial economies. Native Americans, black South Africans, and other indigenous peoples that were stripped of their land by colonial and apartheid dispossession policies also had to alter their traditional forms of work and turn to wage work to survive.[16]

Under industrialization and industrial capitalism, the evolution of work reflects the capitalist drive to make labor more efficient and productive in the pursuit of profits. In contrast to the craft specialization during the previous six thousand years that reflected a *social* division of labor into bakers, blacksmiths, brewers, farmers, and the like, under industrialization, work undergoes a detailed *manufacturing* division of labor in which specific crafts are decomposed into unskilled, repetitive jobs. In the 1800s, skilled cigar-makers like my great-great-grandfather would make a complete cigar by selecting tobacco leaves, rolling and wrapping the leaves, and cutting the finished cigar using their hands and a knife. In the 1900s, molds, bunching machines, and other innovations allowed skilled cigar-makers to be replaced by unskilled machine operators who focused on narrow parts of the production process. In the early 1900s, Frederick Winslow Taylor preached that every job had one best way for doing it and that managers, not workers, should determine how work would be done. This philosophy of scientific management or "Taylorism" therefore reinforced the decomposition of skilled jobs into basic repetitive tasks and created sharp distinctions between managers (who were seen as providing the brains) and laborers (who were seen as only providing brawn).[17] Gendered norms regarding women's work and men's work were adapted to the new industrial workplaces, with women being largely confined to repetitive tasks requiring nimble fingers. In other words, industrialization updated, but did not end, the long-standing sexual division of labor.

In 1913, Henry Ford popularized the moving assembly line, and the mass manufacturing model of work was thus established for much of the rest of the century in industrialized and industrializing countries. As industrialization spread to Russia, Japan, and South Korea, for example, wage work with detailed divisions of labor became more important, albeit with national and cultural variation. Similar trends are currently under way in China, India, Mexico, and elsewhere. In the United States, Britain, and other wealthy, industrialized countries over the last three decades, flexible specialization has replaced mass manufacturing as the industrial catchphrase, employee empowerment rather than scientific management is embraced, the service sector or the creative sector is displacing manufacturing as the employment engine, and globalization is straining employers, employees, unions, and communities.[18]

But the essential nature of modern work—that is, lifelong wage work in specialized occupations outside the household complemented by unpaid caring work within it—remains largely the same for most individuals in industrialized countries and continues to be shaped by gendered assumptions in the workplace and in the home. Recent immigrants and other marginalized groups in industrialized countries also rely on informal work to survive. In other countries, agricultural work is more important but is commonly supplemented by small-scale household production or informal work reminiscent of preindustrial work in today's industrialized countries. Industrialization also continues to expand into new areas in search of low-cost labor, and the end of the twentieth century witnessed a sharp rise in the number of female manufacturing workers in developing countries. Unfortunately, modern forms of slavery, often "hidden behind a mask of fraudulent labor contracts" and enforced by the threat of physical violence, are also a harsh reality for many individuals.[19]

These patterns of work over the past 2.5 million years indicate that work will continue to evolve and change, although it is hard to know what forms these changes will take. At the beginning of the Industrial Revolution, the influential economist David Ricardo predicted that wages would always fall to the subsistence level of workers. At this same time, Luddites revolted against the introduction of machines in the textile industry for fear that automation and other changes would destroy their livelihoods. Toward the end of the nineteenth century, Edward Bellamy and other utopian writers envisioned future paths for work that would end menial labor and create near-workerless factories. More recently, Jeremy Rifkin predicted that the end of work is near as information technology will enable machines to replace labor throughout the economy.[20] None of these predictions came true. One should therefore be cautious about grand projections for the future of work, but it seems safe to assume that work will remain an essential and dynamic element of the human experience, albeit experienced differently by unique individuals, occupations, and cultures and likely shaped by technology, enduring but evolving social norms regarding gender, race, and other identities, and even sometimes by violence.

The Importance of Work

Depending on how old you are when you are reading this, you will likely need to work, are working, or have worked to support yourself and your family. Workerless utopian visions aside, there is little doubt that work is essential for human survival. Ironically, the necessity of work for survival makes it easier to overlook the deeper importance of work. Why study work if it is a preordained fact of life beyond our control? While many academic disciplines study work, it is not a central subject in many of them. Similarly, work-related issues are frequently overshadowed by other concerns in the news media and public policy debates. This is unfortunate and reflects a limited understanding of the true importance of work, which goes far beyond obtaining the twenty-five hundred or so daily calories we need to survive.

We might not even have to work very hard to survive—by some estimates, simple hunter-gatherers can survive by working only three to five hours per day.[21] Even if these estimates are overly optimistic, it is reasonable to assert that many individuals in industrialized countries work more than what is required for maintaining a minimally decent standard of living. In fact, we spend much of our adult lives working, and many of our days are spent mostly at work, a reality that presumably caused the American author William Faulkner to quip, "The only thing a man can do for eight hours is work." There are a variety of potential reasons beyond survival for why we work so much—such as to form an identity, be free, earn money, and serve or care for others—and these visions of work form the foundation for this book. The diversity of these personal reasons for why we work partially reveals the deep importance of work.

It is easy to overlook how fundamentally our lives are shaped by work. Work establishes the basic rhythms of our lives—the size and nature of one's household, meal and sleep patterns, weekends, and vacations are all determined by the demands of work. Work contributed to the creation of written language five thousand years ago because of the need to track the distribution of the surpluses created by agricultural innovation and craft specialization, and continues to be reflected in our literature, art, and culture. Even our conception of time is linked to work—hunter-gatherers link time to tasks; modern industrial societies use the precision of clock time to measure and coordinate work and to sharply divide work time from leisure. In fact, work is the source of the human-made world, and the agricultural, scientific, and industrial revolutions were all produced by workers experimenting with methods to make their work easier or more effective. Martin Luther's theological revolution rested, at least in part, on a revision of the Roman Catholic Church's view at the time that spiritual work was superior to everyday work, and work-related issues continue to appear in the social teachings of the world's major religions. And the extent to which we are truly equal cannot be divorced from questions about employment discrimination and equal access to jobs.[22]

Thinking about work is also a very powerful method for considering fundamental economic, social, and political issues, and some of the sharpest debates in the social sciences are rooted in work. For example, at their core, the tremendous debates over capitalism, socialism, and communism over the past 150 years are not about politics or property, but are about work. Karl Marx's critique of capitalism is based on the control of the means of production by the owners of capital. This control is seen not only as the source of capital's sociopolitical dominance, but as more fundamentally causing the commoditization and division of labor, which in turn leads to the inhumanity of worker alienation. Marx was ultimately a profound social theorist of work whose concern with workers' suffering led him to seek a more humane society.[23] Proposals for socialism and communism by Marx and others thereby emerged from concerns with work.

More generally, whether agricultural, classical, feudal, capitalist, or other societies are judged to represent progress over their predecessors partly depends on the extent to which a society's people work harder than earlier ones. Debates over the work burdens of prehistoric and contemporary hunter-gatherers are not simply about understanding this form of egalitarian social organization but are also about providing a benchmark for evaluating the relative affluence of workers in state- and class-based societies. Variants of capitalism are also evaluated in working terms. Titles like *The Overworked American* and *Modern Times, Ancient Hours* highlight the criticism of today's liberal market economy because of the resulting long working hours.[24] Quality-of-life comparisons between the United States and Europe frequently revolve around shorter working hours (favoring European lifestyles) and lower unemployment rates (favoring U.S. prosperity).

Work is also central to debates in human evolution. A long-standing puzzle in archaeology and anthropology is why Neanderthals, after living successfully in Europe and Eastern Asia for over one hundred thousand years, disappeared after the arrival of our *Homo sapiens* ancestors. Anthropologists Steven Kuhn and Mary Stiner argue that Neanderthal men, women, and children all focused much of their energy on hunting large game, while early humans divided labor along gender and age lines—an important feature of social organization that continues today—with men hunting and women and children gathering. Unlike humans, then, Neanderthals may have "lacked the kind of diverse resource base and labor network" needed to prevent starvation during lean times.[25] In other words, a key element of work—the division of labor—may help explain why *Homo sapiens* displaced the Neanderthals and therefore why we inhabit the earth.

Issues of work are also intimately intertwined with how human societies are organized. The division of labor along gender lines is seen by anthropologists as an important milestone in evolutionary history. The progression over thousands of years from egalitarian bands of hunter-gatherers to transegalitarian agricultural village communities to hierarchical nation-states with extensive social differentiation parallels similarly drastic changes in work from hunting and foraging to subsistence agriculture to specialized production. In fact, changes in work may have helped *cause* the transition to complex societies as agricultural surpluses and craft specialization perhaps promoted social differentiation. In this view, today's political states and socioeconomic inequalities can be traced back to changes in the nature of work. Changes in work are likely not the only cause of the growth of complex societies and may reflect, rather than cause, social differentiation, but the associations between work, social differentiation, and cultural evolution are additional elements of the deep importance of work in theory and in practice.[26]

Work is also intimately intertwined with one of the most important cultural changes of the last two hundred years: the rise of modern consumerism. Beyond the obvious linkage of work providing income for consumer purchases, some theorize that individuals turned to consumer goods as a way of defining and displaying success when changes in the nature of work undermined traditional visions of success in the eighteenth and nineteenth centuries. The ability to purchase nonessential consumer goods is seen as compensation for the burden of long factory hours, the loss of personal control associated with bureaucratic managerial positions, and, for middle-class women, social pressures to work in the home and not outside it. The intensification of a consumer culture in the post–World War II era, in turn, has caused work to be increasingly seen as a narrow economic activity to earn disposable income rather than as an activity with intrinsic value. Individuals see themselves as consumers, not workers, and work has "disappeared from the social imagination."[27] Low prices for consumer goods, not decent working conditions for those who produce, transport, and sell them, are seen as socially desirable.

These examples demonstrate the importance of work for understanding deeply fundamental issues. But of course work is tremendously important for practical reasons, too. Indigenous peoples struggle to survive when industrialization encroaches on their traditional work practices but does not provide adequate jobs for earning income. Poverty-relief efforts in the United States and elsewhere are increasingly tied to work in the form of workfare rather than welfare. Businesses around the globe continually face the challenge of designing human resource management practices that create highly productive workers. Many of the most difficult ethical issues facing business also involve work, such as employee privacy and monitoring, whistle-blowing, and discrimination.[28] And intense debates continue over the costs and benefits of government regulation of work, from local minimum wage laws to the incorporation of labor standards in international trade agreements.

In other words, the importance of work is ubiquitous—in our individual lives, in society, and across a wide range of academic disciplines. Unfortunately, the breadth of work's importance is frequently overlooked by scholars, students, policymakers, business leaders, and the public at large and is instead reduced to oversimplified tenets of work as a necessity or a source of income. But work is too important to be ignored or taken for granted. Work is a fundamental to nearly the entire human experience and merits thoughtful consideration, study, and understanding.

Concepts of Work

Against this backdrop of the fundamental importance of work and the diverse nature of work across time and space, in this book I consider how we conceptualize work by constructing ten key conceptualizations of work (see Table 2). Each chapter of *The Thought of Work* presents one of the ten conceptualizations. Chapter 1 starts with one of the oldest and most enduring visions of work—that is, as a curse. Variations of work as a curse span from ancient Greece to today and in the Judeo-Christian tradition date back all the way to the Garden of Eden. Work as a curse is a useful starting point for thinking about work because it is ingrained in popular culture and because

Table 2   Conceptualizing Work

WORK AS . . .	DEFINITION	INTELLECTUAL ROOTS
1. A Curse	An unquestioned burden necessary for human survival or maintenance of the social order	Western theology, ancient Greco-Roman philosophy
2. Freedom	A way to achieve independence from nature or other humans and to express human creativity	Western liberal individualism, political theory
3. A Commodity	An abstract quantity of productive effort that has tradable economic value	Capitalism, industrialization, economics
4. Occupational Citizenship	An activity pursued by human members of a community entitled to certain rights	Western citizenship ideals, theology, industrial relations
5. Disutility	A lousy activity tolerated to obtain goods and services that provide pleasure	Utilitarianism, economics
6. Personal Fulfillment	Physical and psychological functioning that (ideally) satisfies individual needs	Western liberal individualism, systematic management, psychology
7. A Social Relation	Human interaction embedded in social norms, institutions, and power structures	Industrialization, sociology, anthropology
8. Caring for Others	The physical, cognitive, and emotional effort required to attend to and maintain others	Women's rights, feminism
9. Identity	A method for understanding who you are and where you stand in the social structure	Psychology, sociology, philosophy
10. Service	The devotion of effort to others, such as God, household, community, or country	Theology, Confucianism, republicanism, humanitarianism

we need to reject a vision of work as solely a curse in order to question what work really is, and what it should be. If work is simply a curse, then we should accept rather than question our fate of painful toil, and it is not worth thinking about work very much. But if work is not a curse, then we should think about what it is and how it is structured.

In sharp contrast to visions of work in which humans are trapped by the curse of working to survive, chapter 2 shows how work can be seen as a source of freedom. The rise of liberal individualism in Western thought that started in the sixteenth century placed the individual at the center of many theories and philosophies, including those pertaining to work. Seeing work as an individual-centric, free, creative activity that establishes an individual's independence both from nature and from other humans is therefore the foundation for today's Western conceptualizations of work.

With the exception of work as service (chapter 10), the remaining conceptualizations are largely the intellectual product of Western theorizing in philosophy and in the social and behavioral sciences brought on by the rise of the market economy and industrialization. This does not mean that these conceptualizations apply only to Western or industrialized work. Rather, these ways of *thinking* about work stem from the rise of Western individualism and industrialization, but these lenses can be applied to other contexts, too. In modern market-based economies, work is seen in the abstract as productive effort that has economic value and can therefore be exchanged like other economic goods and services—in other words, work is a commodity. In chapter 3 I describe the importance of this view of work as a commodity in mainstream economic thought and sketch the important critiques of Karl Marx, feminist scholars, and others.

Treating work like any other commodity is rejected by some because it overlooks the deep moral significance of the fact that work is done by human beings. In chapter 4 I therefore develop the conceptualization of work as occupational citizenship—an activity undertaken by citizens with inherent equal worth who are entitled to certain rights and standards of dignity and self-determination irrespective of what the market provides. This conceptualization encompasses scholarship in industrial relations, political theory, human rights, ethics, theology, and related areas and emphasizes the achievement of workers' rights through institutional intervention in the labor market and in the workplace.

This conceptualization, however, is similar to treating work as a commodity to the extent that it does not ask why we work. One important reason to work is to earn income. This is formalized in mainstream economic thought in which individuals are seen as rational actors who maximize their personal welfare ("utility") by consuming goods and services and by enjoying leisure. Work is assumed to reduce utility by requiring painful effort and by taking time away from leisure activities. Individuals are therefore seen as tolerating work only to obtain goods, services, and leisure, either by producing them directly or by earning income to purchase them. And so one of the powerful modern conceptions of work is as disutility—an instrumental, economic activity that is tolerated because of the resulting income and extrinsic rewards but that lacks psychological satisfaction and other intrinsic rewards and is therefore not enjoyed. This mainstream economics view of work is the subject of chapter 5.

In contrast, chapter 6 presents the conceptualization of work as personal fulfillment. When appropriately structured, work can be beneficial for an individual's physical and psychological health. Concerns with workplace safety notwithstanding, this perspective on work is largely rooted in psychological theorizing and emphasizes the potential for work to promote psychological well-being by satisfying human needs for achievement, mastery, self-esteem, and self-worth. Similarly, lousy work—that is, work that involves mindless repetition, abusive co-workers or bosses, excessive physical or mental demands, or other undesirable factors—is seen as having negative psychological effects and is not dismissed simply as a curse or something to be tolerated to earn income. To conceptualize work as personal fulfillment is therefore to emphasize the cognitive and emotional/attitudinal aspects of work that provide personal satisfaction or dissatisfaction. In this chapter I also discuss human resource management, because thinking about work as a source of personal fulfillment provides the intellectual foundations for human resource management, which seeks to enhance worker effectiveness by recognizing the satisfying and dissatisfying aspects of work.

Economic and psychological perspectives on work differ in their emphases on extrinsic or intrinsic rewards but share a focus on the individual— individual rewards, individual effort (even in the context of teams), individual choices about work. Chapter 7 enriches these individual-centric perspectives by emphasizing the social aspects of work that are highlighted by sociologists, social psychologists, and others. Rather than just being an economic exchange, work can be a social exchange built on trust rather than money. Rather than driven by individual attempts to maximize utility or job satisfaction, work can be powerfully influenced by social norms, institutions, and unequal power dynamics between competing social groups. In Marxist and related perspectives that particularly emphasize these power dynamics, the modern employment relationship looks less like an economic contract between equals (chapter 3) and more like a contested exchange characterized by conflict and accommodation, and human resource management appears more like a strategy to control rather than motivate workers.

Particularly enduring and powerful social norms across diverse cultures define the culturally acceptable and unacceptable work roles for men and women. In popular Anglo-American usage, for example, "women's work" is a value-laden, pejorative term used to characterize forms of work not worthy of a man. In this way, feminist thought argues that work is conceptualized differently for women than for men. In particular, women's work is frequently defined as caring for others. By creating a socially constructed myth that caring for others reflects some natural maternal or feminine instinct, modern society devalues women's unpaid household work and justifies paying women less than men in the paid-employment sector. Work as caring for others is therefore the subject of chapter 8. Chapter 9 analyzes the conceptualization of work as part of one's identity. In this chapter I draw on scholarship in psychology, sociology, and philosophy to explore the ways in which work helps us make sense of who we are, where we stand in the social structure, and what it means to be human.

Lastly, work can be considered as a way to contribute to needs or desires that go beyond the individual worker and his or her immediate family. The focus of chapter 10 is therefore work as serving God (including as a calling), one's multigenerational family, community, or country. This thought of work predates the rise of Western individualism but is evident in many time periods and is advocated by some as a contemporary antidote to perceived excesses of individualism. A final chapter provides some concluding thoughts.

These ten conceptualizations of work are important. Individually, they provide the keys to understanding diverse disciplinary perspectives on work. The individual conceptualizations are so ingrained in their respective academic disciplines that they often remain hidden to outsiders. By making them explicit, I hope to make the rich research on work in these disciplines more accessible. Moreover, the thought of work shapes the nature of work in practice. If work is seen as a commodity, it will be left in the hands of the marketplace. If work is seen as an important source of personal fulfillment, it will be structured to provide this fulfillment. If work is seen as caring for others, then care workers will command greater respect. Corporate and public policies such as incentive-based compensation, self-directed work teams, minimum wage laws, and international trade agreements all reflect specific conceptualizations of work. Similarly, different visions of work provide dramatically different assessments of human resource management, labor unions, diversity programs, and other features of the modern workplace. The

ten conceptualizations of work are ideas about work that have real consequences.

The ten conceptualizations of work developed here therefore provide the
basis for thinking about what work means to us as individuals, and what
we value as a society. The twentieth-century emphasis on paid employment in an industrial society and the twenty-first-century narrative of a
"new economy" or a "new capitalism" in a globalized world both serve
to privilege commodity, market, and economic-based conceptualizations of
work as production while marginalizing reproductive work that sustains the
health and welfare of individuals, families, and communities.[29] In this way,
many workers and forms of work are denied the social status, legal rights,
and material benefits accorded to workers and work that are favored by
dominant cultural norms. The long-standing Western vision of work as a
way to achieve freedom from the vagaries of the natural world by mastering it arguably provides the seed for excess consumption and environmental
degradation. How we think about work matters, so we need to think about
it carefully and broadly.

In sum, while the specific nature of work has changed significantly
throughout history, work has always been a central feature of human existence. When we work, we experience our biological, psychological, economic, and social selves. Work locates us in the physical and social world and
thereby helps us and others make sense of who we are, while also determining our access to material and social resources.[30] When we think about work,
our conceptualizations and understandings need to be equally rich, not only
to better understand work but also to value it and structure it in desirable
ways that reflect its deep importance.

CHAPTER 1

Work as a Curse

Work is a necessary evil to be avoided.
—Mark Twain (1835–1910)

Work can be a four-letter word. It can be hard, hot, dangerous, and dull. Day after day, year after year, work can be physically, mentally, and emotionally draining. For centuries, then, work has been seen negatively as a burden. Contemplation and leisure are seen as the ideal human activities; work is "a necessary evil to be avoided." In the words of Sigmund Freud, "The great majority work only when forced by necessity," and in his characterization, this amounts to a "natural human aversion to work."[1] As revealed at various places in this book, some disagree that this aversion to work is natural, but there should be little argument that work can and has been conceptualized as a human burden. The burdensome nature of work is reinforced by the frequency with which work is used as punishment—from Zeus, in Greek mythology, sentencing Sisyphus to an eternity of pushing a large boulder up a steep hill just to watch it roll back down, to the nineteenth-century British penal colonies in Australia, the twentieth-century Nazi system of forced labor, the twentieth-century Gulag system of penal labor in the Soviet Union, and the continued use of forced labor in the Chinese *laogai* system and of chain gangs in the United States. One of the French words for work, *travail,* comes from a Latin word for a torture device. All of these negative views of work are part of an enduring conceptualization of work—that is, as a curse.

God's Curse

"In the beginning God created the heavens and the earth." This first sentence of the Bible, in which God works, cements the importance of work in the Judeo-Christian tradition. Humans were then created in the image of this working God and placed in the Garden of Eden to till, cultivate, or work it, depending on the translation used. Work is therefore seen as God's will and as unavoidable. But then Adam and Eve disobeyed God's order not to eat from the tree of the knowledge of good and evil and were subsequently punished— Eve with painful childbirth and Adam with hard work. God's reprimand to Adam that "Cursed is the ground because of you; through painful toil you will eat of it all the days of your life" is seen in Judeo-Christian thought as making hard work "by the sweat of your brow" humankind's punishment for human imperfection and weakness. Work is therefore popularly seen as a God-given curse, though some theological interpretations note that God technically curses the ground, not Adam, and this is taken to mean that work becomes burdensome but not cursed per se.[2]

This biblical story parallels Greco-Roman mythology. In *Works and Days* (circa 700 BCE), one of the earliest Greek poets, Hesiod, told stories in which humans originally did not have to work (at least not very hard), but a displeased god (an angry Zeus, for example, vengeful because Prometheus had given fire to man) punishes humans with toil. The Roman poet Virgil also told a Garden of Eden–like story in *The Georgics* in 29 BCE. Under Saturn's reign, work was not required and "no settlers broke the fields with their plows" as "Earth herself gave everything more freely when no one made demands." But when Jupiter overthrows Saturn, he does not tolerate human laziness and thereby makes it necessary for humans to labor to satisfy their excessive desires.[3]

Seeing hard work as a divine curse therefore has deep roots in Western thought and has been echoed for centuries. Saint Benedict and others who developed the Western monastic rules starting fifteen hundred years ago emphasized the obligation for monks to work, including manual work for up to eight hours a day depending on the season. The medieval Christian church saw work as penitential activity in which hard work was a way to seek redemption. At the end of the nineteenth century, Pope Leo XIII wrote that because of Adam and Eve's original sin, "bodily labor" is no longer an individual's "free choice" and "delight" but is instead "compulsory, and the painful expiation for his disobedience." In 1981, Pope John Paul II likened each individual's "enduring the toil of work" to Jesus's "work of salvation [that] came about through suffering."[4]

Preaching the acceptance of hard work is also a method for trying to prevent sinful activities that come from having too much free time because, as the old proverb says, "Idle hands are the devil's tools." An emphasis on work thus goes hand in hand with criticisms of laziness and idleness, as in biblical verses such as "If a man will not work, he shall not eat" and "The desire of the lazy man kills him, for his hands refuse to labor." These biblical teachings are echoed in the Benedictine monastic rules: "Idleness is the enemy of the soul. For this reason the brethren should be occupied at certain times in manual labour, and at other times in sacred reading." In the sixteenth century, John Calvin and his followers were "uncompromising" in their "attacks on laziness." Such views would later come to be characterized as part of the Protestant or Puritan work ethic. Slothfulness or laziness continues today as one of the seven deadly or cardinal sins in the Roman Catholic Church. Islam, too, preaches the importance of work over idleness. A Buddhist saying simply states, "One day of no work, one day of no food."[5]

It should be stressed that hard work as a curse is only one side of the religious beliefs about work. Many theologians believe that the Bible provides a dualistic view of work as both a burden and a blessing. Before God "cursed" Adam with hard work, he placed him "in the Garden of Eden to work it and take care of it," an act commonly interpreted as providing "a strong affirmation of the nobility of human work." From Saint Paul and early Benedictine monks to Luther and Calvin to today's Christian theology, work is seen as a means of independence, for charity, and for serving God. Similar themes are found in Islamic thought. The key papal encyclicals on work dating back to *Rerum Novarum* ("On the Condition of Workers") in 1891 and continuing through *Centesimus Annus* ("The Hundredth Year") one hundred years later emphasize social justice and dignity for workers, not the burdens of toil:

> And yet, in spite of all this toil—perhaps, in a sense, because of it—work is a good thing for man. Even though it bears the mark of a *bonum arduum* [difficult good], in the terminology of Saint Thomas, this does not take away the fact that, as such, it is a good thing for man. It is not only good in the sense that it is useful or something to enjoy; it is also good as being something worthy, that is to say, something that corresponds to man's dignity, that expresses this dignity and increases it.

From a popular theological perspective, then, work is "an ambiguous reality: it is both a noble expression of human creation in the image of God and a painful testimony to human estrangement from God."[6] In this book, the noble side of this duality is reflected in other conceptualizations, such as work as freedom from the vagaries of nature (chapter 2) and work as service to the kingdom of God (chapter 10).

This dual nature of work is reflected in a Russian concept of work that is rooted in Christian theology. Russian peasants, in particular, saw their backbreaking toil as akin to the suffering that Jesus endured. But as this toil led to a harvest, and as Jesus's suffering led to his resurrection, "the cyclical relation between the actual peasant experience and the ecclesiastical image nurtured and sustained the Russian peasant's love-hate vision of his work as life-giving and life-taking." The duality between work-as-suffering and work-as-salvation is further echoed in Russian literature as Tolstoy emphasized the salvation aspect of suffering while Chekhov challenged this view and "condemned [this suffering] as a curse."[7]

In spite of a rich theology on the dignity of work in the service of God, issues of work are frequently absent from sermons and other aspects of individuals' worship experiences. Ignoring work in this way signals that it is not a method for serving God or other spiritual goals: "Regardless of the bridges we build, the bodies we heal, the children we educate, the toilets we clean, the food we harvest, and the garments we mend, we amass no credit with the Almighty."[8] This allows the popular conceptualization that (hard) work is God's curse to persist and endure.

The Curse of the Lowly and the Enslaved

Seeing work as the curse of toil that afflicts the human condition is a type of universal conceptualization of work. Alternatively, particular forms of work might be conceptualized as a curse that specific individuals must endure. In classical Greek thought, for example, a sharp division was drawn between proper and improper work. Individuals who worked for others—the precursors to today's wage and salary workers—were seen essentially as slaves: "The artisan who sells his own products and the workman who hires out his services . . . both work to satisfy the needs of others, not their own. They depend upon others for their livelihood. For that reason they are no longer free." Free men, to Plato and Aristotle, use things, they do not make them; using something is seen as part of a free, rational choice and can therefore promote flourishing or happiness, but making things is associated with necessity and therefore indicates a lack of freedom and flourishing.[9]

This view of work rejects an intense work ethic. Work is only good to the extent that it produces things to help you or your family to flourish. Flourishing, furthermore, is not a material ideal. Rather, Aristotle believed that the good life consisted of virtue, contemplation, the pursuit of knowledge, and participation in governance. "Work, as Aristotle sees it, gets in the way of the more proper pursuits of a citizen, not only wasting his time in inferior activities, but corrupting him and making his pursuit of virtue more difficult." While perhaps because of concerns with preparing for war rather than seeking virtue, Sparta even prohibited citizens from working.[10]

The division between proper and improper, or honorable and dishonorable, forms of work persists in later eras. Like Aristotle before him, the Roman orator Cicero wrote about the laborers and craftsmen whose wage work amounted to slavery and vulgarity. This stemmed not only from Aristotelian views of freedom but also from a belief that physical labor (except agricultural work) degrades the body and mind and leaves one ill-equipped for advancing higher levels of human knowledge like philosophy or mathematics. The caste system in India has lasted for centuries and is even more explicit in crafting social hierarchies of occupations. The impoverished untouchables are the lowest caste because their occupations involve contact with "polluted" substances such as dead animals (including leather) or human waste, and this contact makes them, and their offspring, permanently impure. Contemporary Western society also attaches social stigmas to jobs that involve dirty work. Such jobs frequently involve the human body or its products—for example, hospital orderlies, personal care attendants, sex workers, or janitors. The word *villain,* furthermore, should continue to remind us about the extent to which manual laborers have been stigmatized through the ages, as this word comes from *villein*—a member of the serf class at the bottom of the medieval economic and social ladder who toiled the hardest.[11]

This is not to say that these workers do not take pride in or derive meaning from their work. Irrespective of the views of the Greco-Roman elites—which is what mostly survives in written form today—there is evidence that ancient artisans took pride in their work. Examples of ancient pottery proudly signed by their creator have been found; other pottery depicts scenes of people at work; and tombs of craftsmen have been discovered that proudly proclaim the deceased's occupation. Slaves in all eras find ways to achieve some element of dignity, and contemporary workers in dirty jobs are able to construct positive self-identities.[12] But elite segments of societies tend to see these lower forms of work as a curse to be avoided.

Specifically, lousy work can be conceptualized as a curse when it is assumed that God or nature requires some to engage in arduous or dirty work and that it is the natural place of the lowly classes to bear this burden. The creation story of the caste system in India involves a divinely created hierarchy. It is therefore the will of the gods that specific castes must endure lousy work. European colonial policies that dispossessed indigenous populations of their land and coerced them into growing cash crops and extracting natural resources were rationalized on an intellectual basis by a claimed superiority of Europeans. More recently, the controversial book *The Bell Curve* argues that contemporary America is stratified by intellectual ability that is largely genetic in origin.[13] Such an argument implies that the lower classes occupy their natural place in the social and occupational hierarchy and demonstrates the persistence of this line of thinking. The marginalization in contemporary Western societies of some occupations as "women's work" or fit only for minorities or immigrants can similarly reflect a belief in a natural social hierarchy.

Or consider slavery. Slavery and other systems of forced labor are invariably justified by the dominant elite by subscribing to some theory of natural or God-given superiority. Perhaps most famously, Aristotle reasoned that nature creates humans of varying intellectual abilities, and the intellectually inferior are naturally suited to be slaves. Such a view is implicitly echoed across time and culture in that the elites in all systems of slavery embrace a stereotype of slaves as lazy, irresponsible, and in need of masters. Proslavery writers in the nineteenth-century American South, for example, argued that "it is the order of nature and of God, that the being of superior faculties and knowledge, and therefore of superior power, should control and dispose of those who are inferior" and that "the institution of slavery is an essential process in emerging from savage life." Southerners further believed that black skin identified inferiority and therefore revealed natural slaves. American slavery was further justified by reference to the biblical curse of Ham in which Noah cursed some of Ham's descendants with servitude. Nature or God is therefore seen as cursing some not only with the burden of lousy work but also with the "social death" that results from slavery.[14]

Take This Job and Accept It

For thousands of years, work has been seen as painful toil that degrades one's dignity and conflicts with life's more virtuous or pleasurable pursuits. The frustrations of lousy work are succinctly summed up in the song "Take This Job and Shove It" popularized by Johnny Paycheck, while numerous songs, poems, and other pieces of popular culture from many eras lament the curse of work. But since work is required for survival, it becomes, in the words of Mark Twain, "a necessary evil to be avoided." Saint Paul, Saint Benedict, Martin Luther, John Calvin, and other religious figures throughout history have therefore found it necessary to exhort individuals to work. In the first half of the eighteenth century, many British economists believed in the utility-of-poverty doctrine, as captured by this remark from 1771: "Every one but an idiot knows that the lower classes must be kept poor or they will never be industrious." The contemporary drive to make work a requirement for receiving income support or welfare payments reflects, at least partly, an assumption that people need to be pushed to work.[15] And throughout history, violence has been used to force slaves to do a wide range of burdensome tasks.

Beyond the perception that people need to be forced to work, a particularly troublesome implication of seeing work as a curse is that it implicitly or explicitly reinforces the status quo while marginalizing deeper considerations of the nature of work. If hard work—for all, or just for the lowly and the enslaved—is preordained by God or nature, then individuals should simply accept their burdens. In fact, until perhaps Calvin's writings in the sixteenth century, Western conceptions of work did not provide for upward social mobility. Rather, by reference to divine or natural law, political and religious leaders tried to "ensure that individuals did not attempt to trespass beyond the position or 'station' to which they have been allocated." In the thirteenth century, for example, Thomas Aquinas wrote that "the diversification of men for diverse tasks is the result, primarily, of divine providence" and that "in human affairs, in virtue of the order of natural and divine law, inferiors are bound to obey their superiors." Such views are reflected in the hierarchy of Greco-Roman society, the feudal ordering of European medieval society, and the enduring caste system in India. Moreover, the medieval belief that the lower classes "had to work because they were poor, and they were poor because they had to work" and the ancient Greco-Roman belief that "those who must work are unfit to rule" persist today.[16]

When phrased as God's punishment of Adam and Eve or as the necessity of surviving by extracting food and shelter from a harsh natural world, work is "just there":

> In the face of the everyday difficulty of work, in defiance of the distractions we daily seek, we might say: just work! In this tone, the injunction to "just work" demands that we suspend doubt and dissatisfaction, and reconcile ourselves to what must be done, to the task at hand.

We therefore see ourselves as consumers, taxpayers, parents, citizens, and in many other roles, but not as workers. Work is something that we must do, and therefore there is not much to think about. Work is seen as natural, not as a human creation, and therefore unquestioned. "To experience work as *necessary* seems to displace room for its moral evaluation: work is what it is and not what we might wish it to be."[17] Take this job and shove it becomes take this job and accept it as our fate.

But work is not "just there."[18] Work is central to the human condition, and its deep importance must be appreciated. While working to survive is a natural condition, the form that work has taken through the ages is typically a human creation. For example, modern employment under capitalism—working for someone else for pay, frequently in limited-liability corporations—is a societal creation, not a product of God or nature. We therefore should analyze work, consider alternative conceptualizations, and question how work should be structured to serve human and social ends.

Attributing the conditions of specific forms of work to individual choices and personal responsibility rather than to divine creation has the same effect of making society not responsible for the quality of work. In other words, regardless of whether work is seen as a divine curse, if some are naturally meant to be slaves, or if being stuck in a lousy job reflects a lack of personal ambition, there is little urgency to reform the nature of work. In today's conservative political discourse, then, upward economic mobility should be promoted through education and individual effort to move up the occupational ladder, not through the enactment of government standards to improve the nature of work at the bottom of the economic ladder. Seeing work as a curse is therefore a metaphor for accepting work as beyond our collective control. But work is within our control. Society can choose how to conceptualize work, and how to structure it accordingly.

CHAPTER 2

Work as Freedom

> Perfect freedom is reserved for the man who lives by his own work and in that work does what he wants to do.
>
> —R. G. Collingwood (1889–1943)

The *Merriam-Webster Dictionary* defines freedom as "the absence of necessity, coercion, or constraint in choice or action." This leads to two ways of thinking about freedom as it relates to work—independence from the primary demands of surviving in the natural environment, and liberty from the coercion of other humans. For most of human history, it would have been curious to associate work with either sense of freedom. Some slaves might have been able to work hard enough to earn their freedom, but work more generally was likely seen as obligated by God, nature, custom, law, or physical force. The importance of the individual and freedom in modern Western thought, however, alters the conceptual landscape and allows work to be conceptualized as freedom in several ways.

One conceptualization pertains to freedom from nature: work can be seen as a creative activity that either establishes some independence from or is done independently of the daily necessities of nature, though contemporary concerns with environmental degradation suggest that this drive to master the natural world has perhaps been taken too far. The remaining conceptualizations deal with individual liberty from the coercion of other humans. First, John Locke famously argued in the seventeenth century that labor forms the basis of political and economic freedom by serving as the source of private property. In other words, work can be a classical source of liberty—not from nature, but from other humans and human institutions through the ownership of your labor. Second, the legal systems of capitalist economies see work as an activity undertaken by individuals who are free to pursue occupations of their choosing and to quit at will. In other words, employment is a contractual relation between legal equals, albeit with various standards and limitations across countries. Third, critics of the contractual perspective question the extent to which formal legal equality is sufficient for providing workers with true economic and political independence. This criticism raises a more general consideration—how to think about the various degrees to which workers are free or unfree. Conceptualizing work as freedom therefore deserves our attention.

The Freedom to Create

Consider first freedom from nature. Western thought generally embraces a human-centered perspective in which human beings are believed to occupy a privileged position in the natural world. Nature is seen as something to be mastered for human needs. In early Western thought, then, work was viewed as a struggle with nature—only through "painful toil . . . by the sweat of your brow" does God in the book of Genesis allow humans to extract their livelihood from the earth. An increasingly scientific and decreasingly religious view of the natural world during the Middle Ages, however, made nature seem "penetrable and predictable." Work then becomes seen as mastery over nature: "Man, confronting the universe, did not merely accept this external world; he changed it and, with his tools, sought to make of it a humanized world." Work is a method for creating useful products, which are, in the words of Karl Marx, "nature's material adapted by a change of form to the wants of man." In other words, work is a way to create freedom from the vagaries of the natural world and unlock humans from the slavish pursuit of the food and shelter needed to survive, and "to impose culture" on the natural world.[1]

In this way, a worker is a creator—someone who "rebels against nature's dictates." Creative work has occurred throughout history and can take many forms. From some perspectives, creative work is more pervasive than ever before. Urban studies theorist Richard Florida argues that the "creative class" now amounts to 30 percent of the U.S. workforce and includes individuals in "science and engineering, architecture and design, education, arts, music and entertainment, whose economic function is to create new ideas, new technology and/or new creative content" and also includes "creative professionals in business and finance, law, heath care, and related fields [who] engage in complex problem solving." Ideally, creative work allows us "to be ourselves, set our own schedules, do challenging work and live in communities that reflect our values and priorities."[2]

Critics, however, have long contrasted the ideal of work as the free, creative expression of humans with the realities of modern forms of work for many workers. In the nineteenth century, this contrast was the basis for Marx's objection to the alienated nature of work under capitalism (chapter 3). Similarly, the twentieth-century philosopher Hannah Arendt distinguished between what she labeled labor and work. These terms are used interchangeably in this book, but for Arendt, labor consists of those activities required to produce the means of subsistence whereas work creates a durable human world. She criticized the modern emphasis on consumption and mass production for creating a laboring society rather than a working society—that is, for reducing humans to *Animal laborans* (a species that labors to survive like animals) rather than *Homo faber* (a species that works to build and create). This is seen as problematic because it is *Homo faber* for whom work is freedom and creation rather than slavish toil: "*Homo faber* is indeed a lord and master, not only because he is the master or has set himself up as the master of all nature but because he is master of himself and his doings."[3]

The French language reinforces the important contrast between creative work and toil—one French word for work, *travail,* is rooted in a Latin word for a torture device, whereas another word for work, *œuvre,* comes from the Latin *opus* relating to accomplishment and creativity. This is not purely a semantic difference: French sociologists have a strong tradition in their scholarship of distinguishing between work as pain and work as creation.[4]

Working with Rather Than Mastering the Natural World

Conceptualizing work as the freedom to create a means of independence from the harsh necessities of survival or as an expression of human creativity beyond what nature dictates reflects in each case an underlying mind-set of human mastery over nature. This mind-set can be criticized for reflecting a male-dominated perspective. Through childbirth and breast-feeding, women can productively contribute to the maintenance of human society by cooperating with nature rather than needing to master it. Men's bodies, in contrast, are not productive in the same way:

> Men's contribution to the production of new life, though necessary at all times, could become *visible* only after a long historical process of men's action on external nature by means of tools, and their reflection

on this process. . . . Thus, the male self-conception as human, that is, as being productive, is closely linked to the invention and control of technology. Without tools man is no MAN.

To some feminist theorists, these differences in how men and women relate to nature laid the foundation for male dominance in patriarchal societies in many historical eras up to and including modern capitalism. Specifically, man's need to master nature in order to be considered productive is seen as including mastery over women because their reproductive activities are viewed as part of nature. By equating indigenous peoples to uncivilized savages that are part of nature, "civilized" man similarly used his mastery of nature to justify European colonization of Africa, the Americas, and elsewhere between the sixteenth and twentieth centuries.[5]

In contrast to the Western worldview that privileges humans over other living things, consider instead a perspective in which all living organisms are equally valued. In societies that embrace this perspective, activities that modern societies see as work are frequently subsumed into a larger conception of daily life that is inseparable from the natural environment. In other words, indigenous and hunter-gatherer societies typically see themselves as actively engaged within and relating to a holistic environmental system, not mastering or managing it as an external resource. The Mbuti Pygmies in central Africa and the Nayaka in India refer to the forests where they live as father or mother, while the North American Cree see animals as having qualities of personhood. Working the Native American "Navajo way" requires fulfilling "reciprocal obligations with the earth." Work activities such as hunting or farming are therefore not conceptualized in opposition to nature and are instead seen as part of nature. Barbara Mann, a scholar of Native Americans, further argues that Native American Iroquois economics is premised upon assumptions of abundance, not scarcity as in Western economic thought. Work activities can therefore not be separated from spiritual rituals that relate the "workers" to their natural environment. And the Inuit of northern Canada are just one example of an indigenous people whose traditional language lacks a distinct word for work because work is part of life, not a separate activity.[6]

While we should guard against creating an overly romanticized depiction of these societies, they provide an interesting foil for Western conceptualizations of work as freedom that assume, in the words of Leonardo da Vinci, that "God sells us all things at the price of labor." Work need not be freedom from or mastery over nature to be valued; it can instead be seen as an integral part of human participation in the natural environment: "not work as a relationship to nature which is partly one of dominating her, partly one of worship of and enslavement by the very products of man's hands, but work as creation in which man becomes one with nature in the act of creation."[7] Contemporary concerns with overconsumption, environmental degradation, and the need to create sustainable ("green" or eco-friendly) practices lend urgency to the need to rethink Western conceptualizations of work as domination over the natural world.

The Freedom to Own

In contrast to the idea of freedom from nature's constraints, now consider freedom from coercion by other humans. This type of freedom is paramount in political and economic liberalism and is pursued through protections for private property rights. In the political sphere, the right to control yourself and your property serves as a protection against the oppression of others. In the economic realm, the right to buy, sell, and consume commodities allows for individual choice and allocates commodities to their most efficient uses. As classical liberal ideas were being developed in the late seventeenth century, the influential John Locke asserted that these property rights are derived from an individual's work.[8]

Locke's reasoning started from the Western, human-centric worldview in which God gave the natural environment to humans in order to live, and work is required to appropriate nature's products. But rather than stopping there and seeing work as a curse, Locke argued that individuals own themselves and therefore own the fruits of their labor:

> Though the Earth, and all inferior Creatures, be common to all Men, yet every Man has a *Property* in his own *Person*. This no Body has any Right to but himself. The *Labour* of his Body, and the *Work* of his Hands, we may say, are properly his. Whatsoever then he removes out of the State that Nature hath provided, and left it in, he hath mixed his *Labour* with, and joined to it something that is his own, and thereby makes it his *Property*.

Note carefully that this reasoning is rooted in seeing human equality and ownership of your own person as natural, not human-made, creations that stem from the basic fact of being human. Property rights are therefore natural rights that pre-date the formation of civil society. Consequently, Locke asserted that governments are established by the consent of the people to protect their property rights, and governmental action should not infringe on these natural rights. This proved to be a very influential idea, and property rights are enshrined today as a hallmark of modern liberal protections against government oppression.[9] The U.S. Constitution, for example, forbids the deprivation of "life, liberty, or property, without due process of law." Since this began with Locke's theory of labor ownership, work can be conceptualized as a fundamental source of *political* freedom via property ownership.

Locke's theorizing also has important implications for *economic* liberalism and capitalism. By making work one's own property, it becomes something that one has personal control over. Workers are therefore free to sell their labor for pay if they so choose. Moreover, because your work is yours and yours alone, there are no social obligations or limitations on how much you can accumulate through your work. Wage work and unchecked capitalist accumulation are therefore given moral approval, and the foundation is laid for seeing work as an economic commodity to be bought and sold in free markets (chapter 3). Locke's influence is clearly evident in this passage from Adam Smith's famous economic treatise *The Wealth of Nations:*

> The property which every man has in his own labour, as it is the original foundation of all other property, so it is the most sacred and inviolable. The patrimony of a poor man lies in the strength and dexterity of his hands; and to hinder him from employing this strength and dexterity in what manner he thinks proper without injury to his neighbour, is a plain violation of this most sacred property. It is a manifest encroachment upon the just liberty both of the workman, and of those who might be disposed to employ him.[10]

Work is thus conceptualized as the freedom to own not only the fruits of one's labor (property) but also to own and therefore sell what Karl Marx later called one's labor power—that is, the capacity to work.

The Freedom to Contract

John Locke and Adam Smith envisioned a liberal political and economic order in which individuals can freely sell their labor. But to achieve this in practice required changing the conceptualization of work in each industrializing country's legal system. For centuries, the natural social order in Europe was hierarchical—"the superiority of husband over wife, parents over children, and master over servants in the family, ministers and elders over congregation in the church, rulers over subjects in the state." The emergence of Western liberalism reflected a new vision of the natural social order consisting of free and autonomous individuals. The legal regulation of work in Europe and the United States consequently evolved in ways that reflected the emergence of this new imagined social order, and this evolution required a new conceptualization of work.[11]

In the aftermath of the labor shortages caused by the Black Death in the fourteenth century, several English laws prohibited workers from quitting before their agreed-upon ending date and established maximum wage rates at their pre-plague levels. These laws sought to enforce the obligations of duty and obedience that domestic and agricultural servants owed their masters, akin to the obedience that family members owed the master of the domestic household. One-year service periods were common (to ensure adequate workers for the harvest), and workers faced fines and imprisonment if they left prematurely or refused to carry out their work. These "servants" included agricultural laborers and craft workers who lived in the master's household. Though these were the forerunners of today's employees, they were "seen as contributing personal service, conceived not as specific labour duties but as a general contribution to the needs of the enterprise, be it household, farm, or workshop."[12] The legal backing of strict apprenticeship arrangements akin to indentured servitude further reinforced the dominance of masters in the work realm.

On the eve of the Industrial Revolution in mid-eighteenth-century Britain, then, the employment relationship was seen by the legal system as a master-servant relationship. In fact, four "Master and Servant Acts" were passed between 1747 and 1823, and these acts not only reinforced the earlier penalties for work refusal but also expanded the coverage to include more industrial workers. Under these acts, British workers were still being criminally prosecuted as late as the 1870s for abandoning their work. In this way, work was conceptualized as a status relation such that rights and obligations depended on long-standing traditions of social standing. The status of master obligated the head of the household to care for his family, and his dependents owed him obedience. The master was similarly obligated to care for his employees, and they owed him unquestioned service for the duration of their agreement. In continental Europe, the traditionally subordinate status of workers was enforced during the nineteenth century through the workbook system in which individuals could not get a new job until their current master certified that their work was complete.[13]

The shift to free labor markets entailed replacing this conceptualization of work as a hierarchical status relation with one in which work is viewed as a voluntary contractual relation between equals. This is seen most graphically in the case of the United States. Starting from the English master-servant legal regime in colonial times, U.S. judges weakened master-servant principles during the 1800s.[14] During the first half of the 1800s, U.S. workers who

quit working before their agreed-upon ending date might forfeit as punishment several months of pay that they had already earned, but unlike their
British counterparts, they were not forced to complete their terms of service.
As the century unfolded, employees were increasingly seen by the courts as
their own masters capable and deserving of managing their own affairs. At
the same time, employers were increasingly seen as commercial employers of
labor through an economic transaction, not as masters in the traditional sense.
Legal rulings therefore increasingly denied employers the right to physically punish their workers and also freed them from their traditional obligations as masters of dependent servant/employees, such as the responsibility to
maintain them if they were injured. Consequently, by the beginning of the
twentieth century, the master-servant doctrine in the United States had been
replaced by the freedom to contract.

This statement from a Massachusetts politician and lawyer in 1853 captured the emerging legal thought:

> In a free government like ours, employment is simply a contract
> between parties having equal rights. The operative agrees to perform a
> certain amount of work in consideration of receiving a certain amount
> of money. The work to be performed is, by the contract, an equivalent
> for the money to be paid. The relation, when properly entered into,
> is therefore one of mutual benefit. The employed is under no greater
> obligation to the employer than the employer is to the employed. . . . In
> the eye of the law, they are both freemen—citizens having equal rights,
> and brethren having one common destiny.

From the 1880s to the 1920s, U.S. courts invalidated state laws limiting
working hours in bakeries to ten hours per day, specifying minimum wages,
outlawing "yellow-dog" contracts (in which workers promise not to join or
form a union), prohibiting wages paid in company scrip redeemable only at
the company store, and other labor standards, because such laws were seen
as interfering with the freedom to enter into freely chosen employment
contracts. In other words, if employees were willing to voluntarily agree to
long hours, low wages, yellow-dog contracts, or payment in company scrip,
then lawmakers and judges should not deprive autonomous men of their
freedom to control their own lives by banning such terms and conditions of
employment. (As discussed later in this chapter, women were viewed differently.) The freedom to contract in all economic transactions, including but
not limited to employment matters, is also a necessary legal support for the
private economic activity that mainstream economic thought relies on to
produce the optimal allocation of scarce resources.[15] So the development of

the legal area of contracts in Anglo-American law fits squarely into both the political and economic frameworks of Western liberalism.

The voluntary aspect of free contracting in the employment relationship is taken to an extreme in the United States in the form of the employment-at-will doctrine. Though its nineteenth-century origins are still debated, the employment-at-will doctrine emerged with the freedom to contract during the second half of the nineteenth century. As the name suggests, this legal doctrine makes employment at the will or discretion of the employee and the employer. Employees are therefore allowed to quit at any time for any reason. Legal scholar Robert Steinfeld emphasizes how this revolutionized the U.S. employment relationship:

> The employer did continue to enjoy the legal right to command the labor he hired, but that right could not legally be enforced through corporal punishment and could only be exercised so long as the employee wished it to be. The employer did continue to be entitled to the fruits of the employee's labor, but again, only so long as the employee wished him to be. . . . [Now] workers were always physically free to come and go as they wished and to take whatever work was offered.[16]

On the other side of the coin, employees can be dismissed for (nearly) any reason, or no reason at all. Contrary to popular beliefs, a valid reason for terminating an employee is not required.

The ideal of an unrestricted freedom to contract in the employment relationship is based on a conceptualization of work as something that individuals can freely sell at terms of their own choosing to employers as legal equals, not as a status relation. The shift from the master-servant doctrine to the freedom to contract and the employment-at-will doctrine illustrates Sir Henry Sumner Maine's oft-repeated nineteenth-century statement that "the movement of the progressive societies has hitherto been a movement *from Status to Contract.*" Specifically, starting from the earlier master-servant era "in which all the relations of Persons are summed up in the relations of Family, we seem to have steadily moved towards a phase of social order in which all these relations arise from the free agreement of individuals."[17]

The Continuing Tension between Status and Contract

The shift from status to contract in the legal regulation of work, however, has been incomplete. The freedom to contract in the modern employment relationship is rarely unrestricted. While the employment-at-will doctrine continues to provide the legal foundation for the U.S. employment relationship

in the twenty-first century, a variety of exceptions have been created by stat-
ute and judicial precedent. For example, employees cannot be fired because
of their gender, race, ethnicity, union membership status, or other protected
categories. U.S. laws prohibit employers and employees from freely contracting in ways that pay a subminimum wage, ignore basic safety standards, or fail
to provide workers' compensation coverage. Moreover, the legal backing for
employer control of the workplace is an extension of status-based, hierarchical master-servant principles and is not based on contract law.[18] As such, the
legal regulation of work in the United States reflects varying emphases on
status and contract.

The United States is not unique in this regard, and the legal regulation of
work in capitalist countries generally reflects varying emphases on status and
contract. Britain repealed the Master and Servant Acts in the late nineteenth
century, but the increased emphasis on the freedom to contract was tempered by collective representation by labor unions such that an American-
style employment-at-will doctrine did not emerge. The legal regulation of
work in France, Germany, and other European civil law countries experienced a similar trajectory, with the freedom of contract replacing the status-
based feudal order and guild system, but with lingering status influences.
The development of Japanese labor law also followed this general pattern in
which contract principles became more important, but did not completely
displace the importance of status-based principles.[19]

Some elements of status in today's legal regulation of work favor workers.
Unfair dismissal protections are quite common in the industrialized world
outside the United States such that employers need a valid reason to dismiss
employees. These protections are rooted in an underlying sense of fairness
(status relations), not in principles of commercial contracting. Modern welfare states, in their diverse forms around the world, similarly temper the
contractual aspect of employment with safety nets because of status-based
principles of citizenship and dignity. In these respects, the status of workers
has improved since the eighteenth century. But in other areas, the privileged
status of masters is perpetuated through the modern legal regulation of work.
Employees in many countries have a duty to be loyal to their employers.
While this might seem to be a contractual principle, its origins instead lie in
the hierarchies of the master-servant era. The continued legal subordination
of workers who must obey their employers' directives, just like the servants
of the fourteenth century, is therefore criticized by detractors.[20]

The conceptualization of the employment relationship as a contractual
arrangement freely undertaken by employers and employees is a foundational
idea in the legal regulation of work in industrialized countries today, even if

the freedom to contract is limited in various ways by status concerns. Some believe that work should be conceptualized primarily as a contractual activity among free individuals because the resulting legal supports for the freedom to contract will maximize individual freedom and economic efficiency. Others believe that the uniqueness of human labor and power imbalances in the employment relationship mean that the legal principles of contract law do not and should not apply to work.[21] Rather, work should be conceptualized as a status relation among unequal parties in which legal supports for the freedom to contract only make workers free in a formal, technical sense but not in the everyday reality of lived lives. In both cases, the importance of how work is conceptualized is readily apparent, and similar debates over the appropriate conceptualization of work are repeated outside the legal arena (compare chapters 3 and 4).

Free/Unfree Labor

The erosion of the master-servant doctrine, along with the concurrent rise of the freedom to contract, raises the provocative issue of free versus unfree labor. Free workers are "able to enter or withdraw from the labour market at will" and thereby choose their employer. At first glance, this might seem to yield a simple dichotomy—slaves are unfree and everyone else is free. Such a dichotomy has great discursive or rhetorical power—if only slavery is deemed unfree, then all other practices are given "an aura of normality" and are left unchallenged by reformers, as happened in debates over European colonial practices in Africa.[22]

But such a dichotomy is overly simplistic. Various forms of unfree labor in addition to slavery have been prominent in world history up to the present day, such as convict labor, indentured servitude and debt bondage, serfdom, submission to patriarchy, or military impressment and conscription. As workers in these various systems have differing levels of freedom, it is better to think of the concept of "free/unfree labor" as including a continuum of possibilities rather than as representing a simple dichotomy. Wage workers, too, are potentially subjected to various restrictions, such as work permits or immigration limitations, and from some critical perspectives are not free under capitalism even in the absence of formal legal restraints because of a lack of true alternatives to selling one's labor power in the labor market.[23]

The economic and social upheavals brought on by the Industrial Revolution help reveal how workers who are formally free in the eyes of the law can be seen as less than free in practice. The replacement of household-based production—whether agricultural, skilled craft, or unskilled sweated work—with mines, factories, and offices forced workers to commute, interact with strangers, and work in dangerous, noisy, and otherwise unpleasant workplaces exemplified by the fabled "dark Satanic mills." By working for others rather than themselves, workers became dependent on employers for their livelihoods and lost control over their work pace and methods. The Industrial Revolution even redefined the nature of time for modern humans as the time discipline of modern jobs became dominant. Time became your employer's, not your own, and was measured by your employer's time clock, not your own personal rhythms.[24] In these ways, then, the freedom to sell one's labor involves sacrificing numerous other freedoms.

Independence, Work, and Citizenship

The extent to which a worker is free is not just a matter of personal economic liberty; rather, it is also strongly connected to political citizenship and social inclusion. The development of American democratic ideals in the nineteenth century occurred when both slavery and European aristocracies were seen as contrary to the ideals of self-rule by equal citizens. Freely chosen work and the independence that it allows thereby became the key criteria for what it meant to be a citizen:

> To be a recognized and active citizen at all he must be an equal member of the polity, a voter, but he must also be independent, which has all along meant that he must be an "earner," a free remunerated worker, one who is rewarded for the actual work he has done, neither more nor less. He cannot be a slave or an aristocrat.

While the widespread fear of slavery and the aristocracy may have faded, work continues today to be highly valued in this way—not for work itself, but for the independence and self-sufficiency that it creates. Today this is perhaps more visibly recognized when it is absent rather than present: not working creates a "sense of dependence and failure, the loss of others' respect—in short, the individual's sense of exclusion from the community of equal citizens."[25]

These relationships between independence, work, and citizenship can be complex. In the United States in the nineteenth century, wage labor was equated by some to "wage slavery." Just as the black slaves in the southern United States were economically and politically dependent on their owners, so, too, were wage workers seen as economically and politically dependent on their capitalist employers and therefore not full-fledged, free citizens. Advocates of "worker republicanism" therefore championed self-employed skilled craftwork, farming, and other forms of work that provided the independence needed for full citizenship in the self-rule tradition of civic republicanism. At best, wage work was a temporary stepping-stone to becoming independent and therefore free, as captured by a speech by Abraham Lincoln in 1859:

> The prudent, penniless beginner in the world labors for wages awhile, saves a surplus with which to buy tools or land for himself, then labors on his own account another while, and at length hires another new beginner to help him. This, say its advocates, is free labor—the just, and generous, and prosperous system, which opens the way for all, gives hope to all, and energy, and progress, and improvement of condition to all. If any continue through life in the condition of the hired laborer, it is not the fault of the system, but because of either a dependent nature which prefers it, or improvidence, folly, or singular misfortune.

Consistent with this vision, the Homestead Act in 1862 gave free land to settlers of the plains of the United States as a method for wage workers to become independent.[26]

Within the workplace, servile workers who were constantly told what to do were viewed as incapable of self-rule in the political arena. U.S. craft unions therefore pushed for worker and union control of their crafts in the name of republican self-rule. Work rules were developed to regulate apprenticeship standards, the demarcation of job duties between skilled and unskilled workers, work allocation procedures, and other standards. Before the 1900s, these work rules were often established unilaterally by labor unions and enforced by union members refusing to work on any other terms and by unions fining or expelling members who undermined these standards. Skilled British artisans similarly sought to protect the standards of their crafts.[27] While these efforts have economic and psychological aspects (e.g., compensation and pride of workmanship), the political aspect of being seen as free, independent citizens should not be overlooked.

Or perhaps more accurately, as free, independent *white men*. Women, especially white women, were not expected to be economically self-reliant. Rather, they might work for pay until they married, and then they were fired or expected to quit in order to focus on taking care of their husband and family. In 1908, the U.S. Supreme Court upheld an Oregon law prohibiting women from working more than ten hours a day, and other legislation followed that limited women's work opportunities in various ways, all premised on the protection of women's key roles in child rearing. This cemented "a conception of citizenship rooted in motherhood and family life that could and did override women's rights as individuals under the law." Nonwhite men were also viewed as incapable of full economic and political independence.[28] In other words, the American conceptualization of work as a source of freedom and citizenship in the decades before and after the turn of the twentieth century primarily applied to white men.

While "wage slavery" is a nineteenth-century term, concerns with the corrosive effects of economic dependency within the domain of work persist today. Management scholar Bruce Barry argues for free-speech protections for individuals in the workplace because "work is also how people create for themselves economic independence—a necessity if social and political rights are to have much meaning." The coercive power of contemporary employers over employees' freedom in the United States is revealed by cases in which employees have been fired for refusing to engage in illegal actions, and for blogging, smoking, and other off-duty activities. It is not hard to imagine other employees giving in to their employers' demands in order to keep their jobs. This economic dependency not only affects individual lifestyle freedoms but can also undermine democracy. American employers have used "their economic power over people's livelihoods to control the political behavior" of their employees by firing them because they displayed a bumper sticker supporting a Democratic candidate on a private vehicle, asked a question at a political rally, or refused to make a donation to a specific candidate. Such firings might not be pervasive, but the potential for undue employer influence in the democratic process is further highlighted by the sharp increase in the number of employers using their company e-mail systems to inform workers about pro-business political candidates.[29] While such messages are portrayed as neutral, some employees might feel pressured to support the candidates favored by their employers.

In addition to contemporary concerns with dependency, some also criticize contemporary employment practices that undermine the civic republicanism ideals of participatory democracy. When companies reward unquestioned loyalty, conformity, and deference to authority rather than participatory decision making and open discourse, undemocratic ideals are being reinforced. When workers are expected to follow orders without providing input, the deliberative skills needed for self-rule are being undermined. Political scientist Carole Pateman and others have therefore argued that the workplace should be a training ground for participatory democracy, and such an argument is frequently translated into an emphasis on enhancing employee voice (chapter 4). Not everyone shares these concerns, and it is instead more common to argue that not only are companies more efficient when they are undemocratic, but property rights give companies the freedom to structure their work as they see fit.[30] But for those who continue to be concerned with the effects of economic dependency and hierarchal employment practices on individual liberty and participatory self-rule, work is conceptualized as providing, at best, something less than full freedom and therefore something less than full citizenship.

The Spectacular Rise of Labor

To the extent that work frees individuals from necessity, coercion, or constraint, work can be a source of individual freedom. This conceptualization remains important today. Western liberalism has created a "shame of dependence" in which adults are expected to be independent and not rely on others. Working to earn enough income to support you and your family is a key source of this independence. Working does not simply provide money for consumption (chapter 5), but also for self-sufficiency and therefore citizenship. Becoming financially independent is also an important aspect of transitioning to adulthood. The income that work provides helps enable women to escape bad marriages. And while women often experience a reduction in living standards after a divorce, many also experience an increased sense of independence. For some, this comes from having paid work responsibilities and a paycheck for the first time in a long while.[31]

Work as providing the freedom to own and control things also remains an important part of today's Western culture of individual liberty. "I should be able to spend my money or use my physical property as I please because I earned it" is a sentiment that can probably be found among at least a fraction of the population in numerous countries. This sentiment is derived from the same principle asserted by Locke in the late seventeenth century— the natural right to own one's work. Implicitly, this requires continued acceptance of Locke's assumption that an individual "comes into being already equipped with certain needs or desires and the bodily means to set about their satisfaction" rather than needing to be nurtured and educated by others.[32] In this way, the work of the individual is privileged over the importance of the community. For better or worse, then, Locke's theory of labor ownership lives on.

Going back in time several centuries, the development of the conceptualization of work as freedom also had lasting implications for how we think about work. In ancient Greco-Roman thought and under feudalism, hard work was the curse of the naturally inferior classes (chapter 1). In Christian theology before the twelfth century, work was subordinate to religious activity. Individuals worked in order to avoid the temptations of sin that come from idleness, to produce food and shelter that allows one to devote other hours to prayer and worship, and to help the needy. After the twelfth century, with the secularization of work that comes from seeing work as a personal rather than spiritual activity, the door was opened for today's emphasis on the economic aspects of work such as productivity and income. For some, this represented a moral loss. But it also placed work at the center of Western thought:

> The sudden, spectacular rise of labor from the lowest, most despised position to the highest rank, as the most esteemed of all human activities, began when Locke discovered that labor is the source of all property. It followed its course when Adam Smith asserted that labor was the source of all wealth and found its climax in Marx's system of labor where labor became the source of all productivity and the expression of the very humanity of man.

Regrettably, many forms of unfree labor persist today, from modern slavery to debt bondage to forced domestic service, in which individuals labor under despicable conditions.[33] From some perspectives, even formally free workers under capitalism are not truly free. But because of the spectacular *conceptual* rise of labor, work as freedom is seen as the Western ideal for which to strive.

CHAPTER 3

Work as a Commodity

> Labour-power is a commodity which its possessor, the
> wage-worker, sells to the capitalist. Why does he sell
> it? It is in order to live.
>
> —Karl Marx (1818–83)

Over four thousand years ago in Mesopotamia,
Marduk-naçir was hired by Mar-Sippar for a year and paid two and a half
shekels of silver in wages. This and other examples of wage labor in ancient
civilizations demonstrate that paid employment is not a creation of capitalism. But paid employment is unique under industrial capitalism in at least
two ways. First, a greater fraction of individuals work for pay in an industrialized, capitalist economy than in other economic systems. In other words,
paid employment becomes a dominant mode of economic activity for the
first time with the emergence of industrial capitalism. This new dominance
means that work becomes a separate sphere of life activity distinct from
one's family, religious, and community life. Second, paid employment in a
capitalist system is distinctively conceptualized as a commodity.[1] When work
is thought of as purely a commodity, it is analyzed as an abstract economic
quantity independent of noneconomic concerns.

This is a modern conceptualization of work. In ancient Greco-Roman
thought, work was seen as a concrete method for directly satisfying human
needs—for example, by growing food—not as a source of money or of economic value (chapter 1). Medieval artisans sold or exchanged products, not
labor time. The putting-out system several centuries later similarly involved
an exchange of money for completed products, not control over labor effort.
Those who ceded control over their labor effort were seen as slaves or servants.

It is not until the seventeenth and eighteenth centuries that labor effort was conceptualized in the abstract as a commodity that could be bought and sold, beginning with the writings of early British economists that culminated with Adam Smith's famous treatise *The Wealth of Nations* in 1776. This shift was part of the broader emergence of Western liberalism: "What could be more natural in a social universe composed of separate and autonomous individuals whose chief occupation was trading commodities back and forth than that some individuals should sell the property in their labor to other individuals, to whom thereafter it would belong?"[2]

In *The Wealth of Nations,* Smith describes how the division of labor into specialized occupations or jobs creates a situation in which

> every workman has a great quantity of his own work to dispose of beyond what he himself has occasion for; and every other workman being exactly in the same situation, he is enabled to exchange a great quantity of his own goods for a great quantity, or, what comes to the same thing, for the price of a great quantity of theirs.[3]

Conceptually, work thus becomes seen as a source of economic value that is traded in the marketplace. It then just takes a small step to see work as a generic input into a production function such that employers and workers are viewed conceptually as buying and selling generic units of this commodity called work or labor. Individuals become interchangeable, as it does not matter who is actually doing the work, and work becomes an abstract concept because diverse forms of concrete work—that is, ways in which work is actually conducted, such as hammering a nail, driving a truck, or programming a piece of computer software—are all seen as sources of economic value that can be made equivalent by exchanging them via an appropriate set of relative prices. Work, then, is conceptualized as a traded commodity like any other good or service.

As described toward the end of this chapter, Karl Marx was an impassioned critic of the commodification of work—or more accurately, of the commodification of "labor power." Marx explicitly differentiated "labor power" from "labor."[4] Labor power is an individual's capacity to work—that is, his or her physical and mental capabilities. Labor, in contrast, is a person's actual work. For Marx, then, capitalism commodifies labor power. It is the (temporary) control over an individual's capacity to work that is being bought and sold in the labor market, not an individual's actual work. This distinction is important for Marxian analyses because it provides the basis for Marx's theory of surplus value (described in the next section). This distinction also means that Marxist-inspired analyses are concerned with how labor power is converted into actual work via what Marx labeled the labor process (chapter 7). Mainstream economic theorizing from Adam Smith to the present day, however, largely assumes away distinctions between labor and labor power by assuming that employers get what they pay for. From this perspective, it is reasonable to say that "work is a commodity," but it is also useful to remember that Marx would have us say that "labor power is a commodity."

The conceptualization of work as a commodity is an enduring one. In the capitalist economies of the twenty-first century, most working-age individuals sell their labor power as a commodity to earn a living. Mainstream economic theory continues to model work as a commodity, and concerns with how workers are treated are as relevant today as when Marx sharply criticized the commodification of work under capitalism more than a century ago. And employment in capitalist societies is legally regulated as a contractual relationship (albeit a messy one) in which work is exchanged as a commodity (chapter 2).

Labor as *the* Source of Value

A commodity is an object with two values—a use value and an exchange value. A commodity's use value is its utility—the extent to which it usefully serves human needs and desires. A commodity's exchange value is its price— how much it can command in the marketplace. The use value of work captures its worth in being able to produce goods and services; the exchange value of work (technically, labor power) is the compensation earned by a worker. The use value of work was recognized in precapitalist societies, but to conceptualize work (labor power) as a commodity is to see work as also having exchange value (frequently shortened to "value").

When work was first conceptualized as a commodity, from perhaps the late 1600s to the 1800s, it was seen as a special commodity. This began with seeing the productive power of work, such as in John Locke's statement that "for whatever bread is more worth than acorns, wine than water, and cloth or silk than leaves, skins, or moss, that is wholly owing to labour and industry." As this was the era in which capitalism was replacing feudalism, such views on the productive power of work became visions of the productive power of free wage workers in a capitalist system, and work came to be thought of as an abstract source of prosperity:

> A precious new commodity, labour power, is thrown upon the market—
> a commodity which when properly organized, particularly in manufacture, is capable of yielding not only an abundance of material goods to the nation, but also handsome profits to its purchaser.[5]

So labor power is a commodity to be exchanged in markets and consumed like other commodities, but it is also a special commodity that creates other commodities.

In fact, work was seen for a time as the benchmark for valuing other commodities, and even as the source of all value. In dissolving the precapitalist ties that bound individuals together, such as feudal obligations, capitalism created a new ethos in which individuals are interdependent because they are making and exchanging different commodities. In other words, a capitalist society is held together by the need for commodities made by others. Economist Ronald Meek described how this can lead to seeing work as the source of these commodities' exchange values:

> If we regard society as consisting in essence of an association of separate producers who live by mutually exchanging the products of their different labours, we are likely to come to think of the exchange of these products as being in essence the exchange of *quantities of social labour.* And if we begin thinking in these terms, we may well eventually conclude that the *value* of a commodity—i.e., its power of purchasing or commanding other commodities in exchange—is a quality conferred upon it by virtue of the fact that a certain portion of the labour force of society has been allocated to its production.

The result was the eventual emergence of the labor theory of value, which posits that "the value of a commodity, or the quantity of any other commodity for which it will exchange, depends on the relative quantity of labour which is necessary for its production," to quote from the early nineteenth century proponent of the labor theory of value, David Ricardo.[6] In this conceptualization, work is a special commodity because its productive power resides in many other commodities and explains why these commodities generally differ in value.

Mainstream acceptance of the labor theory of value, however, was short-lived. Socialist writers and worker advocates used Ricardo's labor theory of value to claim that labor creates all wealth, and therefore workers deserve most, if not all, of the profits. Even before Marx developed his own labor theory of value in the mid-nineteenth century, then, conservative economists were distancing themselves from this perspective.[7] Before the end of the nineteenth century, the labor theory of value would be replaced in mainstream economic thought by marginal utility theory, in which a commodity's value is determined by the additional utility it provides to the consumers of the commodity, not by the labor embodied within it. Marx's labor theory of value is nevertheless important to consider.

Marx's labor theory of value is a theory of worker exploitation rooted in the previously described distinction between labor and labor power. As Marx saw it, capitalism commodifies labor power—workers sell and employers buy individuals' capacities to work. Since labor power is a commodity, Marx applied the Ricardian labor theory of value to it and argued that the exchange value of one's labor power equals the amount of labor required to produce it—that is, the amount of labor required to provide some subsistence level for the worker and his family. The capitalist pays the worker this amount for his labor power and in return captures the full value of the worker's labor. In other words, the capitalist acquires what Marx called the surplus value—the net worth of the products produced by the worker's labor over and above the low subsistence wage paid for the worker's labor power. For Marx, this surplus value is the basis of capitalist exploitation—it is produced by workers but captured by capitalists because workers do not own the means of production and are therefore forced to accept the capitalist's terms that pay the worker less than the full value of the product of his labor.[8]

Labor theories of value have been widely criticized on both ideological and substantive grounds, and except in some Marxist circles, today labor is no longer seen as a special source of value.[9] Today's capitalist societies recognize the productive power of capital as well as labor, and mainstream economic thought sees prices as determined not by production costs, but by consumption-driven demand that is constrained by scarcity on the supply side. Today, those who see work as a special commodity are likely to do so based on a principle of seeing workers as fully human with psychological and social needs, and perhaps entitled to human or citizenship rights (chapters 4, 6–9), not based on workers' unique productive powers.

Labor as a Commodity in Contemporary Economic Thought

The labor theory of value is important for the conceptualization of work because this theory's development created the idea of abstract labor with economic value. In other words, the labor theory of value commodified work in intellectual discourse. Contemporary mainstream economic theory (that is, neoclassical economic theory) fully embraces this view that abstract labor is a commodity. The difference between classical economic thought of the early 1800s and today's neoclassical paradigm, however, lies in the role of labor in creating value. Specifically, individual pleasure ("utility") is the centerpiece of human behavior in neoclassical economic thought such that the value of a commodity is not seen as determined by how much labor is required to produce it, but by people's willingness to pay for it.

Neoclassical economics thus becomes the science of exchange focusing on utility-maximizing individuals or households, profit-maximizing firms, and other rational, optimizing agents (e.g., investors) who exchange with each other in markets such that prices allocate scarce resources. This "scientific" emphasis on exchange causes labor to be treated as just another commodity. In other words, in neoclassical economic thought, work is not privileged; rather, it is modeled with an emphasis on exchange value, like all other commodities. The field of labor economics thereby analyzes the determinants of labor demand, labor supply, the price of labor (wages), and related topics by applying "the basic principles of neoclassical economic theory [to] the analysis of labor markets."[10]

One way in which this economic scholarship commodifies work is by treating it like any other factor of production on the demand side. Employers are assumed to maximize their profits by using the optimum amounts of labor, capital, and other inputs to produce goods and services for sale. Labor demand—the strength of an employer's desire to hire employees—is thus derived from the employer's profit-maximization problem, and labor demand curves can be drawn that show how many workers (or hours of labor) would be hired at various wage rates. In this way, economists analyze and forecast changes in demand for various occupations and skills based on other changes in the economy, such as increased globalization or the emergence of new information technologies.[11]

Economic scholarship also commodifies work on the supply side by treating work as something that individuals choose to sell in varying quantities in order to earn income and maximize their individual or household utility. Discussion of this labor supply decision is postponed until chapter 5; suffice it to say here that individuals are seen as generating labor supply curves just as employers generate labor demand curves. For employers and employees alike, hours of labor is simply one of a number of quantities to factor into the relevant optimization problem, and the optimum amount of labor to buy or sell in the labor market is determined in the same way as other factors of production of goods and services.

Like beer, computers, or other items of exchange, the allocation of work is seen as governed by the impersonal laws of supply and demand. When the supply of labor is low, its price (simplified as the wage rate, but in reality including diverse forms of compensation and benefits) will be bid up; when the demand for labor is low, its price will fall. The intersection of supply and demand determines the going wage rate, and "the theory of the determination of wages in a free market is simply a special case of the general theory of value."[12] This supply and demand framework therefore provides the basic economic way for thinking about how wages (and other terms and conditions of employment) are determined within a labor market for a specific job or type of worker. And in this model, work is implicitly conceptualized as a commodity.

The Invisible Hand of the Competitive Labor Market

The economic exchange of commodities, including labor, can occur in markets that are perfectly or imperfectly competitive, but *perfect* competition holds a special place in mainstream economic thought. Perfect competition occurs when no individual or organization has market power—all agents have complete information, all transactions are costless, property rights are legally protected, and other requirements are met such that all agents are equals. The power of perfect competition in economic thought stems from a long-standing theoretical result that scarce resources are optimally allocated and economic welfare is maximized by the invisible hand of economic activity in perfectly competitive markets.

Mainstream economic theorizing therefore sees labor unions as labor market monopolies that interfere with the efficient allocation of labor as a commodity and therefore harm the economy. Other labor market interventions such as minimum wage laws or paid parental leave mandates are similarly seen as distorting the optimal operation of free markets in which the commodity of labor should be freely exchanged like all other commodities. Theoretically, perfect competition causes all factors of production—including labor—to be rewarded by the economic value they contribute. As such, there is never "exploitation," because workers are paid according to what they contribute. In neoclassical economic thought, employees do not need labor unions or government regulations to protect against abuse by their employers. Rather, employees' best protection is a competitive labor market, because a substandard employer's employees will quit and work someplace else.[13]

While this is admittedly a stylized portrayal of a sophisticated body of economic theory that recognizes market imperfections, this is the type of simplified thinking frequently found in public policy debates under the banner of the neoliberal market ideology. This neoliberal market ideology emphasizes the importance of economic outcomes and believes that economic outcomes are best served by laissez-faire public policies that support property rights, free markets, and free trade. If the wage is simply the price of labor, then all social connotations regarding subsistence and minimum living conditions are lost, and prosperity equates to business prosperity.[14] This is a source of the old adage "What's good for General Motors is good for the country." Supporters of the neoliberal market ideology therefore oppose minimum wage laws, legal protections for labor unions, proposals for paid parental leaves, and other pro-worker public policies because of perceived negative consequences for economic efficiency. Underlying this neoliberal market thinking is the unstated conceptualization of work as a freely exchanged, generic commodity.

Lastly, from some perspectives, power and conflict are at the heart of the employment relationship (see chapter 7). But the mainstream economics emphasis on self-interested, voluntary exchanges of commodified work in competitive markets reduces power and conflict to sterile constructs that are seen through market-based lenses. Potential conflicts between employers and employees over the terms and conditions of employment are resolved by the labor market. Employers and employees agree to terms that are mutually beneficial, or look for other employees or employers when there is disagreement. Power is seen as what someone can command in the labor market, but this is determined by supply and demand. And when markets are working properly (that is, are perfectly competitive), supply and demand determine fair terms and conditions of employment that reflect economic value, not coercion or exploitation. As such, self-interested, mutually beneficial trades in competitive labor markets, not power and conflict, are central to mainstream economic conceptualizations of the employment relationship. While this perspective critically relies on the presence of labor markets that are perfectly competitive, it is also fundamentally rooted in seeing work as a commodity.

Labor Effort or Materialized Labor?

To conceptualize work as a commodity is to think of work as an abstract quantity that is bought and sold. But how should we think about what is being bought and sold? In a historical comparison of the emergence of wage labor in Germany and Britain, sociologist Richard Biernacki uncovers two distinct ways of imagining that work is a commodity. The dominant perspective in nineteenth-century Germany was that employers purchased "the timed appropriation of workers' labor power and disposition over workers' labor activity"; in nineteenth-century Britain, employers were seen as purchasing "workers' materialized labor via its products."[15] In Britain, when commercial markets that allowed for the free exchange of products developed, the conceptual nature of labor was rooted in the existing independent artisan and putting-out systems. This way of thinking about work was extended into the factory system by continuing to see workers as providing products, not effort or time, because the relaxation of legal restrictions on the free exchange of labor, which might have allowed for a new conceptualization of labor, did not occur until later. In Germany, in contrast, free markets for labor and commercial products developed at the same time, and a new way of thinking about wage labor emerged—that is, as workers selling control over their effort for specific periods of time.

Biernacki further shows how the difference between seeing commodified work as labor effort and as materialized products framed how employers and employees related to each other and experienced work in their daily lives.[16] Nineteenth-century German and British weavers were paid on the basis of piece rates, but German piece rates were based on how many times a worker performed a certain action, whereas British piece rates were based on the length of cloth produced. In other words, the German piece rates sought to measure labor effort, while the British piece rates measured materialized labor via the finished product. Since workers' conceptualizations of work provided their lens for thinking about how they experienced work, it also shaped their grievances. In seeing work as measured by time, German weavers demanded compensation for time spent waiting for materials; in seeing work as measured by the resulting product, British weavers demanded piece rates high enough to make up for time spent waiting for materials. When work is seen as labor effort, profits come from the effective use of this effort, and supervisory practices are seen as important. When work is seen as materialized in products, profits come from being able to sell these products at a higher price than the price at which they are purchased from the workers, and wage rates, not supervisory practices, are key. As a result, German textile strikes were much more likely to include disputes over the production process than British textile strikes, which instead focused primarily on wages. These comparisons not only illustrate different ways of conceptualizing work as a commodity but also reveal that conceptualizations of work are part of the culture that shapes everyday understandings and therefore practices. How work is conceptualized has real effects on how work is structured and experienced.

These two differing ways of imagining work as a commodity persist today. Salaried employment, for example, treats work as materialized in various outputs because salaried employees are rewarded for what they produce, not the time they put in. Hourly employment, in contrast, compensates individuals for time worked and thereby treats work as labor effort. Overtime pay, premium pay for working weekends, paid break time, and other time-related issues are therefore important issues for hourly workers, but not salaried. Some employer-employee disputes can also be seen as clashes between visions of work as labor effort or materialized labor. One such dispute is whether employees should be paid for time spent putting on and taking off safety equipment; another is the extent to which pay should be based on performance. In their research on work, economists tend to focus on the exchange value of labor. This is consistent with seeing work as materialized labor, because the exchange value of work is seen as rooted in workers' abilities to create valuable products. Sociologists are more likely to focus on the labor process, consistent with seeing work as labor effort (chapter 7). Similarly, pluralist industrial relations scholars and activists who advocate for equitable compensation for workers are implicitly seeking decent rewards for materialized labor (chapter 4). Marxist industrial relations scholars and activists who emphasize employee dignity and control in the workplace are implicitly seeing work as labor effort.

The Alienation and Subordination of Fictitious Commodities

One of the most influential critics of the conceptualization of work as a commodity was Karl Marx. In fact, Marx's sharp criticisms of capitalism are ultimately rooted in the capitalist commodification of work, and his landmark *Capital* opens with a discussion of commodities. It is here that Marx emphasized that a commodity has both a use value and an exchange value and argued that capitalism differs from precapitalist systems in valuing exchange over usefulness. From Marx's perspective, capitalism gives rise to a "fetishism of commodities" such that the emphasis on exchange value in a capitalist society is so pervasive that each commodity is seen as having an exchange value independent of how it is produced or used.[17] Just as so-called "primitive" religions endowed physical objects with sacred powers, so, too, does capitalism endow commodities with inherent, almost mystical, exchange values.

But, as Marx chided, "so far no chemist has ever discovered exchange value either in a pearl or a diamond." Rather, the values of commodities are constructed by people through personal desires, social norms of prestige, socially created laws and property rights, and other means. This, then, yields one of Marx's central concerns—endowing commodities with inherent value hides the underlying social relationships. This is particularly problematic for work because abstract, commodified work appears to have some objective value—the going rate of pay, for example—and employment appears to be the impersonal exchange of one commodity (labor power) for another (money). This commodified view covers up the underlying social phenomena that structure work—interpersonal relationships, social norms, and, of particular concern for Marx, unequal property rights and ownership structures. In other words, under capitalism, the narrow vision of work as an abstract commodity exchanged for money "causes the social relations of individuals to appear in the perverted form of a social relation between things."[18] From Marx's perspective, then, not only is work in capitalist systems an unequal power relation between labor and capital (chapter 7), but conceptualizing work as a commodity covers up these unequal power relations and shelters them from being questioned. Marx did not envy the feudal serf but thought that at least the serf would recognize his subordinated position because his compulsory labor was not disguised as an exchange of commodities.

Marx's other major concern with the commodification of work under capitalism is the resulting degradation of work. This is not simply a concern with the substandard physical and material conditions endured by individuals working long hours in dangerous conditions for low pay, but is also a more fundamental objection to the loss of one's essential humanness that comes from the commodification of work. Marx labeled this loss of humanness "alienation." To appreciate this perspective, first note that under capitalism, wage workers do not own the means of production such as tools or machines. Rather than selling the fruits of their labor (as is the case for the self-employed), individuals must sell their capacity for working ("labor power") to a capitalist who then sells whatever the workers produce. This was tremendously problematical for Marx because he believed that self-directed work is the essential quality of being human (chapter 9). The commodification of work therefore means that wage workers are forced to sell a critical part of themselves:

> The putting of labor-power into action—i.e., the work—is the active expression of the laborer's own life. And this life activity he sells to another person in order to secure the necessary means of life. His life-activity, therefore, is but a means of securing his own existence. He works that he may keep alive. He does not count the labor itself as a part of his life; it is rather a sacrifice of his life. It is a commodity that he has auctioned off to another.

In other words, workers are alienated because they lose touch with an essential part of their humanity, a concern eloquently captured by the German poet Friedrich von Schiller's critique of modernization several decades earlier:

Enjoyment was divorced from labor, the means from the end, the effort from the reward. Everlastingly chained to a single little fragment of the whole, a man develops into nothing but a fragment; everlastingly in his ear the monotonous sound of the wheel that he turns, he never develops the harmony of his being, and instead of putting the stamp of humanity upon his own nature, he becomes nothing more than the imprint of his occupation or of his specialized knowledge.[19]

Marx identified four ways in which workers are alienated under capitalism.[20] One, individuals are divorced from the product of their labor because the factory owner owns and controls what the workers produce. Two, because capitalists control how things are made, workers are also alienated from the process and activity of producing. In selling their labor power, workers surrender control of their actions to someone else. Three, creative work is seen as an essential feature of being human. By denying individuals control over what they produce and how they produce it, the previous two elements deprive humans of their essential nature. And four, because humans relate to each other through their work, they are alienated from each other.

It is tempting today to use these elements of alienation for thinking about specific job characteristics (e.g., some jobs allow for greater autonomy than others) and workers' subjective views of their jobs (e.g., some employees are more satisfied than others). Such an approach conceptualizes work as a potential source of personal fulfillment under the right circumstances (chapter 6). But note carefully that alienation in Marx's sense is not a subjective feeling of job dissatisfaction that varies from worker to worker, nor is it something that can be fixed by tweaking a job's characteristics. Rather, Marx's alienation is an objective, fundamental feature of paid employment under capitalism. When work is commodified such that one's labor power is sold to someone else for a wage or a salary, alienation results because "labor is external to the worker, i.e., it does not belong to his essential being; that in his work, therefore, he does not affirm himself but denies himself" and "the external character of labor for the worker appears in the fact that it is not his own, but someone else's, that it does not belong to him, that in it he belongs, not to himself, but to another." In sum, the concept of alienation is used by Marx to "display the devastating effect of capitalist production on human beings, on their physical and mental states and on the social processes of which they are a part."[21]

Or more crudely, by alienating individuals from their work, capitalism reduces humans to animals. From this perspective, the commodification of work is not just a barrier to personal fulfillment (chapter 6). Rather, it is a modern curse for the majority of individuals in a capitalist system who earn their living by working for others. Since Marx's time, the question of how to structure work to avoid alienation and instead achieve some greater purpose on a personal or societal level has been a particular concern in German scholarship and political thought, albeit increasingly dominated in recent years by Anglo-American conceptions of job satisfaction.[22]

Another important critic of the commodification of work was the noted economic historian Karl Polanyi, who saw the Industrial Revolution's commodification of both labor and land as overturning several thousand years of human history in which economic systems had served human and social needs, not vice versa:

> Labor and land are no other than the human beings themselves of which every society consists and the natural surroundings in which it exists. To include them in the market mechanism means to subordinate the substance of society itself to the laws of the market.

Polanyi recognizes that making work a commodity is necessary for creating market-based, capitalist societies, but he argues that work is not truly a commodity because, in a spirit reminiscent of Marx, "labor is only another name for a human activity which goes with life itself, which in its turn is not produced for sale but for entirely different reasons, nor can that activity be detached from the rest of life." To Polanyi, then, work under capitalism is a fictitious commodity, and we fail to recognize this fiction at our own peril.[23]

From these critical perspectives, workers are coerced into commodifying their labor. The enclosure movement in Britain from the fifteenth to the nineteenth centuries in which common lands were turned into private property is seen as impoverishing the peasantry and forcing them into wage work to survive. The dispossession of Native Americans from their land by Euro-American settlers and U.S. government policy similarly forced Native Americans to use "the one resource they still controlled: the strength of their hands and the sweat of their backs" and to start selling "what had not in their own cultures been a commodity: their labor power." The Spanish colonial government's requirement that tributes in sixteenth-century South America be paid in money rather than in kind forced indigenous Indians into wage labor in silver mines. In the indigenous Setswana language of southern Africa, the precolonial word *dira* captures the indigenous, non-commodified idea of productive work creating food and other products that sustain the community; the word *bereka,* derived from the colonizing Afrikaner's word *werk,* refers to paid employment. The former is seen as a form of self-construction, the latter as self-destruction and alienation that is forced by European colonization. From these perspectives, then, the rate of participation in the formal labor market is not a measure of progress but instead measures "the degree of resource loss and dependency" of previously self-sufficient cultures.[24]

Devaluing Noncommodified Work

Industrialization and the widespread commodification of work significantly altered the previously close relationship between the production of goods and the reproduction (broadly defined) of human life as the former was moved out of the household and into the factory. In the process, a popular ideology of separate spheres emerged in the nineteenth century—the male breadwinner's world of public economic activity and the woman's world of private household tasks, at least for white women who could afford to avoid paid employment. Work in these two spheres is conceptualized very differently— paid employment is valued for its economic contributions, while domestic work is characterized by visions of the "unproductive housewife."[25] And in the neoliberal market ideology, there is nothing worse than being labeled unproductive.

Even before the unproductive housewife was cemented in the social imagination in the nineteenth century, Adam Smith pronounced domestic work caring for a household to be unproductive because it does not create valuable commodities:

> There is one sort of labour which adds to the value of the subject upon which it is bestowed: there is another which has no such effect. The former, as it produces a value, may be called productive; the latter, unproductive labour. Thus the labour of a manufacturer adds, generally, to the value of the materials which he works upon, that of his own maintenance, and of his master's profit. The labour of a menial servant, on the contrary, adds to the value of nothing.

That this domestic activity is often unpaid further adds to its devaluing:

> Domestic labour, overwhelmingly women's labour, is unwaged; lacking the wage as a signifier of work, it becomes insignificant. It does not appear as "real" work. It is not "worth" anything monetarily. It is a "labour of love," with all the attendant mystification that is involved.

Women's economic contributions have therefore been devalued by the commodification of work that arises under capitalism and that is embraced in mainstream economic theorizing, in spite of the critiques of feminist economics and other feminist scholarship (chapter 8). At least some industrialized legal systems similarly "treat women's home work as if it were not value-producing labor"; for example, "the U.S. legal system conceptualizes housework as solely an expression of affection, the currency of familial emotions." In these ways, some feminist scholars argue that capitalism is a patriarchal system that exploits women.[26]

The commodification of work can also be criticized for devaluing other forms of work that do not appear related to the key capitalist elements of commodity production, profit, and market exchange. As just one example, consider Euro-American views of Native Americans. In the nineteenth century, Native American work activities like fishing and hunting were seen by white settlers as more like a sport than work and therefore were rendered less important than Euro-American forms of work. By labeling Native American agricultural practices as primitive because they were focused more on subsistence than extraction for profit, white settlers deemed Native Americans as unfit for productive agricultural work, and thereby rationalized the taking of Native American lands. The devaluing of nonwaged work can also occur in noncapitalist systems. In Communist China under Mao, if work "was pursued outside a household-based context and produced social exchange value, it was compensated and valued [whereas] if it either was done in the home or did not produce exchange value, it was uncompensated and devalued."[27] In these ways, a focus on commodified work in the form of stable, full-time paid jobs can make other forms of work invisible within capitalist or noncapitalist societies.

Limiting the Commodification of Work

In modern capitalist societies, work is a commodity. Like other commodities, labor is bought and sold in the marketplace and possesses both use and exchange values. Labor markets are important for allocating labor and are a significant influence on how work is experienced in our daily lives. Our understanding of work would be incomplete, then, without conceptualizing work as a commodity. Economics studies the production, distribution, and consumption of commodities, so it should not be a surprise that work is analyzed as a commodity most frequently in this discipline. Economic theorizing therefore provides a rigorous framework for thinking about labor demand, labor supply, wage determination, and a host of other work-related issues. Furthermore, the theoretical ability of Adam Smith's invisible hand to maximize efficiency when work is a commodity in perfectly competitive labor markets reveals why many economists and adherents to the neoliberal market ideology support laissez-faire approaches to public policies on work. It should be noted that critics argue that neoliberal market supporters favor a neoliberal ideology not because of a sincere belief in overall efficiency, but because it gives legitimacy to the power and wealth they have been able to accumulate.

However, irrespective of the theoretical power of economics and of the true reasons for championing a neoliberal market ideology, we should not fully commodify work. The mainstream economics conceptualization of work as a generic commodity governed by the laws of supply and demand is part of the mainstream economics vision of itself as a value-free, nonideological science of the allocation of scarce resources. But economists have not kept these "scientific" principles of how the economy works from becoming normative principles of how the economy *should* work—such as beliefs that labor should be allocated like any other commodity and economic efficiency should be the primary concern. Contrary to popular claims within economics, this market-based conceptualization of the commodified employment relationship is not devoid of ethical content but instead is rooted very strongly in two specific ethical theories—utilitarianism and libertarianism—that have been widely criticized for their narrow conceptions of human concerns.[28]

When work is a commodity to be optimally allocated, concerns with working and living conditions are marginalized; virtues, communities, relationships, and how individuals are treated are only important so far as they increase aggregate welfare. By focusing on market-based activities, unpaid caring for others is not seen as "real" work, and women's economic contributions are rendered invisible. The full commodification of work can therefore be criticized for the neoliberal market ideology it creates.

Conceptually, then, the commodification of work should be limited. Though it seems that people go "off" to work away from their homes each day, work is too important a human activity to be separated from a worker's family life and community life. Work should not be conceptualized as a purely economic activity undertaken in a distinct sphere of one's life. Work under capitalism has the elements of a commodity, but work is also undertaken by individuals seeking personal fulfillment and identity within employment relationships that are embedded in rich social relations and democratic societies. Work need not be only paid employment exchanged as a commodity, but can also include unpaid caring for others and other forms of work not rewarded by the capitalist marketplace. These additional conceptualizations of work are the subject of many of the remaining chapters and should be used to complement the understandings that derive from seeing work as a commodity, and to temper the neoliberal market ideology that treats workers as just another commodity subject to the vagaries of supply and demand.

CHAPTER 4

Work as Occupational Citizenship

> It is shameful and inhuman, however, to use men as
> things for gain and to put no more value on them
> than what they are worth in muscle and energy.
>
> —Pope Leo XIII (1810–1903)

When work is conceptualized as a commodity, it is seen as governed by the marketplace, with outcomes determined by supply and demand. There is then little basis for considering standards for work that go beyond the freedom for individuals to work in any occupation and quit at will so that work is efficiently allocated. An alternative conceptualization is to reject that work is purely a commodity and to instead emphasize that work is done by human beings who are members of communities and societies. From this perspective, workers are citizens who are entitled to decent working and living conditions that are determined by standards of human dignity, not supply and demand, and to meaningful forms of self-determination in the workplace that go beyond the freedom to quit. In other words, workers are entitled to equity—fairness in the distribution of economic rewards, the administration of employment policies, and the provision of employee security—and voice, which means meaningful participation in workplace decision making.[1] In this way, work is conceptualized as occupational citizenship. That is, work is not a commodity but an activity pursued by human members of a community with inherent equal worth who are entitled to certain rights and standards of dignity and self-determination.

The principle of rights for workers as citizens of human communities dates back at least to the nineteenth century, and the term "industrial citizenship" is usually traced back to sociologist T. H. Marshall, who used it to describe the acquisition of economic and social rights in the workplaces of industrialized societies through labor union representation and collective bargaining. Contemporary treatments replace "industrial" with "occupational" because of the importance of nonindustrial employment and other forms of work, and also incorporate both individual and collective rights. Thus, occupational citizenship is broadly defined here as the achievement of rights to which workers are entitled because of membership in a human community and which are attained by institutional rather than market forces.[2] To see workers as citizens is to decommodify them, to give them a status as more than just factors of production (chapter 3) or individuals seeking personal fulfillment or identities (chapters 6 and 9). The conceptualization of occupational citizenship, therefore, seeks to ensure that equity and voice are achieved for *all* workers without being dependent on the vagaries of supply and demand or managerial goodwill. This conceptualization is a descendant of the nineteenth-century concerns with wage slavery, but the contemporary focus is on adding labor standards to make work consistent with citizenship rather than rejecting paid employment as incompatible with the independence required for citizenship (chapter 2).

Conceptualizing work as occupational citizenship reflects the view of work in the field of industrial relations and of some scholars in law, sociology, economics, political science, history, and related fields. This conceptualization is also closely related to conceptualizations of workers' rights as human rights. Human rights are universal rights that result from the basic quality of being human: "Certain things ought not to be done to any human being and certain other things ought to be done for every human being." Whether from a citizenship or human rights foundation, the lists of desired workers' rights are largely interchangeable, and the justifications for these rights are complementary, though there are some subtle differences. Debates over the technicalities of citizenship versus human rights, however, should not obscure what is intended here as a simple foundation: "Labor is comprised of human beings endowed with economic, physical, psychological, and social needs, who participate as citizens in a democratic society" and therefore should not be treated as a commodity.[3]

This secular perspective is not intended to slight the complementary religious foundations for treating labor as more than a commodity. Buddhism, Hinduism, Judaism, Christianity, and Islam all "share a universal interest in addressing the integrity, worth, and dignity of all persons, and, consequently, the duty toward other people." The source of inherent human dignity, therefore, can just as easily be seen as theological rather than political or moral, and the implications for thinking about work are the same.[4]

More Than a Commodity, Entitled to Citizenship/Human Rights

There are diverse objections to the complete commodification of work (chapter 3). For example, some argue that labor cannot be managed simply as other factors of production because of the psychological and social aspects of human beings (chapters 6 and 7). But central to this chapter is a rejection of the belief that labor is a commodity on the grounds that labor "is embodied in human beings and thus brings to the workplace and labor market a much higher moral significance" than other commodities or factors of production. To treat labor as a commodity is to treat it as a means, in violation of one of the central principles of Kantian ethics: "Act in such a way that you always treat humanity, whether in your own person or in the person of any other, never simply as a means, but always at the same time as an end." Similarly, the theologies of the world's major religions would probably all agree with the words of Pope John Paul II in the encyclical *Laborem Exercens* ("On Human Work"): "The value of human work is not primarily the kind of work being done but the fact that the one who is doing it is a person. . . . The primary basis of the value of work is man himself." Consequently, as set forth in Pope Leo XIII's famous encyclical *Rerum Novarum* ("On the Condition of Workers"), "Justice demands that the dignity of human personality be respected in [workers]. . . . It is shameful and inhuman, however, to use men as things for gain and to put no more value on them that what they are worth in muscle and energy."[5]

Those at the bottom of the labor market, however, are at great risk of being valued as just muscle and energy. Mid-nineteenth- and early twentieth-century exposés—such as books by Friedrich Engels or Henry Mayhew, novels by Charles Dickens, Émile Zola, and Upton Sinclair or the photography of Lewis Hines and Jacob Riis—revealed the dangerous working conditions in "dark Satanic mills" and the horrible living conditions in the urban slums. Modern exposés similarly illustrate the low pay, long hours, dangerous conditions, and tenuous lives endured by workers and their families from London to Minneapolis, and Vancouver to Guangdong.[6] The early exposés created movements within and outside of academia to decommodify labor, and the contemporary exposés underscore the continued relevance of this thinking.

Notable among the early academic efforts were those led by Sidney and Beatrice Webb in Britain and John R. Commons in the United States to craft an institutional approach to economic analysis that emphasized the human qualities of labor. Unlike the radical followers of Karl Marx, the early institutionalists did not seek the abolishment of capitalism but rather, in the words of Commons, "to save capitalism by making it good." But in contrast to neoclassical economists who emphasized efficiency and consumption in allegedly amoral terms (chapter 3), the early institutionalists recognized the moral implications of economic activity and saw the ultimate goal of human activity as "the full and harmonious development in each individual of all human faculties." Efficiency is important in this endeavor, but so is ensuring that workers are treated fairly, can live decent lives, and have opportunities for personal growth. In addition to subscribing to an institutionalist paradigm within economics, the Webbs, Commons, and others founded the then closely related field of industrial relations, which focuses on studying and improving the operation of the employment relationship. The early idea that labor is more than a commodity continues to be embodied in modern industrial relations and institutionalist approaches to labor economics. Similarly, feminist and social economists see work as part of a complex system of social provisioning, not just material production, and therefore reject the mainstream economics view of labor as a commodity.[7]

The rejection of labor as a commodity on the basis of respect for human dignity is closely intertwined with the principles of democracy and civic republicanism—citizenship, political equality, and deliberative decision making. As articulated by an early institutionalist,

> The welfare of wage earners in industrial communities is the concern of everybody. As citizens, as employers, as consumers, as workers, in one way or another all are affected by the prosperity or adversity, the contentment or unrest, the efficiency or inefficiency, the wealth or the poverty of the wage earner. . . . These truths are particularly applicable to a democracy which of its nature is forced to admit the equality of man, to affirm the equal right of access to the good things in life, and to take the measures necessary to the realization of these opportunities. The submergence of any section of the people either by the tyranny of the few or by the unexpected consequences of industrial development is abhorrent to the principles of democracy.

The Webbs thus argued that "if the democratic state is to attain its fullest and finest development, it is essential that the actual needs and desires of the human agents concerned should be the main considerations in determining the conditions of employment." Democratic states have multiple methods for protecting workers' rights and achieving these objectives. Prior to the enactment of such methods, Commons argued, workers "are treated as commodities to be bought and sold according to supply and demand. Afterward they are treated as citizens with rights against others on account of their value to the nation as a whole." The Webbs and Commons, therefore, anticipated by several decades what was to become a central idea of industrial citizenship that continues to endure today—that citizenship rights for workers are intended to avoid the complete commodification of labor.[8]

Labor unions and other reformist organizations have long histories of advocating for a richer conceptualization of work than as a commodity controlled by the marketplace, such as this description of a federation of British miners' unions from 1892: "They held it was a vital principle that a man by his labor should live, and notwithstanding all the teachings of the [neoclassical] economists, all the doctrines taught by way of supply and demand, they said there was a greater doctrine over-riding all these, and that was the doctrine of humanity." Support for this doctrine of humanity at the conclusion of World War I, and a variety of political factors, led to the founding of the International Labour Organization (ILO) based on the principle that "labor should not be regarded as a commodity or article of commerce." The ILO continues its work today as a specialized agency of the United Nations premised on the idea that "all human beings, irrespective of race, creed or sex, have the right to pursue both their material well-being and their spiritual development in conditions of freedom and dignity, of economic security and equal opportunity"—or what the ILO now simply calls "decent work."[9]

Similarly, work-related human rights are enshrined in the Universal Declaration of Human Rights adopted by the United Nations in 1948:

- Adequate pay ("just and favorable remuneration ensuring for himself and his family an existence worthy of human dignity")
- Benefits ("medical care and necessary social services, and the right to security in the event of unemployment, sickness, disability, widowhood, old age or other lack of livelihood in circumstances beyond his control" as well as "periodic holidays with pay")
- Decent working conditions ("just and favorable conditions of work" and "reasonable limitation of working hours")
- Non-discrimination ("the right to equal pay for equal work" and "free choice of employment")
- Rights to unionize ("the right to form and join trade unions for the protection of his interests")

Human rights advocates therefore argue that global corporations and international bodies such as the World Trade Organization are obligated to respect and promote workers' rights, though this obligation is frequently unfulfilled. National governments, too, are sharply criticized by those who see labor rights as human rights, especially for failing to adequately protect workers' rights to unionize and engage in collective bargaining. While not without problems, the human rights perspective therefore provides a complementary way to think about the citizenship standards that should apply to work, particularly if we see "human rights" not as a particular political theory but as an umbrella concept that represents the pursuit of human dignity and the decommodification of work.[10]

Imperfect Labor Markets and Bargaining-Power Inequalities

Debates over how to best provide adequate standards for the working and living conditions of workers and their families are as sharp today as they were over a hundred years ago. One perspective emphasizes individual initiative and the freedom to contract in free markets. In this analysis from 1875, little would be changed if it were written today, except for avoiding the sexist implication that only men are workers:

> Workmen bring a certain valuable service to the market, just such a service as the capitalist wants, and he has to offer just such a service as they want, namely, wages. Now let them come to a free and fair agreement on the terms of the exchange. Let the workmen by all means make the very best terms they can; let them insist to the last penny on all which they can get elsewhere, for the value of their service is determined . . . by what it will bring. . . . The more intelligence and skill and self-respect a workman has, the better prepared he is to strike the bargain and secure his just due. If the employer will not yield him this, let him have done with it at once, and go elsewhere.[11]

This reliance on the labor market to provide fair working and living conditions depends heavily on the labor market being *perfectly* competitive. In economic theory, perfect competition requires a particular set of conditions, such as full information and costless transactions so that buyers and sellers are equally powerful to accept the best deal and equally powerless to impose a bad deal on others (chapter 3).

Institutionalist labor economists, industrial relations scholars, and others reject the neoclassical economics assumption that labor markets are perfectly competitive. If the labor market was perfectly competitive, anyone could always instantly land a job for which they are qualified at the market rate of pay and benefits. But as noted by economist Alan Manning, "People go to the pub to celebrate when they get a job rather than greeting the news with a shrug . . . and people go to the pub to drown their sorrows when they lose their job rather than picking up another one straight away." And, as also noted by Manning, contrary to the implications of the perfect-competition model, all of an employer's workers do not quit if the employer cuts wages by a penny.[12] Rather, there are important "frictions" that render labor markets imperfectly competitive. For example, workers have mobility costs and cannot change jobs without time, effort, and financial sacrifice. Even assuming away problems of unemployment in loose labor markets that make it difficult to find jobs, switching employers might entail starting over at the bottom of the seniority ladder, losing unvested retirement benefits, finding new health care providers under a new insurance plan, and, in the case of geographical relocation, paying for the financial costs of moving and finding new housing and the emotional costs of relocating one's family.

With nontrivial mobility costs and other complications, labor markets are imperfectly competitive, and wages and other terms and conditions of employment are not completely determined by supply and demand. Rather, institutions matter. Employers frequently have the power to set wages and establish other employment practices within some boundaries established by (imperfect) labor market competition. In other words, there is a range of indeterminacy, and the employment relationship is a bargained exchange between employers and employees with (at least some) competing interests such that employment outcomes depend on the elements of the environment that determine each party's bargaining power. Decent working and living conditions, therefore, depend on employees having adequate bargaining power. And even Adam Smith recognized that employers often have the upper hand:

> The workmen desire to get as much, the masters to give as little as possible. . . . In all such disputes the masters can hold out much longer. A landlord, a farmer, a master manufacturer, or merchant, though they did not employ a single workman, could generally live a year or two upon the stocks which they have already acquired. Many workmen could not subsist a week, few could subsist a month, and scarce any a year without employment. In the long-run the workman may be as necessary to his master as his master is to him, but the necessity is not so immediate.[13]

The increased mobility of capital in the twenty-first century that has resulted from information technologies and globalization has magnified, not narrowed, employers' bargaining-power advantages over many workers. With greater bargaining power, employers can pay low wages for working long hours under autocratic and dangerous working conditions. Labor market competition does not provide a check against such practices (as assumed in the neoliberal market ideology) but in fact encourages them, especially in periods of high unemployment. This is one of the central views of pluralist industrial relations thought—substandard wages and working conditions are the result of bargaining-power inequalities in destructively competitive labor markets.[14]

These concerns are reinforced by the theory of labor market segmentation. In the textbook model in mainstream economic thought, the labor market freely adjusts to changes in labor supply and demand, and the main determinant of workers' earnings is therefore their level of human capital (chapter 5). An institutionalist perspective, in contrast, highlights institutional realities that restrict this free adjustment and instead create noncompeting segmented labor markets. Internal labor market theory, for example, posits that economic, social, and political factors cause certain employers to construct job ladders. Workers are hired into these job ladders via specific ports of entry (e.g., management trainee) and then advance up the career ladder via internal training and promotions. For outsiders who, for example, increase their education to improve their earnings, employment opportunities do not necessarily result, because the limited ports of entry shield the "good" jobs from external labor market pressures. Other institutional realities might include the difficulties workers have in changing their skills to match technological changes; discrimination; and differences in the quality of workers' social networks (chapter 7). The end result is labor market segmentation in which there are a limited number of good jobs in the primary labor market and excess workers in a secondary labor market characterized by low wages and job insecurity. Today's concerns with overeducation, the inability of the working poor to break the cycle of poverty, the use of contingent or temporary workers to shield stable core employees, and persistent informal labor markets in developing economies all reinforce the relevance of labor market segmentation for understanding work.[15]

In sum, in contrast to mainstream economic theory in which labor market inequalities simply reflect nonmarket inequalities (e.g., differences in human capital or individual initiative), institutionalist labor economists and pluralist industrial relations scholars see real-world labor markets as *creating* inequality.[16] Returning to the conceptualization of citizenship rights, such inequalities threaten not only material standards for workers and their families but also political freedom (chapter 2). From this perspective, full citizenship rights (or human rights) are therefore denied by the inequalities inherent in the laissez-faire employment relationship.

Employee Voice

Employee voice has long been an important issue in work. Human beings have innate needs for autonomy and self-determination. Citizens in a participatory democracy are entitled to have input into decisions that affect their lives. Nongovernmental institutions should not stifle the values of civic republicanism that underlie our conceptions of democracy:

> Can we accept that democratic government, which requires of the individual independent judgment and active participation in deciding important social issues, will flourish when in one of the most important spheres of life—that of work and economic production—the great majority of individuals are denied the opportunity to take an effective part in reaching the decisions which vitally affect their lives? It does not seem to me that a man can live in a condition of complete and unalterable subordination during much of his life, and yet acquire the habits of responsible choice and self-government which political democracy calls for.

These needs and rights manifest themselves in the workplace as employee voice. Numerous surveys of workers from a variety of countries strongly document that employees want a voice in their workplaces. These surveys also reveal a diversity of views on the most desirable forms of employee voice. An inclusive perspective is therefore appropriate, such that employee voice should be broadly recognized as the ability to express opinions and have meaningful input, both individually and collectively, over the full range of issues confronting workers, from job-related decision making, to the terms and conditions of employment, to business issues.[17]

The most basic form of employee voice is individual voice. In the neoliberal market ideology, this is exercised by one's feet in the form of quitting, and economist Albert Hirschman's popular exit-voice framework slightly broadens this by seeing voice as a complaint mechanism that can be used instead of quitting. A richer conception of individual voice is the ability to make decisions about one's own work, refuse unsafe work, and set working hours. This is partly captured by what is labeled autonomy in human resource management: "substantial freedom, independence, and discretion to the individual in scheduling the work and in determining the procedures to be used in carrying it out." The human resource management perspective is that autonomy is a job characteristic that can provide intrinsic work motivation and should therefore be designed into jobs when warranted by the productivity gains (chapter 6). Similarly, voice in the high-performance paradigm in human resource management is seen as employee involvement in sharing ideas for process improvement (e.g., quality circles) or as working autonomously with others (e.g., self-directed work teams) to improve organizational performance (chapter 6). To see work as occupational citizenship, however, is to go beyond the efficiency aspects of voice to also value human needs, even when employee voice does not improve productivity. Admittedly, the modern employment relationship entails sacrificing autonomy in return for pay, but the promotion of mental health (via task discretion), physical health (via refusing unsafe work), families (via controls over working time), and political discourse (via free speech) demands that individual self-determination should not be solely determined by efficiency concerns.[18]

Against a backdrop of imperfect labor markets that render individual employee-employer relations unequal, industrial relations scholarship traditionally discounts individual voice in favor of collective voice that provides industrial democracy. To start with, industrial relations scholars seek to understand the rules of the workplace. Organizations are therefore seen as industrial governments that can be autocratic, technocratic, or democratic. The ideals of fairness and self-determination inherent in occupational citizenship are best served by the democratic form of industrial government ("industrial democracy") in which unilateral, unchecked managerial authority is replaced by orderly rules, participatory rule-making, checks and balances, and due process in dispute resolution. That (non-Marxist) industrial relations scholars see the employment relationship as analogous to a pluralist political society in which multiple parties (e.g., employers and employees) have legitimate but sometimes conflicting interests reinforces the preference for decision-making and dispute-resolution processes that respect a diversity of rights and interests.[19]

Dating back at least to the Webbs' classic *Industrial Democracy*, industrial democracy in Anglophone countries has traditionally been seen as requiring that employees be represented by labor unions independent of employers and the state. When wages and other terms and conditions of employment are determined by collective bargaining rather than by unilateral employer action, employees have a voice at the negotiating table. Collective bargaining agreements replace managerial whims with orderly rules. A grievance procedure provides due process in the resolution of disputes. Labor unions are seen as essential in all of these activities because imperfectly competitive labor markets and capitalist legal systems favor employers. Labor unions that are legally and financially independent of employers are the needed counterweight to managerial power and are therefore necessary for giving employee voice legitimacy through the negotiation and enforcement of collective bargaining agreements. Consistent with this thinking, labor unions have a long history of promoting collective power as a way to bring democracy to the workplace and to strengthen political democracy by creating independent and responsible rather than subordinate and repressed citizen-workers.[20] As will be discussed later in this chapter, labor unions are also particularly privileged in industrial relations thought because of their ability to equalize bargaining power and achieve decent pay and working conditions for workers who would otherwise be at the mercy of powerful employers in imperfect labor markets.

In Anglophone countries, then, collective forms of *nonunion* voice are controversial. During the welfare capitalism movement of the 1920s in the United States (chapter 6), some companies created nonunion employee representation plans in which a group of employees would meet with managers to discuss employment conditions. While these plans provided more benefits to employees than their critics are willing to recognize, there were notable examples where these plans were manipulated by managers to prevent employees from forming independent labor unions. Consequently, U.S. labor law now treats nonunion employee representation plans as illegal sham unions. Nevertheless, against the backdrop of corporate efforts to create quality circles, joint consultative committees, and other nonunion mechanisms for discussing workplace issues, debates over whether such plans are legitimate (albeit limited) vehicles of employee voice or company-dominated tools for undermining or preventing unionization are again contentious in twenty-first-century industrial relations in North America, Britain, and elsewhere.[21]

In continental Europe, the situation is different. Collective bargaining tends to be a regional or sectoral activity such that employee voice in the workplace occurs instead through systems of codetermination that include works councils and employee representation on corporate management boards as provided by each country's labor laws. A works council is a committee of employees elected to represent all the workers (except senior executives)—skilled and unskilled, blue and white collar, union and nonunion—in dealings with management. In some cases, this workplace representation is intimately connected to unionism (e.g., Spain and Sweden), while in others, workplace committees receive assistance from unions but are legally independent from them (e.g., France and Germany). A company must establish and support a works council if a certain number of employees indicate a desire. Works councils cannot strike, but depending on the specific issue, they have rights of codetermination (joint determination), consultation, or information. Labor unionists outside of Europe tend to see works councils as a substitute for independent unions. But many pluralist academics see statutorily protected works councils as a possible method for enhancing employee voice to at least partly compensate for a decline in union strength, such as in the United States and Australia.[22]

In 1994, a European Union directive required companies with significant operations in at least two European countries to establish European Works Councils so that employees can be consulted and receive information on issues of transnational interest. While European Works Councils have the potential to enhance workers' citizenship rights in multinational corporations, most of the evidence suggests that their actual effects have so far been modest.[23]

Striking a Balance in the Employment Relationship

There are multiple frames of reference for thinking about employer-employee conflict. Human resource management is based on a frame of reference that assumes that employer-employee conflict is the manifestation of poorly designed managerial practices and that the right policies can align employer-employee interests and largely remove conflict from the employment relationship (chapter 6). This is called a unitarist frame of reference because of its emphasis on achieving a unity of interests between an employer and its employees. At the other end of the spectrum, Marxist and other critical perspectives see the employment relationship as inherently characterized by sharply antagonistic employer-employee conflict (chapter 7). A third perspective—the pluralist perspective, most closely associated with (non-Marxist) industrial relations—occupies a middle ground such that employers and employees are seen as having a mixture of conflicting objectives (e.g., higher wages versus lower labor costs) and shared objectives (e.g., productive workers, profitable employers, a healthy economy). This mixture provides the incentive for compromise, but unlike in the unitarist perspective, workers and employers are assumed to have some conflicts of interest that are inherent in the employment relationship.[24]

A central premise of the pluralist perspective on the employment relationship is that these conflicts should be balanced. The pluralist industrial relations paradigm fully respects capitalism and business owners' need to make a profit. Economic efficiency is acknowledged as important for job creation and economic prosperity. But in contrast to mainstream economic thought and the neoliberal market agenda, efficiency is not paramount. Work should be "tempered by more humane considerations" than "a purely Darwinian view of unrestrained labor market competition." A true industrial democracy requires the protection of all stakeholders in the employment relationship—owners, workers, consumers, and the public. Balancing workers' rights and employers' property rights is necessary for striking a balance between efficiency, equity, and voice.[25]

The vision of a pluralistic employment relationship parallels the pluralist political society's acceptance of the legitimacy of multiple stakeholders, and the need to mediate their competing interests. This parallel further reinforces the conceptualization of work as occupational *citizenship* in which the rights of the parties stem from their membership in a pluralistic community. Citizenship also brings obligations, and the parties to the employment relationship have obligations to adhere to the agreed-upon terms and conditions of the employment bargain. By defining rights and obligations, citizenship also legitimizes certain inequalities.[26] In the case of occupational citizenship, Anglophone citizenship rights do not extend to, using a U.S. legal phrase, the "core of entrepreneurial control." This legitimizes the exclusion of employees from processes that make investment, plant closing, pricing, and other business decisions. Occupational citizenship is therefore consistent with the pluralist focus on seeking a decommodified, balanced employment relationship.

But how to achieve this balance? In some cases, high-skilled workers may have sufficient market power to obtain decent wages and working conditions on their own, and some companies may choose a progressive human resource management strategy that treats workers fairly and provides for involvement in decision making. The twin pluralist assumptions of imperfect labor markets and inherent employer-employee conflicts of interests, however, mean that pluralist adherents are unable to rely on markets or managerial enlightened self-interest and competence to protect workers' interests in all situations. This is not to say that all corporations are exploitative, but it recognizes that some corporations put their interests ahead of their employees (and communities), especially when times are tough.

Pluralist industrial relations thought therefore uniquely embraces nonmarket, nonmanagerial institutions for balancing employers' and employees' objectives and for achieving occupational citizenship. Dating back to the late nineteenth century, labor unions and collective bargaining have been central institutions in industrial relations for balancing competing employment relationship objectives by protecting workers. The economic, legal, and political resources of modern corporations are seen as giving employers a significant power advantage over *individual* employees in imperfectly competitive labor markets. The natural solution to this problem is to have employees pool their resources by joining together and forming labor unions. In other words, corporations are essentially unionized shareholders—organized collectives of individual investors who benefit from pooling their resources and hiring experts—so a level playing field is best achieved by unionized rather than individual employees. Pluralist thought therefore has long criticized the anti-union views of business as being hypocritical:

> Stockholders unite their accumulations of capital and knowledge in a particular line of business and create a simple agency called a corporation. The agency secures the best skill and ability money will command to conduct its affairs. Thus, supplied with a sagacious and powerful representative, they stand back and say to their laborers through this representative: "No representative from you will be heard. You each must speak and act for yourself."[27]

In addition to providing economic protection for workers through enhanced bargaining power, labor unions, as mentioned earlier in this chapter, are also seen as an important source of employee voice. Moreover, unlike the neoliberal market ideology and unitarist perspectives, pluralist thought sees employer-employee conflict as a natural part of the employment relationship. Collective bargaining and formal grievance procedures are seen as methods for institutionalizing employment relationship conflict so that it can be handled productively, without excessive efficiency losses. These additional roles for labor unions further reinforce unions' privileged place in the pluralist paradigm as promoting a balance between efficiency, equity, and voice. Pluralist thought and an occupational citizenship conceptualization of work therefore provide the intellectual foundations for legal supports for labor unions and collective bargaining in many countries.[28]

Pluralist industrial relations also favors, as a complement to labor unions, government regulation of the employment relationship to help advance workers' interests.[29] Workers' compensation and unemployment insurance programs can provide important social safety nets that cushion workers and their families against the insecurities of workplace accidents and the business cycle. Minimum or living wage laws are intended to foster at least some minimal level of living standards. Legislated safety standards, antidiscrimination requirements, family leave mandates, mandatory information and consultation procedures, and other regulations are further seen as methods for ensuring that workers achieve occupational citizenship as healthy, respected members of the community. What is called employment law or individual labor law, depending on the country, is therefore a significant area of both research and policy enactment.

Seeing work as occupational citizenship therefore yields views of labor unions and government regulation that are quite different from those generated from other conceptualizations of work. When work is disutility traded in competitive markets (chapters 3 and 5), unions are labor market monopolies that reduce economic welfare by impeding the operation of competitive markets and violating the liberties of individuals to freely enter into economic relationships. Work-related government mandates are similarly seen as impediments to both efficiency and liberty. When work is seen as a human resource (chapter 6), the focus on the individual fulfillment of intrinsic rewards makes labor market institutions that provide collective and material rewards of little interest. Moreover, the unitarist assumption that is central to seeing work as a human resource renders labor unions and government laws unnecessary because corporate human resource management policies are assumed to satisfy workers' needs. The presence of a labor union or employment law is taken as an indication of poor human resource management practices, and unions are further seen as bringing undesirable conflict to the workplace and undermining employer-employee cooperation.[30]

Seeing work as characterized by antagonistic capital-labor conflict that is deeply rooted in hierarchical, capitalist social relations (chapter 7) results in an equivocal perspective on labor unions and work-related public policies. On the one hand, as this critical perspective embraces the importance of human dignity, labor market institutions that aid workers are beneficial. On the other hand, to the extent that the only legitimate interests are those of labor, not capital, the pluralist pursuit of equitable compromises is seen as misguided. Bargaining for or legislating improved wages and working conditions gives legitimacy to the structural inequalities inherent in the capitalist employment relationship and perpetuates workers' acceptance of a system in which they are exploited. Put a little differently, if worker alienation is inherent in capitalism, as Marx believed (chapter 3), then collective bargaining, minimum wage laws, and other methods for achieving occupational citizenship cannot solve this fundamental problem because they leave capitalist social relations unchanged. Critical scholars and activists therefore criticize conservative labor unions for not doing enough to challenge employer power and raise working-class consciousness, and instead advocate for uniting labor unions as part of a social movement that champions social justice for the working class. Seeing work as a social relation also refocuses research attention on unions away from questions of why workers join unions toward issues of how the social relations of work contribute toward collective mobilization.[31]

There are a number of ways, then, for trying to achieve the objectives of the employment relationship. Even within the pluralist approach emphasizing industrial citizenship, there are a variety of national industrial relations models with varying levels of collective bargaining coverage, bargaining centralization/decentralization, legal protections for unions, and mandated forms of consultation. In northern Europe outside of Britain, industrial relations systems tend to follow a variety of corporatist models in which the major employers association, the key labor union federation, and the government negotiate high-level social partnership agreements on social and economic issues. In this way, workers' interests are directly represented in national policymaking. In southern Europe, industrial relations is more highly politicized, with protest strikes used to pressure government policymaking. Anglophone countries follow more of a liberal market model, even when implementing pluralistic attempts to balance employer and employee interests, such as the National Labor Relations Act in the United States. Labor unions therefore operate to varying degrees within the context of the market, class, and civil society. More generally, it is apparent that there are varieties of capitalism rather than a singular model. Much remains to be learned about how these varieties of capitalism affect industrial relations systems and the provision of occupational citizenship in an era of globalization.[32]

Occupational Citizenship under Siege

The conceptualization of work as occupational citizenship is an important one. It forces society to confront difficult questions about the rights and standards that workers should be entitled to as free, autonomous human beings. Ideals of inherent human dignity rooted in secular, humanist, and spiritual belief systems can provide the moral foundation for preventing the complete commodification of workers in a materialist, utilitarian world. In a world increasingly dominated by the neoliberal market ideology's emphasis on individual choice, the conceptualization of occupational citizenship reminds us that "work worthy of choice requires the kinds of work roles that are fitting for free, equal, and proud democratic citizens." The pluralist view of the nature of conflict in the employment relationship also complements the critical perspective in providing important contrasts for the neoliberal market ideology and unitarist views that essentially assume away the most difficult employer-employee conflicts. Recognizing these conflicts not only creates policy imperatives to handle them productively but also focuses our attention on questions of worker well-being independent from employers' interests.[33]

Other conceptualizations of work are critical of labor market institutions, but by incorporating bargaining-power inequalities in imperfect labor markets into the conceptualization of work as occupational citizenship, a different picture emerges. From this perspective, labor market institutions can positively contribute to societal goals, even if they do not enhance economic efficiency. Similarly, employee voice is not simply seen as a method for improving job satisfaction or organizational performance, but also as a way for achieving democratic values. These unique perspectives provide the keys to understanding North American labor law, European corporatism, and debates over adding enforceable labor standards to free-trade agreements.

But these are difficult times for the occupational citizenship aspects of work. Job insecurity, work-related stress, and work intensification appear to be increasing. The average full-time American worker puts in nearly two hundred more hours each year than thirty years ago. With respect to pay, the United States and Britain have both seen a hollowing out of the middle, with increased growth in both low-skilled, low-pay work and highly paid professional work. A number of these low-skilled workers are part of a growing "gloves-off economy" in which employers evade established labor standards and undercut responsible employers. Globally, there is a massive deficit in decent work, such that 40 percent of workers are poor and over a billion are unable to provide more than two dollars a day for their families to live on.[34]

Occupational citizenship is also threatened intellectually. Against the backdrop of the global decline in labor unionism, the academic field of industrial relations needs to figure out how to remain relevant and vibrant. In public policy discourse, the neoliberal market ideology largely dominates. Legislative proposals to improve occupational citizenship, such as minimum wage increases or paid family leave mandates, are opposed because of perceptions that they harm economic competitiveness and reduce jobs. International proposals to incorporate labor standards into trade agreements are similarly seen as harmful restraints on free trade. To business professionals, the pluralist belief in inherent conflicts of interest between employers and employees is seen as inimical to achieving cooperation and is rejected in favor of unitarist beliefs. Industrial relations teachings also seem less relevant to business professionals and policymakers given the global decline in labor union strength. From a feminist perspective, the occupational citizenship focus on paid employment marginalizes specific groups and other forms of citizenship. For example, by linking retirement income, disability insurance, and other important benefits to paid employment rather than to citizenship more generally, nonpaid work traditionally done by women is devalued and women are denied full citizenship rights. The traditional focus on paid employment also marginalizes the broader realm of reproductive work that includes creating and sustaining communities, such as civic participation.[35]

Nevertheless, occupational citizenship remains important, and the quest for occupational citizenship should be expanded to embrace all forms of work.[36] When the world's major religions or institutions like the United Nations call for checks and balances in the modern economy, they are subscribing to a pluralist, occupational citizenship conceptualization of work, even if this conceptualization is not explicitly articulated. To see individuals as truly free when markets work according to the laws of humanity rather than the law of the jungle continues a long tradition dating back to the early institutionalist economists of over one hundred years ago. When workers want to be treated with respect and have a voice not because it makes them more productive but because that is what they feel they deserve as human beings, they are implicitly looking for citizenship rights in the workplace. Conceptualizations of work must therefore include work as occupational citizenship.

But to truly understand the full intellectual breadth of work, and to understand work's deep importance for the lives of workers and their families, conceptualizations of work must go beyond occupational citizenship. While the conceptualization of work as occupational citizenship rejects the conceptualization of work as solely a commodity, these perspectives share a lack of attention to the specific nature of work. The remaining chapters therefore consider why we work and how work is experienced.

CHAPTER 5

Work as Disutility

> Work is what you do so that some time you won't
> have to do it any more.
>
> —Alfred Polgar (1873–1955)

One obvious reason why people work is for money. In the popular 1960s song "Five O'Clock World," an individual laments another day toiling at work while longing for the end of the workday:

> Tradin' my time for the pay I get
> Livin' on money that I ain't made yet
> Gotta keep goin', gotta make my way
> But I live for the end of the day
>
> But it's a five o'clock world when the whistle blows
> No one owns a piece of my time
> And there's a long-haired girl who waits, I know
> To ease my troubled mind, yeah[1]

Work is portrayed here as something done for money to support one's real life, a life that occurs when the workday or workweek is done. This idea of working solely to earn a living is a powerful one, and it forms the core of an important conceptualization of work embraced by mainstream economic thought. Specifically, in addition to being seen as a commodity (chapter 3), work in neoclassical economic theorizing is viewed as a way of supporting what is assumed to be each individual's fundamental objective—the consumption of goods, services, and leisure in a way that maximizes one's personal utility. But work itself does not provide utility. In mainstream economic thought, work is generally seen as *reducing* utility—that is, work is disutility.

There are two distinct ways in which economists see work as a reducing an individual's utility. First, the nature of work is seen as painful. The nineteenth-century economist W. Stanley Jevons, for example, defined work as "any painful exertion of body or mind undergone with the view to future good." Admittedly, Jevons, and the prominent economist Alfred Marshall after him, allowed that work could occasionally be pleasurable. But the focus was nevertheless on work's negative aspects. Second, work is seen as conflicting with leisure. With a fixed number of hours in a day, the more you work the less time you have for leisure activities. By assuming that leisure is pleasurable and provides utility, work becomes disutility. From this second perspective, the disutility of work is not a pain cost, but an opportunity cost.[2]

So why work? To obtain goods and services. This view of work is frequently found in songs, comics, and other forms of popular culture and dates back to at least the beginning of today's mainstream economic paradigm. Jevons, for example, offered a procurement-focused view of work by stating that "we labor to produce with the sole object of consuming."[3] We work to produce objects for our own consumption or to trade with others, and we work to earn income to purchase goods and services. We only work for compensation, and even the word *compensate* reinforces the disutility of work—we need to be paid to make up for, make amends for, or counterbalance the undesirable act of working. This conceptualization continues to dominate mainstream economic theorizing today. From the beginning of modern neoclassical economics up to the present day, then, work has been seen as disutility—a lousy activity tolerated only to obtain goods and services that provide pleasure.

Labor Supply

Conceptualizing work as disutility underlies mainstream economic approaches to analyzing how much one wants to work. Economists call this "labor supply"—the quantity of work that individuals want to sell in the labor market. Labor supply is typically analyzed by applying one of the hallmarks of modern economic theory, marginal analysis. In general, optimal decision making is seen as that which spends resources on something up to the point where the benefit of adding one more unit equals the cost of that additional unit; in other words, up to where the marginal benefit equals the marginal cost. Jevons cemented the concept of work as disutility by applying marginal analysis not only to consumption decisions, but to work as well: a utility-maximizing individual "will cease to labor just at that point when the pain exactly equals for a moment the corresponding pleasure acquired" by consuming the goods and services obtained by working.[4]

Contemporary economic theorizing takes a similar approach but implicitly assumes that the disutility of work stems from the reduction of leisure time rather than the painful exertion of work. Specifically, individuals are modeled as maximizing a utility function that depends positively on consumption and hours of leisure. Your ability to maximize your utility, however, is limited by budget and time constraints such that you can consume only as much as you earn by working, but every hour worked is an hour less that can be spent on leisure. An individual's (or a household's) labor supply decision therefore reflects a decision to sell the optimum number of hours of labor in order to consume the basket of goods and leisure that maximizes that individual's (or household's) utility.[5] Note that not only does this utility maximization problem reduce labor to a commodity to be optimized and exchanged (chapter 3), but it again reflects the disutility conceptualization by explicitly treating work as a source of income that competes with leisure in one's schedule. Moreover, one could weaken the sole focus on income by broadening the labor supply problem to allow for work to provide various rewards, such as pleasure from interacting with co-workers. But as long as one retains the mind-set that these rewards are part of the compensation required to induce individuals to work, then work is still being conceptualized as disutility.

Conceptualizing work as disutility further raises concerns with the extent to which unemployment benefits and government welfare programs implicitly create incentives for people to withhold their labor supply and avoid working. Specifically, if individuals prefer not to work, and work only to obtain income, then individuals are assumed to prefer publicly provided income. When work is painful or conflicts with leisure, why do it unless you have to? Partial income replacement for a limited duration is therefore seen as a necessary part of an optimal unemployment insurance program, and many countries have seen movements to require individuals to work if they want to receive publicly provided income support or welfare payments.[6]

Lastly, note that labor supply is generally analyzed with little concern for the conditions of work.[7] By seeing work as a source of income that conflicts with leisure, an individual's labor supply decision reduces to a calculation of the optimal number of hours to work to obtain a desired amount of income and leisure. In this way, work is not even part of the labor supply decision—rather, individuals are simply choosing between consumption and leisure. Once the worker is on the job, however, a different research stream in economics, described later in this chapter, concerns itself with how hard that worker will work. The end result is that individuals are implicitly modeled as proceeding in two discrete steps: first deciding how many hours to work, and then deciding how hard to work in those hours.

Human Capital Theory

Since economists see work primarily as a source of income, a major topic of interest in the field of labor economics is understanding why compensation levels vary across workers and jobs. One obvious difference across workers is in their level of skills, which one might naturally expect to be related to wage differences. Economists refer to acquired skills as "human capital." One method for acquiring human capital is through formal schooling. In deciding how much schooling to complete, individuals are assumed to maximize (the discounted present value of) their lifetime earnings by weighing the costs (e.g., college tuition and lost income opportunities while attending school) and benefits (e.g., higher earnings potential in the future) of additional years of schooling. A huge literature exists that uses sophisticated econometric methods and clever natural experiments (e.g., identical twins, differences in compulsory-schooling laws) to estimate the economic returns to schooling, and the accumulated research suggests that individuals can expect to earn an additional 9 percent for each additional year of formal schooling completed. Considering this earnings advantage in combination with the tremendous increase in overall education attainment during the twentieth century, at least in the United States, economists Claudia Goldin and Lawrence Katz label the twentieth century the "Human Capital Century" and ascribe the long-run success of the American economy to human capital.[8] At the same time, the earnings differentials between those with higher and lower levels of education have drastically widened in the past two decades.

Human capital can also be acquired through training. In this regard, it is common to distinguish between general training that enhances widely applicable skills, and specific training that enhances skills that are useful in specific occupations, jobs, or organizations. In the simple competitive model of the labor market (chapter 3), employers will not provide general training unless workers accept a below-market training wage, because the trained employees will be poached by competitors. However, labor market imperfections (such as mobility costs) that bind workers to firms more than in the competitive model provide employers with the opportunity to recoup their investment. In such situations, employers should be more likely to provide training and to encourage the formation of human capital through tuition reimbursement programs. Empirical research generally supports this model of training in imperfect rather than competitive labor markets and also finds evidence of strong economic returns for training, perhaps even larger than for education.[9] For mainstream economists, then, human capital is a key element of work opportunities and income levels. In fact, the standard neoclassical economics answer to concerns with the plight of low-wage workers or the unemployed is to recommend additional education and training.

Complementing human capital theory is another longstanding theory of wage determination, the theory of equalizing differences. Jobs vary across a number of dimensions, such as the mix of salary and benefits in total compensation, the amount of travel required, or the risk of job loss or physical injury. Start by assuming that these characteristics affect everyone's utility in the same way. The theory of equalizing differences implies that employers will need to offer monetary compensation to make workers indifferent between jobs with different amenities and stressors. For example, an employer will need to offer a wage premium for a risky job in order to fill that position. This wage premium is called a compensating wage differential. If we relax the assumption that job characteristics affect everyone in the same way, then workers have differing tastes for various job attributes. In this scenario, economic theory predicts that workers will sort themselves into jobs with the preferred characteristics, and, in the extreme, compensating wage differentials will not be necessary. If it is costly to search for new jobs and to learn about a job's true characteristics, then compensating wage differentials also might not emerge. The empirical evidence on compensating wage differentials is subject to debate. The early research often did not find supportive evidence, but more recent studies with improved information on risks of fatality and occupational illness have estimated significant differentials.[10] In either case, this theorizing reinforces the economics conceptualization of work as an activity driven by utility-maximizing behavior and monetary rewards.

Principal-Agent Problems, Shirking, and Incentives

The conceptualization of work as disutility is also readily apparent in the scholarship of personnel economists and organizational economists that applies the tools of economic analysis to work-related topics within organizations. In mainstream economic theory, the simple competitive model of the labor market sees employees and employers engaging in mutually beneficial transactions to buy and sell labor (chapter 3). But as recognized by Karl Marx, the employer buys labor power (the potential effort of workers) and must figure out how to get workers to exert this effort.[11] Sociological scholarship on this problem highlights the role of social relations in getting workers to work (chapter 7), while psychological scholarship emphasizes structuring work to provide personal fulfillment (chapter 6). Economic scholarship instead focuses on monetary incentives, because work is seen as disutility tolerated to earn income.

Economists view the employing of a worker as a form of contracting, since it involves an understanding of mutual expectations and performance obligations, regardless of whether these expectations and obligations are written or legally binding. If it were possible to write a complete contract that was legally enforceable, then worker effort would be achieved through enforcing such a contract by firing or fining workers who fail to live up to it. But there are numerous reasons why this is impossible—for example, the inability to foresee every possible work contingency, and the difficultly and cost of observing employee effort.[12]

So what happens in the employment relationship under incomplete contracting? Economic models of workers in organizations fall back on seeing work as disutility and assume that "the worker likes income but hates work" or "dislikes effort." It is then straightforward to show that if the employer pays a fixed wage, employees will exert the least amount of effort that keeps themselves from being fired. A lack of work effort is referred to as "shirking" in the economics literature and is called "counterproductive work behavior" in the psychology literature. Shirking can be seen as effort avoidance if work is painful, or as a form of on-the-job leisure if leisure is assumed to be preferable over work.[13]

In either case, the employer faces what economists call a principal-agent problem: how to get the agent (in this case, a worker) to act in the interests of someone else (a principal—for example, the owners of the organization). One possible solution is monitoring. For example, information technology can be used to track the call length and time between calls of call-center employees, and to listen in on their conversations. But for many occupations, information asymmetries, in which the worker has much better information about his or her effort than the employer, can be very expensive to overcome via monitoring. Economists therefore generally emphasize solutions to the principal-agent problem that include monetary incentives.[14] In short, if individuals act as if they are maximizing utility functions that desire consumption but not work, then monetary incentives can elicit effort by making additional effort utility-enhancing by allowing higher consumption levels.

As a consequence, research in personnel and organizational economics is full of rich models analyzing the optimal incentive schemes under various assumptions. For starters, suppose workers are risk neutral (that is, uncertainty does not affect one's utility), and measurable work output allows pay to be tied to it. It can then be shown that the optimal compensation scheme is to sell the worker a franchise in his or her job for a fixed fee and allow the worker to capture the entire output he or she generates. For example, a taxi company should rent taxis to its drivers and allow the drivers to keep all the revenue they generate. However, for many jobs it is not feasible to require workers to pay a fee for their jobs, and the optimal incentive scheme when such fees are prohibited is a pure commission-based system with no fixed payments and all revenues shared equally. But if workers are risk averse, then this is seen by employees as an excessively risky compensation scheme, and some combination of a fixed payment and commission is preferred. Identifying the optimal combination of fixed and contingent pay can be seen as trying to find the best "compromise between insuring the agent against risk and imposing sufficient risk on him to provide a stimulus to meet the principal's objectives."[15]

Another model for trying to overcome the principal-agent problem is efficiency wage theory. The name of this theory comes from the idea that raising the wages of low-paid, malnourished workers in developing countries above the competitive level can increase profitability by increasing their health and physical stamina. This logic was then adapted to industrialized countries as a possible explanation for the observed puzzle of why wages do not fall when there is persistent unemployment, contrary to the predictions of the textbook model. Employers might pay above-market wages to attract high-quality workers, to induce higher effort through a gift exchange, or of greatest relevance here, to create a penalty for shirking when effort is hard to monitor. If workers are paid more than they can obtain in the labor market, then if they are caught shirking and are fired, they will have to forfeit this wage premium by accepting a job elsewhere at the market wage rate. The threat of this financial penalty is theorized to provide an incentive to work hard rather than shirk.[16]

Another incentive mechanism that is prominent in the economics literature is the use of tournaments. Consider a situation in which only a single worker can be promoted to a position with a higher salary. If this "prize" is known in advance and will be awarded to the employee with the highest performance relative to his or her peers, then the competition for this promotion is a tournament. An economic model of optimizing behavior can then show that if the prize is sufficiently large to compensate for the risk of losing, then this tournament elicits additional employee effort. An intuitive application of tournament theory is to top executives in a corporation, such as when several top executives are competing for the CEO position; but tournament theory has also been applied to numerous situations in which relative employee performance is important.[17]

Lastly, while employee shirking is the classic application of principal–agent models in the work arena, the logic of these models can be applied more generally to situations in which workers and organizations have differing goals. A university might want its faculty members to work equally hard at research and teaching, but an individual professor might prefer research over teaching, or vice versa. A corporate manager might try to keep high-performing employees in his division rather than sharing them with other divisions. A CEO might pursue a corporate merger to garner publicity for herself even if the long-term prospects for success are slim. During the age of sail, navy ship captains might have preferred to seek out enemy merchant ships to capture wealthy prizes rather than engaging the enemy's navy in battle.[18] Economic theorizing suggests the same solution in all these cases— monitoring and monetary incentives that make it in the agent's interest to act in the principal's interest.

The theories sketched in this and the previous section portray an employment relationship that is more enduring and complex than a simple spot market for labor in which employers and employees are continually searching for mutually beneficial transactions and adjusting the terms and conditions of employment. In fact, long-term, implicit contracts between employers and employees can be better than short-term spot market transactions in motivating employees, allocating risk, and encouraging investment in human capital. The economics perspective on work, then, should not be reduced to a simple labor-supply, labor-demand framework. Nevertheless, this mainstream economic theorizing on work consistently embraces a rational, optimizing model of behavior in which competitive concerns are constantly in the background. For example, optimal incentive schemes not only need to elicit appropriate levels of effort, but also need to be sufficiently competitive to retain the appropriate workers and keep the organization profitable.[19] More fundamentally, whether exchanged in spot markets or through long-term implicit contracts, work is consistently conceptualized as disutility.

Disutility or Marginal Disutility?

Economist David Spencer emphasizes that economists have (sometimes carelessly) used two different assumptions in seeing work as disutility: work as painful, and work as competing with leisure. Neither assumption necessarily rules out the ability to get any pleasure from one's work. Economists are primarily concerned with optimal outcomes, so their attention is focused on the margin—with respect to work, this is the number of hours (or some other unit of time) where the marginal cost matches the marginal benefit of additional effort. So what is critical from an economic theory perspective is not whether work is always painful or always competes with leisure, but whether it is painful or competes with leisure on the margin when one is deciding to work one more hour after already having worked, say, forty-five hours that week. To the extent that work *at this point* is tiresome, painful, or simply less pleasurable than leisure, then there is a *marginal* disutility of labor.[20] In other words, mainstream economic theories do not require a universal disutility of labor in which work is always lousy, just a marginal disutility of labor in which the last extra unit of work is not enjoyable.

The technical distinction between universal and marginal disutility is frequently glossed over in practice, however. The theoretical assumption that workers might shirk on the margin becomes a practical belief that workers might always be tempted to shirk. Managerial policies designed to combat the marginal disutility of labor end up creating a mind-set in which workers are seen as *always* inclined to shirk and therefore always needing and only responding to financial incentives. In the words of the famous industrial engineer Frederick Winslow Taylor, "The natural instinct and tendency of men [is] to take it easy."[21] Even within economics, similarly broad and unqualified remarks are common, as reflected in the assumptions quoted in the previous section: "the worker likes income but hates work" or "dislikes effort." Work then is seen as disutility in a general sense, not just on the margin. This is unfortunate because it creates an excessively negative view of work and workers and also places the disutility conceptualization in sharp conflict with some other conceptualizations of work, such as personal fulfillment, identity, or service, rather than allowing these approaches to be complementary.

Beyond Paid Employment

It is easy to mistakenly see economic theorizing on the disutility of work as applying only to paid employment in industrialized countries—that is, to see work as a source of income in which a worker earns a salary or a wage. But the disutility of work is a more general conceptualization of work, and this conceptualization applies equally to issues of work beyond paid employment. Consider unpaid housework—cleaning, cooking, and the like. An economic model of the household sees unpaid housework as producing domestic goods (e.g., a clean house, meals) that provide utility.[22] The effort or time required to produce these goods is seen as painful or as conflicting with leisure—in either case, unpaid housework is conceptualized as disutility analogous to paid work. As in the case of paid work, the optimal decision is to engage in unpaid housework up to the point at which the marginal cost of this effort/time equals the marginal benefit of the utility generated from the consumption of the domestic goods that result. An individual who derives little pleasure from a clean house but a lot of pleasure from reading is predicted to not devote many hours to housework, just as a paid worker who values leisure over income is predicted to not work many hours in paid employment.

A similar model can be applied to agricultural households.[23] A subsistence household is seen as optimally devoting effort to growing its own food up to the point where additional effort is more costly than the consumption value of the food produced. More complicated situations in which the household can grow cash crops as well as staples, and in which members of the household can also work in outside paid jobs, do not change the basic result: decisions about work reflect the optimal trade-off between consumption and leisure because work, whether paid or not, is conceptualized as disutility.

Another example from outside the domain of formal, paid employment is sharecropping. Economic theorizing frequently analyzes sharecropping in a principal-agent framework and sees sharecropping arrangements as a method for providing incentives to work when landlords cannot observe effort.[24] This approach is very similar to economic theorizing on shirking among paid employees within organizations, because embedded in economic models of sharecropping is the same assumption that work is disutility. Conceptualizing work as disutility is therefore a general perspective that is not limited to paid jobs in modern capitalist or industrialized economies.

The (Dis)Utility of Work as Disutility

The analytical foundations of mainstream economic theorizing consist of individuals and organizations that act to maximize their objective functions (e.g., utility or profits) by optimizing on the margin, and of prices adjusting to supply and demand and allocating resources. Within this approach, a number of analytical variations can be accommodated. While these variations have important theoretical implications, they do not change the fundamental economics approach that conceptualizes work as disutility that is tolerated to support consumption. For example, while departing from the standard neoclassical economics model in important respects, scholarship in the new institutional economics nevertheless emphasizes the importance of economic incentives to compensate for the disutility of work and elicit worker effort.

When the textbook competitive model is altered such that risk-averse workers are hypothesized to prefer an implicit contract of constant, predictable wages over time as insurance against the vagaries of the business cycle, this preference is rooted in the desire to maximize utility by smoothing *consumption* patterns across time. And models that diverge from the competitive paradigm by allowing for labor markets to be imperfectly competitive continue to embed the disutility of work in the labor supply decisions of individuals.[25]

However, this conceptualization of work need not be reduced to a caricature in which all work is distasteful. The key assumption in mainstream economics scholarship is that work is burdensome (either directly or by conflicting with leisure) such that it reduces one's utility *on the margin*. Work can provide positive intrinsic rewards, but the disutility aspect becomes important when deciding how hard to work, say, in your eighth or ninth hour of the working day, not the first. In other words, an economic approach to work need not rule out positive aspects of work, but it is distinctive in also recognizing the disutility of work on the margin. For example, when work is seen largely as providing intrinsic rewards (chapter 6), analyses of employee discretion highlight the benefits of giving employees autonomy in their jobs—such as the ability to exercise creative powers, make on-the-spot decisions, and use particular knowledge. In contrast, adding disutility to the problem means that employee autonomy can also be costly in that it provides greater opportunities for employees to shirk. An economic approach that singularly focuses on disutility might design jobs to minimize autonomy to prevent shirking, but a more nuanced approach is to maximize performance by balancing the costs and benefits of autonomy when designing jobs.[26]

Consequently, conceptualizing work in this way provides unique insights. Seeing work as disutility highlights the importance of monetary desires and alternative uses of one's time in deciding how much to work, especially on the margin. Focusing on the optimal use of labor fosters an understanding of the determinants of the demand for workers by organizations, and how to deploy various forms of labor and capital efficiently. Whether or not one agrees with the necessity of economic incentives for eliciting work, understanding that some see work as disutility provides the key to realizing why economic incentives are promoted by economists and adopted by companies, and provides the basis for debating such efforts.

However, treating all forms of work as disutility perpetuates the negative views of work that originally arose by seeing work as a curse, and it "universalizes the badness of work." This can also be condemned as a convenient ideology for those in power. Social hierarchies that might be inconsistent with democracy or fairness are disguised by a perception that everyone, from CEOs to janitors, has to endure the toil and disutility of work. Furthermore, popularizing the idea that workers are prone to shirking justifies hierarchical work structures and deflects pressures for granting workers greater autonomy over their work.[27] As is the case with the conceptual commodification of work (chapter 3), conceptualizing work as disutility is not a purely intellectual exercise and instead has important consequences for how work is experienced.

Scholars from a variety of disciplines also disagree with the utility-maximizing and work-as-disutility foundations of mainstream economic analyses of work. Marxist economics criticizes mainstream economics for its omission of the role of structural capitalist power in enforcing incomplete contracts. Feminist economists object to the marginalization of women and family that results from the mainstream economics emphasis on self-interested, atomistic individuals and market exchange. Behavioral and institutionalist economists, industrial relations scholars, and psychologists believe that cognitive limitations, concerns for fairness, and other factors mean that human action is not best described by selfish utility maximization, and that the ultimate objective of economic activity is not consumption. Sociologists object to the failure of mainstream economic theorizing to see economic activity as embedded in social structures. Theologians and religious leaders criticize the "Gospel of Mammonism" created by an emphasis on the selfish pursuit of material wealth.[28] With respect to work, then, many heterodox economists, psychologists, sociologists, philosophers, industrial relations scholars, theologians, and others see work as a source of human fulfillment (defined in various ways), not disutility. It is to these conceptualizations of work that we turn in the remainder of this book.

CHAPTER 6

Work as Personal Fulfillment

> To find out what one is fitted to do, and to secure an
> opportunity to do it, is the key to happiness.
>
> —John Dewey (1859–1952)

Rather than a burden, work can be fun. In the words of guitarist Ace Frehley from the rock band Kiss:

> I got involved with rock 'n' roll because it's fun. It's not really work to me. When I'm having fun, at the end of the day I say, "Wow, I'm having a great time. I can't believe I'm getting paid to do this." That's the way it should be. When you're on tour you should be having a great time. That's what it's all about.

Work can be intrinsically rewarding, not just a source of income. A 1930s union organizer in the John Steinbeck novel *In Dubious Battle* is asked whether he gets any pleasure out of his work advocating for farm laborers. In spite of the low pay and the likelihood of being seriously injured or killed in battles with growers, he replies,

> More than most people do. It's an important job. You get a hell of a drive out of something that has some meaning to it, and don't you forget it. The thing that takes the heart out of a man is work that doesn't lead any place.

Instead of being a curse for sin, work can provide spiritual satisfaction, as captured by this description of a Chicago carpenter:

He feels called by God to work as a carpenter. . . . Transforming a raw material like wood into a finished cabinet brings pure joy to Ed. His deep satisfaction comes from a belief that his work is an expression of what God wants him to do with his talents.

And while work can be physically exhausting or dangerous, it can also promote physiological and psychological health when it involves appropriate levels of physical activity.[1]

In other words, work can be conceptualized as a source of personal fulfillment. Ideally it promotes physical health and psychological well-being by satisfying human needs for purpose, achievement, mastery, self-esteem, and self-worth.[2] But seeing work as personal fulfillment does not mean that work is always healthy. Lousy work—whether because of mindless repetition, abusive co-workers or bosses, excessive physical or mental demands, or other factors—can have negative physical and psychological effects. Work, then, can be a source of personal satisfaction, or dissatisfaction. Work can bring joy, or stress. Work can help you flourish, or burn out. To conceptualize work as personal fulfillment is to emphasize these positive and negative individual physical and psychological aspects.

Except for a concern with workplace safety, however, the emphasis among those who see work as a source of personal fulfillment is generally on the psychological aspects.[3] In other words, this conceptualization particularly embraces the ways in which work is inherently psychological. All work, including manual labor, is directed by the brain, both cognitively and emotionally. Mental states such as attitudes, moods, and emotions can affect what you put into your work, while the nature of your work—including your job tasks, rewards, relations with co-workers, and how you are supervised—can affect your mental states. The foundation of the conceptualization of work as personal fulfillment, then, is seeing work as an activity that arouses cognitive and affective (emotional/attitudinal) functioning.

This conceptualization is important not only for understanding work but also because it provides the intellectual foundations for modern human resource management. The millions of workers worldwide whose employment is shaped by a variety of human resource management practices are therefore directly impacted by this way of thinking about work. Consequently, in addition to developing the conceptualization of work as personal fulfillment, in this chapter I also devote significant attention to human resource management, including its main principles, practices, and criticisms.

From Joy to Job Satisfaction

As reflected in the quotes that open this chapter, the personal fulfillment that one can potentially derive from work has a variety of sources and forms. In religious thought, the possibility of attaining fulfillment through work is counterposed against the burdensome sense of work as a curse (chapter 1) and against the materialist sense of work as a source of economic production and income (chapters 3 and 5). The modern Catholic Church, for example, embraces work as ideally allowing humans to fulfill their full human potential and achieve self-actualization. In the words of the Second Vatican Council,

> When a man works he not only alters things and society, he develops himself as well. He learns much, he cultivates his resources, he goes outside of himself and beyond himself. Rightly understood this kind of growth is of greater value than any external riches which can be garnered.

In religious writings, this self-actualization or fulfillment is frequently expressed in terms of achieving a sense of inner joy that comes from serving God. The Pietism movement within eighteenth-century German Protestantism, for example, "maintained that work performed in conscious fulfillment to help one's neighbor could be expected to give rise to a sense of blessedness, a feeling of joy." The contemporary theologian Matthew Fox similarly emphasizes the importance of joy in one's work that results when work is experienced as "a kind of [divine] bestowal, a grace, a gratuitous fit of our gifts to others' needs and their gifts to our needs." The Episcopal priest Armand Larive describes joy in work as a delight that is charged with intrinsically shared spirituality. These characterizations are not limited to Western religions, as illustrated by this passage from the ancient Hindu scripture Bhagavad Gita:

> They all attain perfection when they find joy in their work. Hear how a man attains perfection and finds joy in his work. A man attains perfection when his work is worship of God, from whom all things come and who is in all.

Achieving joy can also be characterized as being liberated from the cursed nature of work: "When we find our match between our joy and the world's need, the place God wants us to be, [work] does feel more like liberation than imprisonment."[4]

The theme of joy in work is also evident in secular philosophy. During the Enlightenment in the eighteenth century, German philosophers idealized work as "free, creative, intellectually stimulating, socially useful, personally fulfilling." During industrialization, then, an ongoing concern was maintaining "joy in work" (*Arbeitsfreude*). This is perhaps most famously reflected in Karl Marx's exaltation of work as the highest form of human activity (chapter 9). In the nineteenth century, the ideal of joy in work is also apparent in the writings of the French utopian philosopher Charles Fourier and the French author Émile Zola. *Joy in Work* is also the title of Henri de Man's 1927 book in which he argued that work provides joy by fulfilling a variety of human needs or instincts, including activity, creation, and self-worth, and in which he analyzed workers' attitudes toward their work to assess the factors that related to their realization of joy in their work, or lack thereof.[5]

These ideas continue today. Sociologist Richard Sennett, for example, emphasizes the "special human condition of being engaged" that results from craftsmanship, and the importance of the fulfillment that results from the pride one takes in doing one's work well. But the idea of joy in work has largely been supplanted by a concern with job satisfaction. A well-known definition of job satisfaction is "a pleasurable or positive emotional state resulting from the appraisal of one's job or job experiences." One enduring theory of job satisfaction is the job characteristics model developed by organizational behavior scholars Richard Hackman and Greg Oldham in which five characteristics determine how satisfying a job is: skill variety, task identity, task significance, autonomy, and feedback. Workers in jobs with high levels of these characteristics are generally found to have high levels of job satisfaction.[6] Job satisfaction is arguably today's dominant (nontheological) way to conceptualize the extent of personal fulfillment derived from work, and it provides an important basis for modern human resource management. That job satisfaction has both a cognitive aspect ("the appraisal of one's job or job experiences") and an affective aspect ("a pleasurable or positive emotional state") underscores the importance of mental processes in the experience of work.

On a deeper level than job satisfaction, work can also provide fulfillment through a sense of identity (chapter 9). And while job satisfaction and the earlier German concern with joy in work are largely focused on paid employment, personal fulfillment can be achieved through diverse forms of work. Caring for others—such as a parent caring for a child, or an adult child caring for an elderly parent—is work (chapter 8). It can be stressful, but it also can bring joy and positive mental and physical health consequences. Volunteering can also be a source of enhanced life satisfaction. These diverse forms of work, from everyday paid jobs to unpaid caring or volunteer work, are typically also included in religious perspectives that emphasize the pursuit of joy in work.[7] Personal fulfillment is therefore an important conceptualization for all forms of work, not just paid employment.

Mental Processes at Work

To think of work as a source of personal fulfillment raises more general questions concerning the importance of cognitive and affective mental processes for understanding work. Such questions are emphasized most strongly by scholars in industrial-organizational (I-O) psychology, organizational behavior, and human resource management. A thorough review of the relevant research literature is not possible here, but a brief description of four major topics can reveal the importance of incorporating mental processes into the understanding of work. These four topics are individual differences, job attitudes, organizational justice, and work motivation. The common denominator among these topics is the influence of mental processes on how work is experienced, and therefore conceptualized. How the scholarship in these areas is applied to the practical challenge of effectively managing human resources is described later in this chapter.

Research on individual psychological differences has shown that the strength or weakness of psychological attributes varies from individual to individual. Seeing work as a cognitive and affective activity then suggests that these individual differences are important for understanding work. One major example is general cognitive ability, also called general mental ability, or simply g. There is strong evidence that an individual's general cognitive ability level is one of the most valid predictors of his or her job performance and is the best available predictor of job-related learning. Personality is another category of individual differences. A standard model of personality is the "Big Five": extraversion, agreeableness, neuroticism (emotional stability), conscientiousness, and openness to experience. Conscientiousness is the only dimension that has been found to be consistently related to job performance, but other dimensions might predict other work behaviors such as organizational citizenship behaviors, or work outcomes such as job stress. The overall usefulness of these general personality measures for understanding work, however, continues to be debated. How individuals feel about themselves—measured by a mixture of perceived self-esteem, self-efficacy, emotional stability, and locus of control that has been labeled "core self-evaluation"—is another individual difference measure that has been shown to be related to job satisfaction and job performance. Personal integrity is also an individual difference that is related to a variety of work-related behaviors.[8]

This research on individual differences is applied to the work world through selection tests. If a particular psychological attribute is related to desirable or undesirable work outcomes, then organizations want to be able to measure this attribute and use these measurements to distinguish among individuals when making hiring and job promotion decisions. These applications are not without controversy, however. For example, the use of individual difference measures to select employees can be controversial if a cognitive ability test has adverse consequences for members of minority groups, or if a personality test is perceived as weeding out those who might support a labor union.[9]

Individual differences in personality, attitudes, and values also underlie the Attraction-Selection-Attrition (ASA) model. This theory argues that individuals are attracted to organizations with goals and cultures that match their own personal dispositions, organizations select employees who appear to fit with their goals and cultures, and employees leave organizations when there is a bad fit. Organizations therefore reflect the personalities, attitudes, and values of their workforces. Related to this is a large literature on person-organization fit that finds that congruence between individual and organizational needs and characteristics helps explain a number of work-related phenomena.[10] Seeing work as a source of personal fulfillment in which work involves a number of mental stimuli brings these issues to the fore.

Research on job attitudes is a second area that reveals the importance of incorporating mental processes into the understanding of work. The most researched job attitude—and one of the most researched topics in I-O psychology, organizational behavior, and human resource management—is job satisfaction. Job satisfaction receives so much attention by academics and practitioners alike because it is intuitive to believe that job satisfaction affects job performance—a happy worker is a productive worker, or so it would seem. Empirical research suggests that there is strong support for a modest relationship, but job performance is notoriously difficult to measure, so the extent to which happier workers are more productive continues as a subject of debate. Many other work-related attitudes have been studied, and a popular one is affective organizational commitment. Individuals who have strong emotional attachments to their organizations appear to be less likely to quit and to have higher levels of job performance. This further hints at the importance of a number of other emotions in the workplace, such as envy or mood.[11]

A third prominent topic is organizational justice, or, more simply, fairness in the workplace. It is common to distinguish between distributive and procedural justice. Distributive justice focuses on the perceived fairness of outcomes. An enduring theory in this regard is equity theory, developed by psychologist J. Stacy Adams, which posits that workers alter their behavior to establish equitable outcomes with some reference group. For example, if you believe you are working harder than your co-workers but getting paid the same, equity theory predicts that you will reduce your effort to match that of your co-workers, or seek higher compensation. Procedural justice focuses on the perceived fairness of procedures. For example, the use of consistent standards and objective information in determining pay increases, and giving employees the opportunity to voice their side of a dispute, are believed to enhance individuals' perceptions of procedural justice. Organizational justice is important for understanding work because a large research literature finds that perceptions of both distributive and procedural justice predict employee attitudes, such as job satisfaction and organizational commitment, and work-related behaviors, such as job performance and organizational citizenship behaviors.[12]

Last, but certainly not least, is the topic of work motivation. As will be discussed in the next section, the problem of how to motivate workers has challenged employers and masters for centuries. Economic theorizing generally emphasizes the importance of extrinsic rewards such as pay and promotions (chapter 5). In contrast, theorizing from a psychological perspective generally emphasizes the significance of intrinsic rewards. Psychologist Abraham Maslow's famous hierarchy of needs asserted that humans seek first to satisfy their most basic needs—physiological needs of food, water, and air—and once these are satisfied, attention is turned to safety needs, and then to love, esteem, and finally self-actualization. Psychologist Frederick Herzberg theorized that a lack of extrinsic rewards can cause dissatisfaction, but it is intrinsic factors like achievement, competence, challenge, and opportunities for personal growth that motivate individuals.[13]

As noted above, concerns with fairness and justice can also be motivating factors. Hackman and Oldham's job characteristics model is also a model of intrinsic motivation. For example, individuals in jobs with higher levels of skill variety, task identity, and task significance are believed to experience a sense of meaningfulness, and this intrinsic reward provides motivation. Psychologists Edward Deci and Richard Ryan also developed an influential model in which motivation is rooted in innate human needs for competence and self-determination. From more of a sociological perspective, enhancing one's self-identity, especially as defined through the eyes of others, can be another powerful intrinsic motivator. Even if these perspectives on intrinsic motivators are culturally biased toward high-income countries where basic needs are easily filled by many, or toward Western cultures that value individual fulfillment, they vividly reveal how work can be seen as rooted in mental processes and should not be seen as just an economic or survival activity.[14]

While these examples are premised on a conceptualization of work as personal fulfillment (broadly defined to include a variety of cognitive and affective elements), there is a recurring theme of individual and organizational performance. In other words, the pull to translate personal fulfillment and positive affective states into productivity, job performance, and competitiveness is a powerful one. I-O psychology, organizational behavior, and the academic field of human resource management are ultimately rooted in not only understanding but also improving job and organizational performance.[15] These fields are closely tied to the business vision of workers as human resources—productive assets that, along with physical resources such as machinery, contribute to a company's bottom line. The overarching question in the academic and practitioner fields of human resource management, therefore, is what set of management practices optimizes employee performance. Contemporary answers to this question emphasize understanding the mental elements of work and therefore rely heavily on principles from psychology and organizational behavior.

From the Drive System to Psychological Motivation

Dating back at least to Sumerian slaves, temple builders, and soldiers five thousand years ago, workers have been managed by others. How to effectively manage workers is therefore a long-standing issue. Writing in the first century, the Roman farmer Columella observed that "care is demanded of the master . . . most of all in the matter of the persons in his service" and goes on to discuss the desired characteristics of overseers (e.g., should "exercise authority without laxness and without cruelty, and always humor some of the better hands") and other techniques for managing slaves (e.g., "make it a practice to call them into consultation on any new work" because "they are more willing to set about a piece of work on which they think that their opinions have been asked and their advice followed").[16] Some ideas in human resource management have therefore been around for centuries. But the modern concern with managing workers can be traced back to the shift from a household-based workforce to an industrial workforce that was brought on by the Industrial Revolution.

On the eve of the Industrial Revolution, much of the British population was engaged in agricultural work, with some households supplementing their incomes by small-scale household production ("cottage industries") as artisans or as part of the putting-out (or outwork or sweated) system. In all these activities, the households autonomously controlled their own activities, including choosing the type of work, when and how hard to work, and the techniques used. The transition to the discipline of the factory system in eighteenth-century Britain, and elsewhere later on, was therefore a difficult one. Fixed working hours and days, punctuality, and constant work effort conflicted sharply with the autonomous work habits—and indeed the entire cultural fabric—enjoyed by household-based agricultural and protoindustrial workers (and still enjoyed today by students, consultants, and others). The informal weekly holiday of "Saint Monday," for example, was widely observed by many workers, much to the frustration of industrial employers seeking to impose regular workweeks. Armed with the attitude that their "own rise to wealth and power [was] due to merit, and the workman's subordinate position [was] due to his failings . . . with the essential qualities of industry, ambition, sobriety, and thrift," most factory owners sought to impose discipline and managerial control through extensive work rules, direct supervision, threats, punishments including monetary fines, and incentives based on piece rates.[17] Workers were forced to adapt to the new forms of work, not the other way around.

Fast forward to the late nineteenth century, and most American workplaces were similarly characterized by managerial regimes based on the foreman's empire—the supervisor's unquestioned authority to hire, fire, pay, discipline, and motivate employees, typically through a drive system of "close supervision, abuse, profanity, and threats." This was part of a broader pattern of unscientific managerial methods in both Britain and the United States. Around this time, the need to coordinate increasingly complex production operations and reduce waste led to the emergence of the systematic management movement, especially in the United States. This included the development of modern accounting methods and simple improvements in formal recordkeeping to better coordinate the production process. Engineers also devoted some attention to systematizing the human element of production and thereby started laying the groundwork for modern human resource management.[18]

The most famous application of the systematic management movement to work was Frederick Winslow Taylor's scientific management, also called Taylorism. Taylor and others sought to improve efficiency and predictability by "scientifically" determining the one best way of completing a task. Taylor, for example, spent four months around the turn of the century timing and measuring the amount of coal a worker could shovel to determine that the optimal shovel load was twenty-one pounds. More generally, time and motion studies were used to reduce jobs to their most basic components, and the resulting instruction cards specified exactly how to complete each task, sometimes down to the fraction of a second. Taylorism thus created a sharp separation between the conception and execution of work.[19] Managers, not workers, determine each job's one best way. Workers are cogs in a standardized machine, or just a set of hands. In fact, *hand* means laborer, as in farmhand, factory hand, deckhands ("all hands on deck"), kitchen hands, and the like.

Taylor saw scientific management as a way for these "hands" to maximize their earnings, but this embodies a narrow view of workers' interests and psychological needs. As such, the quest to improve, if not humanize, the management of labor, increase cooperation, and reduce absenteeism, employee turnover, and strikes continued, especially in periods of low unemployment. Diverse initiatives emerged, including civil service reform, the industrial safety and vocational guidance movements, and Progressive-era social reforms. By 1900, notable companies such as Krupp Steel in Germany, Cadbury in Britain, and National Cash Register in the United States had adopted a paternalistic strategy of welfare work. Welfare work attempted to harmonize relations between workers and their employers by creating a family-like company spirit and providing for the enhanced welfare of workers via attractive company housing, recreational programs, libraries, landscaped factory grounds, profit sharing, and pension plans. In the aftermath of the labor shortages and unrest of World War I, welfare work grew into the American welfare capitalism of the 1920s.[20] Welfare capitalism sought to increase efficiency (and avoid unionism) by improving employment conditions through the training of supervisors, using careful hiring and firing procedures, providing wage incentives and protective insurance benefits, improving the physical work environment and safety, enhancing job security, and providing employees with a nonunion voice in the workplace.

The 1910s also witnessed the founding of industrial psychology—now called industrial-organizational psychology in the United States, occupational psychology in Britain, and work psychology elsewhere—by Hugo Münsterberg and Walter Dill Scott in order to "round-out scientific management by giving it the psychological theories and tools necessary to optimally prepare and utilize the labor input." Two ideas were key, and they remain central to I-O psychology today. The first is that workers are psychological beings driven by more than economic incentives. Early efforts in industrial psychology therefore sought to uncover what motivates workers and to use these findings to improve employment practices and redesign jobs accordingly. The second key idea is that humans are characterized by important individual psychological differences, such as differences in cognitive ability or personality traits. Early industrial psychologists therefore also developed tools to distinguish types of individuals and used these tools to create methods for selecting the right employees for the right jobs.[21] All these initiatives are seen by their supporters as mutually beneficial—for employees through improved working lives and for employers through enhanced productivity and profitability.

A decade later, the famous Hawthorne experiments of the late 1920s and early 1930s further undermined the traditional view of a worker as a machine. At first, researchers altered the lighting for several work groups in a Western Electric plant near Chicago. Much to the researchers' surprise, productivity increased for both the control and the test groups, even when lighting was reduced. A number of follow-up experiments were then conducted to examine the determinants of worker productivity, and the results were interpreted as revealing the key roles of personal attitudes, job satisfaction, and social relations with co-workers. From this perspective, managing human resources, then, is not a problem of finding the right economic incentives or adjusting the technical conditions of work to provide good lighting or avoid fatigue, but is a problem of "diagnosing human situations" to manage employee attitudes and create cooperative work groups. While initially analyzed under the banner of the "human relations movement," this focus on attitudes and group dynamics continues to be an important area of scholarly inquiry in I-O psychology and organizational behavior and has grown into key elements of contemporary human resource management.[22]

Unifying Employer and Employee Interests

As psychology was being incorporated into management in the first half of the twentieth century, an equally powerful management philosophy arose—the unitarist philosophy that employer and employee interests can be aligned in a win-win fashion. In the nineteenth and early twentieth centuries, radical critics of capitalism such as Karl Marx argued that employers and employees have distinctly opposing interests because employers need to accumulate profit at the expense of workers (chapter 7). Antagonistic conflicts are therefore unavoidable. Others argued that labor unrest is not inherent in capitalism but rather that employer-employee conflicts stem from poor managerial practices such as abusive supervision or a lack of profit sharing. If labor unrest stems from poor managerial practices, then labor problems can be corrected by improved methods of management. Frederick Winslow Taylor, for example, saw employer-employee conflict as rooted in management's habit of reducing piece rates every time workers figured out how to produce more. Taylor thought that a "scientific" method of determining job standards would end such conflicts and yield "the maximum prosperity for the employer, coupled with the maximum prosperity for each employee." In other words, scientific management "has for its very foundation the firm conviction that the true interests of [employers and employees] are one and the same."[23]

A leading American human resources executive of the 1920s, Clarence Hicks, also saw autocratic management as problematic: "A barren ground for developing real cooperation, autocracy breeds resentment in those who come under its domination." While lamenting the persistence of poor managerial practices—"even today, one finds many remnants of seventeenth-century stupidity"—Hicks championed an approach in which management "brings employee, owner, and consumer together in a mutually beneficial relationship" and creates "a unity of interest." This perspective was echoed by the influential management consultant Mary Parker Follett's call for replacing a power-based conflictual mind-set with what today would be called a win-win (integrative) problem-solving approach in order to make business an "integrative unity" such that the "employer and employee are engaged in a common enterprise. They jointly assume the risks and share the burdens and the benefits of the enterprise." Several decades later, management professor Douglas McGregor again echoed the desirability of integrative approaches to the managing of human resources—"the creation of conditions such that the members of the organization can achieve their own goals *best* by directing their efforts toward the success of the enterprise."[24]

Whether phrased as aligning employer and employee interests, promoting cooperation, or seeking mutual gains, this *unitarist* emphasis is widespread in contemporary human resource management. This is not to say that aligning employer and employee interests is an easy task. The history of modern human resource management, in fact, can be seen as a struggle to find the appropriate policies to unify employer-employee interests and achieve employee cooperation against a backdrop of short-sighted behavior and changing influences such as competitive pressures, employee demographics, social expectations, and laws. But to those who see workers as human resources, the alignment of goals is the ideal state to strive for. In the words of the CEO of retailing giant Target Corporation, "When we're all aligned, we can achieve harmony and drive results for the common good of the company."[25]

Note carefully that this unitarist approach is not simply a strategy for managing people, but is also more fundamentally a belief system about work founded on the very important assumption that employer-employee conflicts of interest are not inherent in the capitalist employment relationship. Scholarship in I-O psychology, psychologically oriented organizational behavior, and human resource management certainly recognizes that diverse forms of conflict are present in the workplace, but this literature frequently focuses on conflict among employees. The flare-up of such conflict is largely perceived as an opportunity for improved human resource management interventions to resolve it—for example, by improving employees' communication skills or weeding out "bad" team members. Moreover, if *employer*-employee conflict exists in a particular organization, it is seen as stemming from poor human resource management practices that need fixing. Sustained conflict is at odds with the unitarist conception of work, and contemporary human resource management therefore tries to manage conflict away rather than embrace it as an inherent part of the employment relationship. Human resource management is therefore typically hostile toward labor unions (chapter 4), and while there are notable exceptions, I-O psychology research typically ignores labor unions.[26] Moreover, while human resource management principles can certainly be pursued in unionized workplaces, the ideal state of human resource management is typically seen as nonunion.

The unitarist assumption also has important ramifications for how one conceptualizes power in the employment relationship. Specifically, when the employment relationship is seen as primarily characterized by a win-win unity of interests among employees and employers, power is unimportant. When goals can always be aligned, there is no need for a party to exploit a power advantage. But managing according to the unitarist principle does not make it true, and debates over this unitarist perspective should be seen as conceptual debates over the true nature of the modern employment relationship, and therefore over the importance of power. Those who reject the validity of the unitarist assumption do not necessarily question the human resource management ideal of treating employees well, but they question whether this always truly benefits employers and employees alike. Specifically, these critics are more inclined to see employer interests as trumping employee interests, especially in challenging economic times, because of the inevitability of conflicts of interests that cannot be resolved by human resource management policies. Protecting employee dignity in these challenging environments therefore requires more than good human resource management policies (chapter 4).

As a brief aside, the unitarist perspective is also an important element of how work is conceptualized under communism. For those who see antagonistic conflicts of interests between capital and labor as a fundamental feature of capitalism, communism is supposed to resolve these conflicts by removing the ownership structures that give rise to them. Under communism, then, common ownership of the means of production (theoretically) achieves a unitarist employment relationship in which everyone shares common goals.

As with human resource management, however, a unity of interests under communism is not easy to achieve. Mao Zedong, for example, clearly stated that conflicts (he called them "contradictions") would persist under communism, but these contradictions result from temporary imperfections and are not antagonistic.[27] With discussion, persuasion, and a recognition of a unity of interests, it was believed that these conflicts could be resolved in ways that served everyone's interests. As such, Mao might very easily have echoed a slightly modified version of the Target CEO's unitarist human resources philosophy: "When we're all aligned, we can achieve harmony and drive results for the common good."

Managing Human Resources for Personal Fulfillment

The evolution in thinking about work and the employment relationship described in the previous two sections gave rise to today's human resource management school of thought. Human resource management is the scholarship and practice of management that seeks to improve individual and organizational performance by recognizing the human factor inherent in employees and by aligning employee-employer interests. This definition includes what used to be called personnel management (to the extent that it recognized the human factor), what some advocate today as strategic human resource management, and other variations. While the specific practices and emphases differ, these approaches are all rooted in organizational performance, the human factor, and the alignment of employee-employer interests. At the same time, not all contemporary approaches to managing employees, such as market-driven low-road strategies, fit within this personal fulfillment–oriented definition of human resource management. As defined here, human resource management approaches are the most extensive in the nonunion sector of the United States; cultural differences, market factors, legislated employment standards, mandatory employee consultation requirements, and the strength of labor unions have affected the extent to which employers (and scholars) have embraced this perspective and implemented various practices and policies elsewhere.[28]

Human resource management builds from the conceptualization of work as personal fulfillment by assuming that to be effective, human resource management practices must satisfy workers' psychological needs by managing their cognitive and affective functioning, and their physical needs by providing a safe workplace. Alternative perspectives and critiques will be discussed in the next section, but adherents to this view see this as a win–win situation. Psychological needs can be fulfilled through fair treatment, intrinsic

WORK AS PERSONAL FULFILLMENT   103

rewards, and placement into appropriate jobs; employees will reciprocate by being hardworking and loyal, and high levels of organizational performance, including profitability and shareholder returns, will result. Employees can gain further psychological rewards from identifying with a high-performing organization, and the virtuous cycle of psychological rewards and profitability continues. This results in a conceptualization of work as a *human* resource—a productive activity undertaken by humans with individual differences seeking psychological satisfaction who require managing and coordinating to align employee and organizational interests for mutual gain.

Contemporary thought on managing the performance of employees therefore embraces a host of strategies that ultimately target the management of the cognitive and affective functioning of employees to promote job satisfaction, organizational commitment, and productivity.[29] Cognitive ability tests, personality tests, interviewing techniques, and other selection devices are recommended in order to identify job candidates who are a good fit and likely to be productive. Jobs and work teams are designed to promote the efficient and effective completion of tasks. This might involve an analysis of skill variety, autonomy, or other job characteristics as well as team dynamics and other social factors that might create or impede job satisfaction, cooperation, and high performance. The use of performance appraisals is rooted in goal-based, mental models of motivation. Policies and procedures are designed and administered with an eye toward promoting fairness.

The importance of the personal fulfillment conceptualization of work for human resource management is also evident in the area of employee compensation. Much of the traditional thinking in this area stems from economics, such as the importance of competitive pay packages for recruitment and retention and the use of financial incentives to motivate performance. Seeing work as personal fulfillment rather than purely as a commodity or as disutility, however, brings the potential importance of intrinsic motivators to the fore. Behaviorally based scholarship suggests that extrinsic rewards can crowd out intrinsic motivators and therefore cautions against an overreliance on extrinsic pay incentives. The practitioner literature in human resource management therefore suggests rewarding employees in many ways. Recognition of the human factor also serves as a warning for diverse employee reactions to compensation practices. Employees do not necessarily have common perceptions about the extent to which their pay depends on performance, and these perceptions can influence attitudes and performance. Differences in merit-based compensation are seen by economists as providing incentives for work effort, but organizational justice theories indicate that this desired behavior requires that employees see these compensation differences as fair.[30]

Alternative Perspectives on Human Resource Management

When work is thought of as a source of personal fulfillment in a unitarist employment relationship, human resource management is seen as an important method for creating productive employment relationships that benefit employers and employees alike. But when work is conceptualized differently, perspectives on human resource management similarly change.[31] When work is thought of as a commodity governed by competitive markets (chapter 3), human resources practices are seen as dictated by the labor market. A firm's compensation cannot lag behind its competitors' or employees will quit; if compensation is overly generous, the employer will suffer from a cost disadvantage when trying to sell products or services. Similarly, to remain competitive, companies must match the efficiency of their competitors' employment practices. The emergence of the division of labor, for example, is seen as coming from market competition, not managerial choice. From this perspective, then, human resource management practices are largely administrative mechanisms for implementing the dictates of competitive labor markets.

In contrast, if work is seen as occupational citizenship in which the employment relationship contains a plurality of shared and conflicting employer-employee interests (chapter 4), then human resources practices reflect this mixture of employer and employee interests. An internal bidding system for job transfers, for example, might represent a compromise between the employer's goal of freely selecting the best applicant and the employees' interests in transparency and objectivity. Moreover, while the unitarist perspective is generally comfortable relying on employer self-interest to promote both employee and employer objectives (since by assumption these can be aligned), the pluralist perspective rejects a sole reliance on employer goodwill (since by assumption there are some interests that clash)—"recessions, depressions, and major industrial downsizings are a mortal threat to advanced, mutual gain [human resource management] systems and can quickly transform employees from high-valued human resource assets to low-valued disposable commodities." When work is conceptualized as occupational citizenship, then, human resource management is seen as useful for aligning those employee-employer interests that are shared, but insufficient for balancing competing interests. From this perspective, human resource management scholarship and practice can also be seen as sophisticated union-avoidance strategies to prevent employees from gaining more power by unionizing. As part of the employee selection process, for example, personality tests can be used to identify "troublemakers" who might be likely to support labor unions.[32]

Lastly, if work is a social relation characterized by antagonistic conflicts of interests and power imbalances (chapter 7), then human resource management practices, and the scholarship that supports them, are seen as disguised rhetoric that quietly undermines worker power and perpetuates managerial control. A mentoring program, for example, is seen not as a method for enhancing job satisfaction and promotion prospects but as a hierarchical means of shaping and disciplining the attitudes of junior employees to serve the employer's interests. Performance appraisals are seen not simply as tools for rewarding and improving employees but also as a means of establishing discipline and control through rankings that "determine who is to be seen in relation to whom." The need for complex motivational systems is interpreted as an indictment of the poor state of work under capitalism. Scientific management is interpreted not as an effort to improve efficiency but as a method for de-skilling jobs that shifts the balance of power in the workplace from skilled workers to managers. The emphasis on unity of interests is seen not as a win–win ideal that truly benefits workers but as the continuing vestiges of medieval master-servant relations in which dissent was illegitimate because a master could "demand unquestioning obedience from his servants."[33]

These and similar critiques are generally rooted in beliefs about antagonistic conflicts of interests associated with neo-Marxist thought, or the manipulation of identity associated with postmodern, Foucauldian thought, and are therefore explored in more detail in chapters 7 and 9. Suffice it to say here that from these perspectives, human resource management practices are viewed as manipulative managerial tools for shaping the ideology and structure of the workplace to strengthen employer control and power at the expense of workers, not to their benefit. Again, conceptualizations of work are very important for how work-related issues are interpreted and understood.

The Difficulty of Deriving Personal Fulfillment from Work

Research in psychology and related areas has uncovered a rich range of cognitive and affective elements of work, from individual differences in mental ability to the importance of attitudes, emotions, and moods. In this way, work involves a variety of cognitive and affective processes. In some respects, then, work occurs in one's mind (and heart). The brain directs our mental and physical actions while also processing what happens to us at work—a compliment from a supervisor, a nasty e-mail message from a co-worker, the completion of a challenging assignment, or a raise and promotion. Viewing work as personal fulfillment therefore highlights the cognitive and affective elements that individuals experience when they work. This conceptualization allows us to see work as a source of psychological well-being, stress, and maybe even joy, and to learn much about these aspects of work from research in I–O psychology and organizational behavior.

Thinking about work in this way is also important because of the insights it provides into the vexing problem of managing workers. The significance of the human factor in this regard was succinctly captured by Henry Ford when he reportedly asked "Why is it that when I hire a pair of hands, I get a human being as well?" Seeing work as personal fulfillment emphasizes the psychological aspects of human beings at work and thereby provides the intellectual foundation for human resource management.

But is work actually fulfilling in practice? Karl Marx, Charles Fourier, Thomas Carlyle, and numerous others in the nineteenth century harshly criticized the Industrial Revolution for its degradation of work that deprived workers of pride, creativity, and other intrinsic rewards. Today, industrialization is taken for granted, but concerns with the separation of the hands and the brain in modern work remain. Forms of work that allow for autonomous decision making, rich interpersonal interactions in effective work teams, and the use of supportive supervision or leadership and other practices are therefore praised for their promotion of psychological well-being. But such policies are far from universal, and work stress, work intensity, and insecurity appear to be on the rise. Human resource management policies are difficult to implement effectively and are criticized by some for being disingenuous schemes to maintain corporate power. How work is experienced by many is therefore criticized for its failure to provide the intrinsic rewards that humans need and deserve.[34] It is hard work making work fulfilling.

CHAPTER 7

Work as a Social Relation

> If hard work were such a wonderful thing, surely the
> rich would have kept it all to themselves.
>
> —Lane Kirkland (1922–99)

More than twenty-five hundred years ago, the
Greek poet Hesiod gave social approval to hard work and described a lack of
acceptability for laziness:

> Both gods and men are angry with a man who lives in idleness, for in
> nature he is like the stingless drones who waste the labor of the bees,
> eating without working; but let it be your care to order your work
> properly, that in the right season your barns may be full. Through work
> men grow rich in flocks and substance, and working they are much
> better loved by the immortals. Work is no disgrace; it is idleness that
> is a disgrace.

In modern Japan and Korea, it is socially unacceptable to leave work before
your boss. The resulting very long work hours take such a physical and psychological toll that there are specific words for death from overwork—*karoshi*
in Japanese, *gwarosa* in Korean. In the early 1600s, the settlers of Jamestown,
the first permanent English colony in America, had the opposite problem.
These colonists did not expect each other to work very hard, and the colony
almost died out because the colonists were more interested in bowling in the
streets than plowing fields and planting crops.[1] In a casual conversation about
why people work, an acquaintance revealed to me that she works so that she
is not seen by others as lazy.

These examples highlight that work occurs within a social context. Work is not shaped simply by economic markets (chapter 3) or human resource management policies (chapter 6), but also by the social structure—that is, by a set of social institutions (social norms, conventions, rules, and procedures) and socially constructed power relations—which determines what is acceptable and what is possible. Work does not only provide income (chapter 5) or psychological satisfaction (chapter 6), but also social approval and status. Work is not just some abstract quantity of productive value (chapter 3), but is an activity that requires human interaction within networks of bosses, co-workers, customers, and others. In these ways, work can be conceptualized as a social relation—a human interaction experienced in and shaped by social networks, social institutions, and socially constructed power relations. From this perspective, work is seen not as something that people simply do, but as a societal creation that "positions us in the power structures of societies" by defining social status and access to resources.[2]

Thinking of work as a social relation encompasses three partially overlapping approaches. First there is a social-exchange approach that emphasizes the consequences of seeing work as a set of interpersonal interactions. A second approach highlights the role of social institutions, especially norms, in shaping work choices and behaviors. A third approach focuses on socially constructed hierarchies and power relations that are seen as critical for understanding work. All these approaches reject the conceptualization of work as simply a free choice made by atomistic individuals, and, in the domain of paid work, as simply an economic transaction between employer and employee. Instead work is seen as a social exchange among various social actors constrained by social norms. Many sociologists, social psychologists, anthropologists, historians, and others therefore see work as embedded in, and defined by, complex social phenomena in which individuals seek approval, status, sociability, and power.[3]

The three approaches to work as a social relation differ in the degree to which they emphasize systemic power differentials and sharply conflicting interests between employers and employees. This emphasis is generally not a central feature of the first approach, it is sometimes the case in the second, and it is a centerpiece of the third. Scholarship that highlights power differentials and conflicting interests stems from Marxist, materialist, feminist, and other schools of thought that for convenience can be grouped together and called critical perspectives. Critical scholarship on work is important not only in sociology but also in history, law, industrial relations, anthropology, archaeology, geography, and, to a lesser extent, economics. Critical scholars see work as particularly characterized by structural and normative struggles for control between employees and employers. From this perspective, then, bureaucracy, employee empowerment, corporate culture, and the division of labor are all seen through this lens of employer control and worker resistance. Unequal power across gender, race, and class is further seen as leading to stratified employment opportunities and gendered and racial divisions of labor (chapter 8). This is a provocative way to conceptualize work.

Thinking about work as a social relation is not limited to paid forms of work. Systems of slavery and other forms of unfree, unpaid labor are stark examples of socially constructed hierarchical work systems that rely on clear power differentials. Volunteering is influenced by social norms.[4] The sexual division of labor of "men's work" and "women's work" affects both the paid and unpaid work roles of men and women in many societies. While many of the examples in this chapter pertain to paid employment, these broader applications should not be overlooked, and they are also explored elsewhere in this book (e.g., chapter 8).

Social Exchanges through Social Networks

Mainstream economic theory sees work as it sees other forms of economic exchange—as an impersonal, financially oriented transaction between calculating, self-interested actors (chapters 3 and 5). In contrast, work can instead be conceptualized as a social exchange. Unlike economic exchanges, social exchanges are characterized by open-ended, ongoing relationships based on trust and reciprocity that have imperfectly specified obligations and a multiplicity of objectives—not only money, but perhaps status, respect, and other socioemotional items.[5]

One example of seeing work as a social exchange is the quintessential corporate employment relationship of the post–World War II period—long-term employment at an organization in which the employer and employee trust and expect each other to do what is necessary for the other's success. In return for their loyalty, employees expect to be rewarded and taken care of in the long run, but they are less concerned with how their daily effort ties explicitly to specific rewards. Employees develop emotional attachments to their organization and feel proud to work for that organization. In fact, these perceived mutual obligations among employees and employers are believed to be sufficiently strong to warrant thinking of them as forming a psychological contract. None of this is to say that financial compensation is not important; rather, if work is (partly) a social exchange, then the bonds between employee and employer are more complex than short-term financial self-interest. Besides an overall employee-employer bond, social exchange relationships can also develop among various individuals or groups, and this has created a veritable alphabet soup of theories: LMX theory (leader-member exchanges), CMX theory (co-worker exchanges), TMX or WGX theory (team or work-group-member exchanges).[6]

Seeing work as a social exchange helps explain workplace behaviors that are difficult to understand if work is only an economic exchange. For example, if work is disutility, then workers are only expected to complete their assigned job tasks. But a large research literature documents the existence of what behavioral scholars call organizational citizenship behaviors (OCBs). OCBs are discretionary actions that help co-workers or the employer but are not formally part of the employee's regular job duties; in other words, lending a helping hand. OCBs are predicted to arise if work is a social exchange because of the ongoing, reciprocal nature of a social exchange—helping another employee, for example, might occur because of help previously received, or potentially needed in the future.[7]

This discussion of various forms of work-related social exchange relationships reinforces the fact that very few people truly work alone. This is partly structural—the division of labor necessitates the use of multiple forms of labor to create a product. But this also reflects the importance of social ties in human behavior. Individual workers, work groups, and organizations "are embedded within networks of interconnected relationships that provide opportunities for and constraints on behavior."[8] In other words, work is conducted through social networks within and across organizations.

How individuals experience work can therefore depend on the characteristics of their social network, or what is frequently called social capital. A particularly strong form of social capital is the Chinese idea of *guanxi*; but social capital can be important in many contexts. With respect to work, social capital is believed to be important for finding new jobs and for being successful in them, with the effectiveness of one's social capital being dependent on the structural nature of one's network as well as the quality of information that is exchanged. Individuals who fill a structural hole by connecting otherwise unconnected individuals can use this advantageous network position to gather and control information; such workers are more likely to be promoted and receive higher bonuses. In contrast, members of disadvantaged socioeconomic groups can suffer from low levels of social capital if their networks do not extend to individuals with greater resources. Note carefully that social networks provide not only opportunities, but also constraints. To maintain a network that is valuable for finding new jobs, for example, individuals must convey positive work qualities consistent with the norms of their occupation. Networked social relations, then, can be a source of normative control that, in essence, punishes individuals who significantly deviate from accepted norms.[9]

Norms, Social Institutions, and Organizational Culture at Work

Dating back to the founders of sociology such as Émile Durkheim and Max Weber, social and behavioral scientists from varied disciplines have believed that social norms fundamentally shape human behavior via social sanctions such as group acceptance for those who abide by the norms and exclusion for those who violate them.[10] Applying this perspective to work is to see work as defined, constrained, and facilitated by sets of norms (that is, by social institutions). This provides a sharp contrast to nonsocial theories in which behavior and roles are rooted in satisfying one's individual economic or psychological needs.

The distinctiveness of the social institution perspective is illustrated by the idea of a career. To a layperson, an economist, or a psychologist, a career is likely seen as a set of jobs chosen by an individual over his or her working life. But a sociologist likely sees the concept of "career" as a social construction that grew out of the rise of corporations and white-collar work. In the social imagination, careers then became associated with a working life of stable, upwardly mobile paid jobs in a chosen profession, which in turn marginalized those working in the so-called secondary sector without job security and benefits, and also those engaged in unpaid work—primarily women caring for others (chapter 8). So in the words of the sociologist Phyllis Moen, "careers are more than shorthand encapsulations of personal biographies; they are located within—and serve to sustain—a social structure that defines a repertoire of expected behaviors and relationships."[11] This perspective can only come from seeing work as a social relation.

Work is affected by various levels of social norms. The importance throughout history of social norms at a cultural level is illustrated by the examples that opened this chapter. Accordingly, there is now a large body of research that analyzes cross-cultural work behaviors. One of the most well-known approaches is Geert Hofstede's five dimensions of national culture: power distance (the extent to which the less powerful accept inequality), uncertainty avoidance (tolerance for uncertainty), individualism/collectivism (strength of group ties), masculinity/femininity (assertiveness and achievement versus caring and cooperation), and long-term/short-term orientation. Hofstede scores countries on these dimensions—for example, power distance is high in the Philippines and Mexico, uncertainty avoidance is high in

Greece and Portugal, and individualism is high in the United States, Britain, and Australia—and then compares these scores to cultural work trends. For example, work is more hierarchical in countries with high power distance and uncertainty avoidance scores, cooperative teamwork is emphasized in feminine countries, individual rewards are more important in individualistic countries, and labor unions are stronger in collective cultures. Contemporary research on cross-cultural work behaviors is more likely to be authored by psychologists than sociologists.[12] National culture is therefore likely to be seen as a set of values rooted in individual mental processes, but to the extent that cultural values are socially constructed and influence behavior through pressures for conformity, they should also be seen as norm-based, social institutions.

At a cultural level, social norms also exert powerful influences on the appropriate and inappropriate work roles for men and women (chapter 8). The social dynamics that make work a social relation are also apparent within work groups and organizations. Frederick Winslow Taylor famously critiqued what he saw as the universal work practice of "soldiering," that is, workers purposely working slower than their full capability. Why was this practice so widespread? Not because of laziness, but because

> it evidently becomes for each man's interest, then, to see that no job is done faster than it has been in the past. The younger and less experienced men are taught this by their elders, and all possible persuasion and social pressure is brought to bear upon the greedy and selfish men to keep them from making new records which result in temporarily increasing their wages, while all those who come after them are made to work harder for the same old pay.

The famous Hawthorne experiments of the 1920s and 1930s and other studies reinforced Taylor's observations and led the Hawthorne researchers to emphasize social dynamics as the key determinant of work behaviors. The workers who were studied in these experiments ignored the official production standard and instead "had an informal standard of a day's work which functioned for the group as a norm of conduct, as a social code."[13] Workers who violated this group norm were given derogatory nicknames, harassed, and ostracized, while adherence to the group norm provided the basis for solidarity against unfavorable supervision and employer policies.

Organizations are social systems, too. The set of norms governing work in a particular organization can therefore be seen as a form of a social institution and is popularly referred to as corporate or organizational culture. Corporate culture is a frequent topic in the popular business press. Whenever two companies announce a proposed merger, questions over the compatibility of the two corporate cultures are raised; whenever there is a corporate scandal, there are questions about what type of corporate culture allows such scandals to occur. Analyzing the effect of organizational culture on work behaviors is also a major research topic in psychology and organizational behavior. It is important to remember that organizational culture is a social phenomenon:

> To warrant the label, "culture," some number of individuals, via mutual influence processes, must come to share a set of values, sentiments, and understandings. Their "collective consciousness," itself conveyed through networks, then constrains the actions of others. In this way, culture both emerges from the confluence of individual actions and is simultaneously experienced by individuals as an exterior and constraining social force.

Moreover, when organizations are seen as networks of *hierarchical* social relations, organizational culture reflects the power differences that underlie these relations.[14] In this way, organizational culture not only shapes work behaviors in a functional manner, but also becomes a normative device of workplace control and the site of employer-employee struggles for how work will be defined, structured, and experienced.

The Normative Control of Work

To get workers to serve their employer's goals to their greatest ability, mainstream economists focus on monetary incentives, psychologists emphasize intrinsic rewards, some authoritarian bosses might favor aggressive supervision and monitoring, and human resources professionals are trained in the importance of performance appraisals, feedback, training, and coaching. But if work is a social relation, then norms, social institutions, and organizational culture can be important determinants of worker effort and cooperation. "By winning the hearts and minds of the workforce, managers [can] achieve the most subtle of all forms of control: moral authority."[15] Theories of the *normative* control of work therefore reveal how norms, culture, and identities can be manipulated to regulate employees, in contrast to the emphasis on rewards in economic and psychological theories and to the *structural* forms of control discussed later in this chapter.

Workers are more likely to consent to employer authority if this authority is seen as consistent with workplace or societal norms and therefore viewed as legitimate. The nature of a workplace's norms can therefore be quite important to employees and employers alike. An employer that wants to speed up production, for example, is unlikely to be successful if this violates accepted effort norms in that workplace. Clashes in interests between employees and employers, therefore, likely manifest themselves as struggles over defining and refining these norms. In other words, if there is a contest over workplace control, it might not be over who has the legal authority to rule the workplace, but "over specific norms and standards defining the nature of work and the employment relation, such as job security, safety, and protection from arbitrary supervision."[16]

Psychological contracts can also be seen as a form of normative workplace control. Employees who feel that they have established a psychological contract will be hardworking, loyal, and committed because they believe their employers have a reciprocal obligation to live up to "their end of the bargain" by providing the employees with job security, promotion opportunities, and other rewards. But in reality, employers have no such obligation, and employees frequently report perceived violations of their psychological contracts. The true power of psychological contracts, therefore, might be in making a hierarchical employment relationship seem balanced to employees and thereby providing legitimacy for the existing social order.[17]

Organizational culture can be another mechanism of normative control. A corporation's culture is not something that simply exists. Rather, organizations actively use training sessions, mentoring programs, company communications, social events, and other activities to intentionally create a shared set of employee values and norms. Behind this are important psychological and social forces. Psychologically, when employees internalize these values, they identify with the organization, form emotional attachments, and serve the organization's interests as if they are their own. In Foucauldian terms, workers become self-disciplining.[18] Sociologically, culture shapes work behaviors by sanctioning those who violate these norms. For example, a culture of "work hard, play hard" causes employees to embrace long hours to further the success of their organization and therefore their personal success; the threat of disapproving managers and co-workers further reinforces a culture of long work hours. A culture of teamwork similarly regulates employee behavior by equating team success with personal success and by creating peer pressure to work hard and not let the team down.

The normative control aspects of organizational culture can be assessed in two very different ways. On the one hand, if workers' true interests largely align with corporate interests (recall the unitarist employment relationship from chapter 6), then employer efforts to create organizational cultures can be seen as win-win situations for employers and employees. On the other hand, if work is a hierarchical social relation with conflicting interests, then these efforts can be seen as sophisticated campaigns to coerce workers into serving corporate rather than personal needs and goals. From this latter perspective, organizational culture is more accurately described as "organizational ideology," as it is crafted to serve one group's interests over another's, and organizational communication should be seen not simply as information sharing, but as a strategic method of controlling employees by shaping their perceptions and understandings.[19]

In fact, various ideologies can be used to promote employers' interests. Creation of a culture of individualism and merit-based rewards can be used to weaken worker support for labor unions. An ideology of marketplace business competition can reduce worker resistance to wage and benefit concessions and other forms of organizational change in the name of organizational survival. Case studies reveal how leaders in multinational corporations are able to stimulate competition between plants or divisions by manipulating workers' loyalties, national identities, and economic insecurities while also using investment decisions to reward compliance and punish resistance.[20]

Lastly, in considering the role of social norms in work, it is important to guard against reification—or what more crudely can be called "thingification." Reification occurs when a socially created concept is transformed into a concrete object and therefore treated as natural and immutable. For example, the neoliberal market paradigm that privileges economic efficiency and shareholder returns over other interests, emphasizes individual over collective employment relations, justifies corporate downsizings, cuts in employee benefit packages, and increased contingent work as necessary for efficiency, and accepts economic inequality as fair because it is market-driven is such a strong part of the twenty-first-century global culture that it is often seen as an objective, unchangeable truth. Workers therefore accept—and even expect—a lack of job security, the threat of wage and benefit concessions, and demands to be constantly connected via e-mail, cell phones, and other means. As a second example, the Japanese culture of paternalism and mutual trust is learned at an early age and generates worker compliance through devotion to their employer. This is seen as an immutable character of Japanese society.[21]

Seeing work as a hierarchical social relation means that the neoliberal market paradigm and a paternalistic work culture both are socially constructed normative methods of workplace control reflecting unequal power dynamics in society, not immutable facts of life or a natural state of affairs. The reification of these norms so that we accept them as unchangeable truths, however, hides the true nature of these norms and maintains the status quo, and thus should be avoided. Rather, we need to better understand how social institutions develop and are perpetuated, including the importance of language, discourse, and communication in shaping views on work.[22]

The Unequal Power and Class Relations of Capitalist Work

In nonmarket societies, work is "embedded in the total cultural fabric" and cannot be separated from kinship and political obligations, spiritual practices, beliefs about nature, and other essential elements of daily life. In industrial societies, however, we often go "off" to work, and work is seen as occupying a distinct sphere of our lives. In this way, it is easy to lose sight of the socially embedded nature of work in industrial societies. Moreover, mainstream economic thought sees the capitalist production system not as a social system, but as a separate technical system that generates economic efficiencies by optimally allocating inputs through the price mechanism of competitive markets. The existence of this system is so ingrained in Western culture that it is taken for granted and seen as a thing (that is, it is "reified"). Marxist and related schools of critical thought instead emphasize that capitalism is not a thing separate from society but is a set of social relations that are created by society. In the words of Karl Marx, "Nature does not produce on the one side owners of money and commodities, and on the other men possessing nothing but their own labor power." Rather, socially constructed laws define the rights of an employer to sell the products of its workers. As such, capitalism defines the "rights and power over resources" in a particular way, and "these rights and powers are attributes of social relations" because they control not how people relate to things, but to each other.[23]

From this Marxist perspective, work is seen as embedded in an unequal capitalist social structure in which workers' rights and power over resources are defined as the right to sell one's labor power as a commodity with no claim to the product of that labor power or to the means of production.[24] This view of work falls within the conceptualization of work as a social relation because the rights and power of capital and labor are socially constructed. Replacing (or supplementing) capitalism with patriarchy such that male-dominated institutions are seen as structuring work to favor men over women yields another example of work as characterized by a socially constructed, unequal power relation. These perspectives have important implications for how we think about the employment relationship and class or gender, with an emphasis on unequal power relations. This section and the one that follows focus on Marxist-inspired analyses of the capitalist employment relationship and class; feminist theories of patriarchy and gender are discussed in chapter 8.

First consider the capitalist employment relationship. Marx distinguished between "labor" and "labor power." Labor is one's actual work; labor power is the potential to labor. The employer buys labor power but then faces the problem of getting the workers to actually work and create something of value through what Marx called the labor process. For Marx, the basis of capitalist exploitation is that the value of what labor creates in excess of the wage paid for labor power ("surplus value") accrues to the capitalist, not the worker. This creates a highly conflicted labor process:

> The directing motive, the end and aim of capitalist production, is to extract the greatest possible amount of surplus-value, and consequently to exploit labor-power to the greatest possible extent. As the number of the cooperating laborers increases, so too does their resistance to the domination of capital, and with it, the necessity for capital to over-come this resistance by counter-pressure. The control exercised by the capitalist . . . is consequently rooted in the unavoidable antagonism between the exploiter and the living and laboring raw material he exploits.

The result is the abusive nature of work under capitalism that Marx so harshly critiqued:

> Within the capitalist system all methods for raising the social produc-tiveness of labor are brought about at the cost of the individual laborer; all means for the development of production transform themselves into means of domination over, and exploitation of, the producers; they mutilate the laborer into a fragment of a man, degrade him to the level of an appendage of a machine, destroy every remnant of charm in his work and turn it into a hated toil; they estrange from him the intellectual potentialities of the labor-process in the same proportion as science is incorporated in it as an independent power; they dis-tort the conditions under which he works, subject him during the labor-process to a despotism the more hateful for its meanness; they transform his life-time into working-time, and drag his wife and child beneath the wheels of the Juggernaut of capital.[25]

It bears repeating that these conditions were seen by Marx as stemming from *socially defined* power relationships between employers and employees, not something natural. Capitalism is a social relation, not a thing. And thus, work is a social relation.

Socially created power relations not only define individual employment relationships (see the next section) but can also be seen as defining a society's classes on an aggregate level. In other words, while there are multiple theories of class, the Marxist perspective defines classes by the rights and power they possess in the social relations of production. In this framework, then, under capitalism there are only two main classes—those who own the means of production (capitalists) and those who do not (the working class)—and they possess sharply divergent interests. By placing the social relations of production at the center of society, Marx made class conflict a key social dynamic that reaches far beyond the workplace. The persistence of capitalism for two centuries undermines Marx's famous belief that this class conflict would inevitably lead to the collapse of capitalism, but it is still useful to analyze social institutions through a lens of capitalist reproduction. Specifically, this perspective highlights that employers and other ruling elites need to work hard at maintaining their power in the face of working-class resistance. As one example of the provocative lens this creates for thinking about work-related issues, government-funded job-training programs that emphasize positive attitudes such as a strong work ethic and submission to authority can be seen as reinforcing employer power by teaching workers to accept lousy working conditions and to not question the authority of employers. As a second example, the male-breadwinner social norm that accompanied industrialization can be seen as a disciplinary device that required men to be the good workers that employers required: "reliable, steady, and willing to work long hours, conform to rules, and put up with dangerous conditions."[26]

The Structural Control of Work

The human resource management approach to work sees work as structured to promote efficiency that benefits workers, their employers, and society (chapter 6). This thinking is rooted in a unitarist vision of the employment relationship in which employers and employees have mostly shared interests. In the various strains of critical thought that descended (to varying degrees) from the Marxist view of the social relations of production, however, employers and employees are seen as having sharply antagonistic interests. Compared to other perspectives, critical thought sees the employment relationship as more antagonistic because of the capitalist drive for profit at the workers' expense, and because the assumption that workers are alienated under capitalism (chapters 3 and 9) means that psychological fulfillment is impossible and workers therefore have little to gain from their work:

> In a situation where workers do not control their own labor process and cannot make their work a creative experience, any exertion beyond

the minimum needed to avert boredom will not be in the workers' interest. On the other side, for the capitalist it is true *without limit* that the more work he can wring out of the labor power he has purchased, the more goods will be produced; and they will be produced without any increased wage costs.[27]

Labor process theory focuses on how labor power is transformed into productive work effort against this backdrop of antagonistic interests. Mainstream economics has been criticized for assuming this problem away by seeing the employment relationship as a transaction in which explicit or implicit contracts specify the details of the wage-effort bargain. Labor process theory instead sees such contracts as impossible in the complexities of the real-world employment relationship, and the resulting indeterminacy of the transformation of labor power into labor provides the space for conflicts between employer control and worker resistance. Sociologist Frank Dobbin's description of Marx is a good way to think about this critical perspective: "Like [mainstream] economists, Marx argued that self-interest shapes economic behavior. But for Marx, self-interest leads people to try to shape the world to their advantage rather than to merely achieve the best price in every transaction." Employers and employees are therefore seen as trying to structure work to their own advantage at the other's expense, and the workplace becomes "contested terrain."[28]

The seminal work on labor process theory is Harry Braverman's *Labor and Monopoly Capital*. Frederick Winslow Taylor and other proponents of scientific management saw scientific management as a method for regularizing work to make it efficient to the benefit of both employers and workers (chapter 6). Braverman developed a very different interpretation—that scientific management was an intentional employer strategy to control the workplace:

> That management had the right to "control" labor was generally assumed before Taylor, but in practice this right usually meant only the general setting of tasks, with little direct interference in the worker's mode of performing them. Taylor's contribution was to overturn this practice and replace it by its opposite. Management, he insisted, could be only a limited and frustrated undertaking so long as it left to the worker any decision about the work. His "system" was simply a means for management to achieve control of the actual mode of performance of every labor activity, from the simplest to the most complicated.

From this perspective, scientific management's decomposition of jobs into simple tasks is seen as a strategy not just for removing inefficient steps, but for eliminating worker discretion. The separation of conception and execution is seen as a strategy not just for designing better processes, but for ensuring employer knowledge of how work should be done. Knowledge is power, and scientific management de-skills jobs by shifting knowledge from workers to employers. This facilitates employer control over how each job is done. It also increases employer control over the workforce, because lower-skilled workers are easier to replace than higher-skilled workers. By replacing worker discretion and thought with mind-numbing repetitive tasks, this detailed *manufacturing* division of labor—in contrast to the *social* division of labor into different occupations common throughout history—is also seen as degrading and dehumanizing work.[29] This is a perspective on the division of labor much different from mainstream economics' emphasis on maximizing efficiency and Taylor's win-win vision.

The literal implementation of scientific management was perhaps limited to the first decades of the 1900s, but its mind-set for routinizing the structure of work was "the bedrock of all work design" for much of the twentieth century. The "mental revolution" of scientific management, to use Taylor's phrase, can therefore be seen as an employer control device over many types of work that continues to be very relevant. As just one example, service workers can be controlled by scripts that they must follow in interacting with customers. That these scripts are written by employers reflects Taylor's separation of conception and execution, and sociologist Robin Leidner's study of McDonald's and a large insurance company shows how these scripts regulate employee decision making and emotional displays, threaten workers' identities (chapter 9), and control customers' decision making by routinizing their choices.[30]

More generally, economist Richard Edwards identifies three employer control strategies found in capitalist enterprises: direct control, in which immediate supervisors closely monitor workers and drive them with threats; technical control, in which machinery such as assembly lines or computers determine how work is done; and bureaucratic control, in which organizational rules and hierarchies structure work. Within a system of bureaucratic control, "the definition and direction of work tasks, the evaluation of worker performances, and the distribution of rewards and imposition of punishments all . . . depend upon established rules and procedures." Today, we call these established rules and procedures human resource management practices. From a critical perspective, these human resource management practices are intentionally designed to extract and direct workers' efforts solely for corporate gain.[31] Organizational hierarchies also serve as control devices by making it seem like power comes from the formal, bureaucratic organization rather than from unequal social relations of production.

These three control strategies can be viewed as a progression—from direct control in the 1800s, to technical control in the early 1900s, to bureaucratic control in the post–World War II period—while also recognizing the continued presence of all three forms in various situations. For example, very small enterprises might still be characterized by direct control. But given the movement away from bureaucratic work structures over the past three decades, a fourth control strategy can now be identified—"concertive" control through work teams. To counter perceived problems of organizational inflexibility and individual tedium, the strategic human resource management movement emphasizes high-performance, team-oriented, flexible practices that empower employees to make decisions. From a unitarist perspective, this is an improved win-win situation, but through a critical lens, this represents another method of employer control of the workplace:

> The empowerment granted is first and foremost in the interests of management rather than for the job satisfaction of employees. . . . Employees may have increased discretion at [an] operational level, but subject to accountability to managerial standards derived from an agenda firmly set by management.[32]

It might seem that members of self-managed work teams are empowered, but team-based performance norms, enforced by peer pressure, control employee behavior as if they were supervisors' rules. Since control resides in the teams, organizational power becomes less visible, but also more powerful. Employee involvement initiatives can also strengthen employer control by weakening employee support for labor unions. Admittedly, the line between structural control through how work is organized and normative control through norms becomes quite blurry in the "empowered" workplace, but the key point is that the critical perspective of labor process theory provides a unique lens for analyzing the "dark side of flexibility," which is seen as inherent in the capitalist labor process.[33]

Conceptualizing employer strategies in terms of controlling the workplace is a very important approach, but a singular focus on employer control can make it seem that workers are passive. Marxist/materialist perspectives on worker agency therefore draw attention to the nature of worker resistance and noncompliance in defense of their interests against employer control devices. Worker noncompliance or "misbehavior" can take many forms, including absenteeism, soldiering, misuse of company resources, or forming labor unions, depending on whether employers and employees are struggling over the appropriation of time, work, product, or identity. The Foucauldian labor process theory perspective, however, does not assume that workers have an objective understanding of how their material interests clash with those of their employers, and this type of scholarship therefore emphasizes the importance of subjective worker perceptions of their identities as preconditions for how they will act (chapter 9). Emerging work is starting to bring these perspectives together by seeing work-related interests and identities as complements rather than strict alternatives.[34]

A singular dichotomy of "control versus resistance" unfortunately reduces the employment relationship to a solely conflictual relation. In reality, employment is also characterized by worker consent. It is therefore now common for labor process theorists to think in terms of a "dialectic of control and accommodation."[35] This reflects a nuanced conception of the labor process in which conflict *and* consent are both important, and in which workers *and* employers have agency as active participants in the labor process. The inherent tensions between conflict and consent further make the employment relationship a dynamic social relation in which employers and workers are constantly readjusting their control strategies, resistance tactics, and areas of accommodation. Again, this element of work reflects a social relation conceptualization of work because it only becomes apparent when the social character of work is recognized.

These social relations of conflict and consent go beyond single workplaces. Scholarship from geography reveals how the spatial locations and the spatial mobility of employees and employers are important aspects of the labor process. For example,

> The development of a particular "spatial division of labour" not only reflects how the labour process is organized but also then shapes its further development—the geographical splitting up of the various parts of the production chain may allow for continued functional integration, even as it helps divide workers spatially and so reduces the kinds of contacts between them that might facilitate oppositional politics.

It is also important not to lose sight of the state's role in the structural control of work. While workplace contests over effort, rewards, and the structure of work appear to be private matters between organizations and workers, the state underlies these interactions by defining important legal rights that shape workplace authority and power structures, particularly pertaining to property, hiring and firing, and unionization. Sometimes the state is even more actively involved in the labor process. In China, the government denies residency permits for rural laborers while also providing them with temporary dormitory accommodations adjacent to urban factories. This directly affects the labor process by ensuring a supply of fresh labor reserves of young workers who work long hours and who are replaced before they can demand higher wages or develop solidarity with their co-workers.[36]

State intervention in the labor process such as this can be seen as serving its economic development interests while also serving as a mechanism for controlling troublesome segments of the populace. In the words of the philosopher Friedrich Nietzsche,

> Fundamentally, one now feels at the sight of work—one always means by work that hard industriousness from early till late—that such work is the best policeman, that it keeps everyone in bounds and can mightily hinder the development of reason, covetousness, desire for independence. For it uses up an extraordinary amount of nervous energy, which is thus denied to reflection, brooding, dreaming, worrying, loving, hating; it sets a small goal always in sight and guarantees easy and regular satisfactions. Thus a society in which there is continual hard work will have more security.

Along these lines, Aristotle argued that Egyptian rulers used the building of the pyramids to prevent rebellion by keeping their subjects working too hard to have time to conspire against them. Contemporary examples in which states deploy forced labor—such as Stalin's Soviet Gulag system, forced labor under the Nazis, China's *laogai* system of forced labor, or convict labor in the American prison system—can be seen in similar terms.[37] While most of the research attention appropriately focuses on the workplace and organizational levels, the structural control of labor is a multilevel phenomenon.

How Important are Social Relations for Work?

It is hard to deny that social relations are an important aspect of work. In fact, some social relations even reproduce and perpetuate themselves. Occupational norms, for example, shape the actions of individuals in those occupations, and these actions reinforce and perpetuate these same norms. The culture of computer programmers encourages programmers to pull all-nighters to finish a project, and every time a programmer follows this norm and pulls an all-nighter, this culture is reinforced. In the first part of the twentieth century, statisticians in the U.S. Census Bureau recoded the occupational information of individual women and minorities to lower-status occupations when the self-reported occupation seemed to be of a higher status than allowed by the statisticians' assumptions about "women's work" and "minority work."[38] The official "statistics" then reproduced the norms about "women's work" or "minority work" by "showing" that women and minorities were frequently in low-status jobs. To a lesser extent this continues today, as gender is one factor used by the Census Bureau to fill in missing occupation codes.

Other social relations aspects of work might be more difficult to maintain, particularly employers' control over workers. The history of modern management—from the beginning of the factory system, to scientific management, bureaucratic control, human resource management, and most recently, employee empowerment—can therefore be seen as a long wave of struggles for control of the social relations of the workplace. This view is not universally shared, but those who reject the idea that social institutions, norms, and employment practices are purposefully manipulated by a dominant group should recognize that "all human societies tend to be structured as systems of group-based social hierarchies," perhaps because of psychological predispositions to favor in-group over out-group members in order to feel good about oneself while reducing uncertainty and threats to one's well-being. And even in the absence of explicit manipulation or discrimination, the social relations of work can be hierarchical, and unequal levels of social capital can perpetuate work-related inequalities. Such inequalities undermine the popular belief that Western workplaces and societies are meritocracies.[39]

In terms of the importance of the social relations conceptualization of work, sociologist Mark Granovetter's warning against oversocializing one's view of human behavior applies to the conceptualization of work. Mainstream economic theorizing contains an undersocialized conceptualization in which social relations have minimal effects on workers; rather, agents are assumed to freely choose whatever course of action maximizes their individual utility (chapter 5). To emphasize the contrasts with previous chapters, in this chapter I emphasize the social relations aspects of work, but this is not intended to imply that we should see work as oversocialized. Work is not completely determined by social forces, because individuals have what social scientists call agency—the ability to act, determine their futures, and shape the social structure.[40]

For example, workers can act to redress dissatisfactory working conditions. Mainstream economists emphasize the ability of employees to quit a lousy job, but seeing work as a social relation opens up additional possibilities. Individuals can be "job crafters" by altering their work tasks and co-worker interactions to shape the nature of their own jobs. Workers can renegotiate workplace norms. Workers can try to appropriate time, work, resources, and identity. And workers can mobilize with their co-workers and form labor unions or participate in other social movements.[41] It is important to remember that these and other forms of worker resistance to dissatisfaction, as well as the opposite side of the same coin (consent), are central topics in sociology and related disciplines because of a specific conceptualization of work—work as an unequal, hierarchical social relation.

While workers have agency, their actions are also affected by norms, values, power, and other elements of the social structure. The ability to craft one's job is not unlimited and varies across individuals and occupations, while efforts to form unions are constrained by attitudes and labor laws. A study of factories taken over by workers in Argentina shows that while workers replaced hierarchical work structures with more egalitarian ones, competitive market pressures on the business side limited the extent of these changes. In the words of Karl Marx, humans "make their own history, but they do not make it just as they please; they do not make it under circumstances chosen by themselves, but under circumstances directly encountered, given and transmitted from the past." This duality between structure and agency remains a central tension in modern sociology.[42] The challenge, therefore, is to find a conceptual balance in which work as a social relation means that social interactions shape the nature of work, but not in a completely deterministic fashion, and perhaps in differing ways across time, space, and level of analysis.

CHAPTER 8

Work as Caring for Others

> Man's work lasts till set of sun; woman's work is never done.
>
> —Proverb

In George Elgar Hicks's painting *The Sinews of Old England* (1857), a sturdy man is about to leave for work, pickax over his shoulder, while his wife is portrayed as staying behind to tend to the household chores and care for their son. In Grant Wood's *American Gothic* (1930), a man dressed in overalls holds a pitchfork, and his workplace (a barn) is visible behind his left shoulder, while a woman, perhaps the farmer's unmarried daughter, is framed by her workplace (a house), and an apron covers her dress. These paintings portray a sexual division of labor in which men engage in physical work outside the home while women focus on domestic labor in it.[1] In fact, if these paintings came to life, the women likely would promptly disappear back into their homes to resume their work.

Industrialization frequently renders this domestic work invisible. An emphasis on producing commodities and contributing to economic development or corporate profitability prioritizes paid employment (chapter 3). Using wages to indicate worth denies unpaid domestic work the appearance of value. Treating childbirth, child care, and other domestic activities as part of a woman's biological nature makes them appear to be instinctual activities done out of love, in contrast to the "real work" of earning a living. Using statistics such as per capita income, the unemployment rate, and gross domestic product to measure economic prosperity signals that unpaid household work is not a valuable activity. This is not solely a Western phenomenon;

China's emphasis on economic development after the Communist revolution similarly prioritized paid employment and devalued unpaid housework. In a classic work on Africa and Asia, economist Ester Boserup shows how women bear the greater burden of economic development by being confined to unpaid household work and the lowest-paid sectors of the labor market.[2]

Feminist thought rejects this devaluing of household work and emphasizes that it is indeed work. Specifically, it is work as caring for others—"the physical, mental, and emotional activities and effort involved in looking after, responding to, and supporting others." Caring involves serving others (chapter 10), but not all forms of serving others involves caring for them in a deeply personal, physical, and emotional way. Building a house for someone could be an example of serving others; personally helping them around that house when they are ill is caring work. Caring for others is not limited to unpaid household work, as demonstrated by paid jobs in the health care and educational sectors; and except for childbirth, it need not be the exclusive domain of women, as indicated by male nurses and stay-at-home dads. But for reasons that likely have much more to do with social norms and power differentials than with biology, caring for others is seen as "women's work" in many societies, albeit with differing norms across cultures and socioeconomic status. In fact, the idea of caring has been constructed to fundamentally define women's roles and identities:

> The experience of caring is the medium through which women are accepted into and feel they belong in the social world. It is the medium through which they gain admittance into both the private world of the home and the public world of the labour market. It is through caring in an informal capacity—as mothers, wives, daughters, neighbours, friends—and through formal caring—as nurses, secretaries, cleaners, teachers, social workers—that women enter and occupy their place in society.[3]

Caring for others is therefore an important conceptualization of work. It highlights the importance of forms of work that are frequently unpaid, while simultaneously providing for a gendered understanding of work that questions the universality of other conceptualizations of work. In other words, work as freedom, a commodity, fulfillment through paid employment, or occupational citizenship might be male-dominated conceptualizations that fail to fully understand how women experience work. To see work as caring for others also deepens our understanding of work by uncovering the social roots of the sexual division of labor and thereby forcing us to confront the hierarchical nature of many societies. These hierarchies are reflected not only in the realities of gender discrimination in the workplace but also in the gendered cultural norms that define appropriate work roles for men and women within the home and the workplace. Lastly, including an appreciation for work as caring for others in the full range of conceptualizations of work fosters a more holistic understanding of work in which one's home life and work life are inseparable.

The Sexual Division of Labor and the Cult of Domesticity

Many societies throughout history and in all regions of the globe have been characterized by a sexual division of labor. Anthropologists George Murdock and Caterina Provost analyzed 185 societies representing diverse geographical regions, time periods, prevailing descent rules (e.g., matrilineal), political complexity, and linguistic families. In an overwhelming majority of the cases, activities such as hunting large animals, smelting ore, metalworking, and woodworking were done exclusively by males, while cooking, spinning, laundering, and fetching water were predominately female activities. In China, the continuing norm that women's work is "inside work" (domestic chores, spinning, weaving) and men's work is "outside work" (farming, wage work) is probably more than two thousand years old. In the Turkish working class, "a 'good' woman knows how to clean, cook, serve, embroider, knit, and crochet," while men are "deemed incapable of living in a household without a woman to look after their needs."[4]

On the eve of industrialization in Britain, the United States, and elsewhere, many households survived by combining small-scale agriculture with household production for consumption and sale. While there was a sexual division of labor, there was not a clear physical distinction between the spheres of production and reproduction (broadly defined). In other words, the "home and economy were the same," and "men and women often worked side by side in the production of foodstuffs and handicrafts."[5] This is not to deny the patriarchal nature of these male-dominated families, but it is to suggest that women's economic contributions to the household were visible.

Industrialization moved commodity production out of the household and into the factory and created sharp physical boundaries between the economy and the home. Various changes in household work patterns could have emerged—women could have worked for wages while men stayed home (as was the case for early textile mills), men and women could have worked in and out of the home equally (as is the case for some households today), or men and women could have assumed fluid work responsibilities over the course of the life cycle. But the social norm that triumphed was the cult of domesticity—the ideology that a woman's natural place is in the home taking care of her family, and because these nurturing activities are part of a woman's nature, they are not really work. In other words, at the start of the nineteenth century, women's household activities were valued as productive labor; by the end of the century, women were seen as dependents of male breadwinners—a vision most-pronounced in the socially constructed view of unpaid, unproductive housewives whose domestic responsibilities have no economic value.[6]

This vision did not simply emerge—it was actively created through photography, novels, homemaker manuals, reform campaigns, and other intentional displays emphasizing women's "proper" domestic roles. Labor leaders similarly contributed to the creation of this ideology by championing the vision of the male breadwinner entitled to a family wage. Admittedly, many women worked for pay outside the home, especially young women who had not yet married and women from poor families that could not live on a single income. But gendered norms implied that such work was preparation for or part of a woman's responsibility for caring for her family rather than serving her personal needs or aspirations.[7]

In Britain, Canada, the United States, and elsewhere in the twenty-first century, caring is still seen primarily as women's work:

> Wherever care is provided, whether paid or unpaid, it is overwhelmingly women who provide it. Women comfort, feed, bathe, toilet, record, clean for, shop for, do laundry for, manage and supervise those needing care, often combining these tasks with more clinical interventions.

Even children express this gendered view by associating women with housekeeping, child care, nursing, and teaching. Admittedly, men do more domestic caring today than in the past two centuries. But this is typically considered "helping out"—in other words, women are still ultimately responsible for household work, and the cult of domesticity persists. Expectations of domesticity continue to apply to women regardless of whether they also work outside the home. So-called "working women"—a term that itself reflects the invisibility of domestic work—frequently must work a "second shift" or a "double day": a full complement of domestic responsibilities after a day of paid employment.[8] In the workplace, women confront gendered expectations about appropriate occupations and work behaviors that are frequently rooted in idealized visions of caring, domesticity, and femininity.

On a broader scale, the cult of domesticity further reinforced important dichotomies in the social imagination: the public economic realm versus the private household, production versus consumption, competition versus nurturing, and work versus leisure.[9] These dichotomies still affect contemporary Western conceptualizations of work and continue to marginalize the contributions of those who care for others.

Caring: A Labor of Love?

It is common to see caring as a labor of love. This characterization highlights the mixed nature of and the debates over caring. An emphasis is placed on love by those who see caring as reflecting some natural female instinct for nurturing others. In this way, it is not seen as real work with legitimate economic value. The U.S. legal system, for example, "conceptualizes housework as solely an expression of affection, the currency of familial emotions"—there are no benefits such as workers' compensation, no direct entitlements to social security (only as a spouse), and only a limited recognition of economic value in divorce proceedings.[10] From this perspective, the sexual division of labor reflects "natural," innate biological or psychological differences between men and women.

For decades, feminist scholars and activists have challenged this implication that caring for a household is not a productive, economic activity. Over one hundred years ago, feminist writer Charlotte Perkins Gilman argued that

> although not producers of wealth, women serve in the final processes of preparation and distribution. Their labor in the household has a genuine economic value. For a certain percentage of persons to serve other persons, in order that the ones so served may produce more, is a contribution not to be overlooked. The labor of women in the house, certainly, enables men to produce more wealth than they otherwise could; and in this way women are economic factors in society.

Feminist scholarship similarly rejects the claim that caring is a natural maternal instinct rather than real work. In the words of Gilman again, "It is not motherhood that keeps the housewife on her feet from dawn till dark; it is house service, not child service. Women work longer and harder than most men, and not solely in maternal duties."[11]

In contrast to the assertion that the sexual division of labor reflects "natural" differences, research indicates that the physical and psychological characteristics of men and women are more similar than different. Variation in the sexual division of labor across time and culture also undermines the natural explanation. In Murdock and Provost's study, there are frequently exceptions to the general patterns, such as working with wood being a female task among the Native American Pawnees, and many activities are done by both men and women in a single culture, or assigned differently across cultures. Crop planting, for example, is almost equally likely to be a male-dominated activity, a shared activity, or a female-dominated activity. There are also examples of societies that exhibit minimal degrees of a sexual division of labor, such as the Qhawqhat Lahu of southwest China. By way of a modern example, clerical office work was seen as a man's job in the mid-nineteenth century but was reconstituted as women's work in the early twentieth century and continues to be a female-dominated occupation today.[12]

Feminist scholars, therefore, typically assert that gender is socially, not biologically, constructed. The *social* significance of being male or female—expectations regarding career choice, family responsibilities, cultural interests, and the like—is defined through social norms. Gender "puts reproductive differences into play" because it is the way in which "our social conduct does something with reproductive difference." In other words, gender is the "social organization of sexual difference"—culturally produced understandings that establish "meanings for bodily differences." Differences in gender arrangements across countries and history demonstrate that this is much more complicated than a simple expression of biological differences. Even within cultures, "social practices sometimes exaggerate (e.g., maternity clothes), sometimes deny (many employment practices), sometimes mythologize (computer games), sometimes complicate ('third gender' customs)" differences between male and female bodies.[13] Feminist thought therefore sees the equation of caring to women's work as a social construction forced by men, not nature.

But how is this social construction created and sustained? There are several important streams to the theorizing on this question. Radical feminism emphasizes patriarchy—"a system of social structures and practices in which men dominate, oppress and exploit women." Patriarchy might have various roots—for example, institutionalized heterosexuality, vulnerabilities that result from the biological aspects of reproduction, and physical coercion or violence by men—and take various forms, but the common result is that men appropriate women's labor within the domestic household. From the perspective of radical feminist thought, patriarchy is a nearly universal system that characterizes societies across many cultures, economic systems, and eras. In contrast, Marxist feminist thought sees patriarchy as a byproduct of capitalism's creation of the private-public divide between unpaid domestic work and paid employment. From this perspective, women are seen as serving capital (not men per se) as a class by reproducing and maintaining wage workers. Capitalist structures are also emphasized in analyses of gender discrimination in paid employment that highlight occupational segregation and labor market segmentation.[14]

As a third approach, dual systems theory marries the radical and Marxist approaches by blending patriarchal and capitalist elements in analyzing women's subordination in contemporary industrial societies. Finally, liberal feminism and poststructural feminism are less concerned with underlying causal explanations and instead emphasize the various ways in which women are subordinated through inequalities in economic and political structures (liberal feminism) and through cultural elements like language, discourse, and symbolic representation (poststructural feminism). This latter perspective is part of the larger "cultural turn" in the social sciences and emphasizes a diversity rather than a universality of women's experiences.[15] From all these feminist perspectives, caring is more labor than love. It is real work that is not freely chosen.

In recognizing the labor aspects of caring, one should also see that women's experiences with caring roles can vary by race, ethnicity, and class. Women in higher-income families, for example, can pay others (typically low-income and minority women) to do their cleaning, child care, and other domestic tasks and will also have better access to formal health care services when family members are sick. As paid caregivers, minority women might be treated more like domestic servants. Some scholars therefore prefer the term "ethgender" over gender to emphasize the intersections between gender and race/ethnicity, though this term overlooks the intersections with class that also affect how women experience work. More frequently overlooked is the issue of age. Child labor laws in many countries restrict paid employment opportunities for youths. Such laws are enacted in the name of protecting child welfare, but the effect is to limit children's work efforts to unpaid domestic chores and, much like the work of their mothers, render it invisible.[16]

Seeing caring for others as a labor of love is therefore useful only if both elements—"labor" and "love"—are recognized. The "labor" element reinforces that caring is real work that varies across individuals and groups and should be valued as such. But it is also work of a different sort—the "love" element underscores the complex emotional attachments and obligations involved in caring for others, and the risks of devaluing family life by reducing caring to just another form of work. Work as caring for others is therefore a challenging conceptualization full of "tangled experiences."[17]

The Ethics of Care

In contrast to feminist perspectives that focus on the subordination of women through their caring responsibilities, some feminist perspectives embrace the positive aspects of caring for others. Psychologist Carol Gilligan, for example, argues that a concern with human relationships is a feminine strength and that as a result the feminine voice consists of "defining the self and proclaiming its worth on the ability to care for and protect others." From this springs a feminist ethics of care that recognizes "for both sexes the importance throughout life of the connection between self and other, the universality of the need for compassion and care." The ethics of care therefore "stresses the moral force of the responsibility to respond to the needs of the dependent."[18]

From this perspective, the conceptualization of work as caring for others should be embraced as morally desirable. This stands in sharp contrast not only to other feminist perspectives that seek to free women from the burdens of caring for others, but also to views on work that are derived from other Western ethical theories. Utilitarianism, by defining ethical actions as those that maximize aggregate welfare or utility, highlights the productive aspects of work. Libertarianism, by seeing actions that infringe on others' freedoms as unethical, conceptualizes work as a freely chosen activity. These two ethical theories provide a justification for the individual and economic focus of the neoliberal market paradigm. Kantian ethical theory (in which individuals have a duty to respect human dignity) and Rawlsian justice ethics (in which there is an ethical concern for the least well-off) both highlight a concern with how workers are treated.[19] These two ethical theories imply that work should not be experienced in such a way as to undermine human dignity and citizenship (chapter 4).

Aristotelian ethics privileges virtue. The result is similar to the ethics of care in promoting human flourishing, and therefore in seeing work as an activity that should foster human fulfillment. But the ethics of care uniquely highlights the special relationships involved in nurturing others. This provides a vision for a post-patriarchal society that would value work differently than at present:

> Instead of seeing the corporate sector, and military strength, and government and law as the most important segments of society deserving the highest levels of wealth and power, a caring society might see the tasks of bringing up children, educating its members, meeting the needs of all, achieving peace and treasuring the environment . . . to be that to which the greatest social efforts of all should be devoted.[20]

The Gendered Body at Work

In practice, work cannot be separated from the human body. Some work is physically draining or even dangerous; other forms of work might provide levels of physical activity that are rewarding. Even work that is largely cognitive requires some physical activity and stamina. But conceptually, work is frequently disembodied.[21] When work is conceptualized as a commodity or a source of income, labor power is a generic, interchangeable, and exchangeable quantity; individual physical sensations, physiological needs, or concerns with our appearance or what we touch are replaced by abstract dimensions like effort and skill (chapters 3 and 5). A conceptual focus on the labor process (chapter 7) or the material conditions of workers (chapter 4) similarly relies on abstract concepts like control and effort instead of a consideration of the intimate effects on individual bodies, excepting concerns with occupational safety. Seeing work as a source of psychological fulfillment focuses our attention on mental sensations, not the corporeal body (chapter 6).

Conceptualizing work as caring for others brings the human body to the fore because caring work frequently involves bodily interaction. Numerous occupations, including nurses and other health care occupations, child care workers, fitness coaches, beauticians, and sex workers, involve paid body work—"employment that takes the body as its immediate site of labour, involving intimate, messy contact with the (frequently supine and naked) body, its orifices or products through touch or close proximity." The corporeal element is important for how this work is conceptualized, albeit in ambivalent ways. On the one hand, the more intimate or dirty the contact, the lower the status of the work in general. On the other hand, working on, and therefore controlling or altering, someone else's body can provide a sense of individual empowerment. Body work is also highly gendered because it is "constructed around gendered assumptions about women" as maternal, subordinate, emotional, and sexually passive rather than predatory.[22]

The human body at work is also front and center in visual representations of work and workers, whether in Victorian Age paintings or contemporary photographic exhibits. Artistic portrayals of work help bring the everyday physical and emotional aspects of work to life and seem particularly powerful in portraying a sense of loss, such as the loss of independent craftsmanship with the rise of industrialization, or the more recent loss of good-paying manufacturing jobs through the deindustrialization of the United States and Europe. Visual representations of work also embody gendered conceptions of work. This chapter opened by noting the strong masculine and feminine work roles reflected in two well-known paintings. Sculptures and other visual representations of work commissioned by nineteenth-century American elites and civic leaders frequently focused on muscled men hard at work in industrial settings and thus promoted conceptualizations of work dominated by masculine ideals. Women were either invisible, or subordinate in the presentations of their domestic roles. In the 1700s, in an annual confirmation of the inside/outside distinction between men's and women's work in traditional Chinese thought, the Chinese emperor ceremonially plowed a field while the empress publicly honored the goddess of silk weaving.[23] Art and other visual presentations, therefore, do not simply reflect gendered visions of work—they also construct and reinforce them.

The gendered body can also be seen as playing an important role in conceptualizing paid work in the modern corporate organization. Mainstream accounts prefer to see organizations as gender neutral. Corporations routinely proclaim to be equal opportunity employers. Human resources practices are seen as measuring tasks, competencies, and performance without regard to personal characteristics; "jobs and hierarchies are abstract categories that have no occupants, no human bodies, no gender," and "the abstract, bodiless worker, who occupies the abstract, gender-neutral job has no sexuality, no emotions, and does not procreate."[24]

Feminist scholars, however, critique this gender-neutral portrayal and argue that it disguises the true, gendered nature of modern organizations. Management scholar Rosabeth Moss Kanter reveals the allegedly masculine nature of the personal traits believed to be necessary for corporate success: "a tough-minded approach to problems; analytical abilities to abstract and plan; a capacity to set aside personal, emotional considerations in the interests of task accomplishment; and a cognitive superiority in problem-solving and decision-making." These norms of masculinity not only shape the differing career paths open to men and women but also provide the basis for sexual harassment in the workplace. Sociologist Joan Acker attacks the gender-neutral portrayal of jobs and hierarchies:

> The closest the disembodied worker doing the abstract job comes to a real worker is the male worker whose life centers on his full-time, life-long job, while his wife or another woman takes care of his personal needs and his children. . . . The woman worker, assumed to have legitimate obligations other than those required by the job, did not fit with the abstract job. . . . Hierarchies are gendered because they are also constructed on these underlying assumptions: Those who are committed to paid employment are "naturally" more suited to responsibility and authority; those who must divide their commitments are in the lower ranks.

In other words, good jobs are designed for the ideal employee—the male breadwinner—who works full time without interrupting his career. The feminization of jobs—for example, in the garment and other labor-intensive manufacturing industries of developing countries—is done within a gendered discourse in which men and women are seen as particularly well suited to certain types of work. Women are channeled into jobs that are perceived as requiring dexterity and docility but not heavy labor and in which peak productivity is easily reached so that turnover or absenteeism, assumed to stem from maternity leave and household caring responsibilities, are not as costly.[25]

The importance of the gendered body in the corporate world is also reflected in the importance of physical appearance for success. In fact, female workers in customer service occupations such as flight attendants and waitresses are expected to sell their attractiveness and their sexuality.[26] Beliefs about the gendered body in the workplace therefore lead to employment-related discrimination as men and women are treated differently—they are segregated into different occupations, given distinct roles and levels of responsibility, expected to sell or tolerate differing levels of sexuality, and paid unequally for comparable work.

Employment Discrimination

In considering employment discrimination experienced by women, it is useful to also include discrimination against racial and ethnic minorities. This is because just as gender is a socially constructed identity, so, too, are race and ethnicity. What does it mean to be black? Or white? Or Hispanic? In 1850, the U.S. Census included three racial categories: white, black, and mulatto; in 1880, Chinese and Indian were added; and in 2010, there were fifteen categories, and respondents could check off as many categories as they felt applied. These changing categories show that race and ethnicity are fluid ideas, not biological facts. Similarly, the "one drop rule" was part of American culture for many years—anyone with any African American heritage was considered African American and treated accordingly. This distinction is not based on any scientific principles—it is socially constructed.[27]

As is the case for gender, then, cultural norms that specify socially acceptable or unacceptable work roles on the basis of race and ethnicity are not derived from biology but from social dynamics and prejudices. For those who see work as a social relation (chapter 7), well documented patterns of wage discrimination or occupational segregation by gender, race, and ethnicity are not viewed as the result of individuals freely choosing jobs or occupations but as a product of social norms and unequal power dynamics across the intersection of gender, race, and ethnicity. From this perspective, "illegal" (as in illegal or undocumented immigrant) can be seen as a new racial category in the United States, because undocumented workers are discriminated against and treated in certain ways based on the assumed characteristics of undocumented workers created by prejudiced groups with higher social standing and greater power.[28]

Economist Richard Anker identifies thirteen common stereotyped characteristics of women that affect their work roles. For example, their allegedly caring nature makes women appear better suited for caring professions; their allegedly nimbler fingers make women appear better suited for occupations involving sewing, knitting, or typing; and their allegedly greater docility makes women appear better suited for low-skilled occupations. The result of these socially constructed stereotypes is occupational segregation in which many jobs are largely dominated by either men or women. In industrialized Western economies, for example, nearly 90 percent of nurses and more than 95 percent of typists are women, while over 90 percent of construction workers and protective service workers are men. More generally, Anker carefully studies forty-one countries and concludes that "occupational segregation by sex is extensive and pervasive and is one of the most important and enduring aspects of labour markets around the world."[29]

A report by the International Labour Organization (ILO) found that in 2004, only 28.3 percent of legislative and managerial jobs were held by women worldwide. In North America, this percentage was 41.2 percent, but in the Middle East, North Africa, and South Asia it was 11 percent or less. Even where women are in management positions, they might face a "glass ceiling" that blocks their promotions to executive positions.[30] Such barriers might stem from beliefs that women are less committed to their careers because of allegedly natural caregiving concerns.

Another aspect of employment discrimination is pay discrimination. The ILO report mentioned above found that "significant gender inequalities in pay were among the most resilient features of labor markets across the world." In industrialized countries, the gender pay gap after adjusting for a wide range of observable control variables appears to be in the 5 to 15 percent range, and larger in developing countries. In the context of the cult of domesticity, it is common to justify paying women less than men by alleging that women are primarily caregivers, not breadwinners, and therefore are not entitled to a family wage. In China, against the backdrop of the gendered norms of women's inside work and men's outside work, women were traditionally paid less than men for outside work "not because they labored less, but because some of their labor was defined out of the sphere of work for compensation," particularly their "uncompensated household-based labor of cooking, cleaning, and [for rural women] feeding the pigs and chickens."[31]

Statistical studies similarly demonstrate that "ethnic penalties"—disadvantaged employment outcomes for minority individuals, including high unemployment rates, occupational segregation, and pay discrimination—are widespread. In the United States, nearly 60 percent of African American and Hispanic women would need to switch to occupations dominated by white men in order to eliminate gender and racial occupational segregation. In Britain, ethnic minority workers are employed at significantly lower rates than whites of the same education level, and large pay gaps are observed for most categories of ethnic minority men. Field experiments in which equally qualified job applicants of different ethnicities applied for jobs revealed significant discrimination in interview and job offer rates in four European countries. An ambitious project that studied unemployment rates and occupational status of ethnic workers across thirteen countries—Australia, Austria, Belgium, Canada, France, Germany, Great Britain, Israel, the Netherlands, Northern Ireland, South Africa, Sweden, and the United States—concluded that "in all countries there is clear ethnic stratification" and that in each country, workers with non-European origins tend to be at "the bottom of the ethnic hierarchy."[32]

From the perspective of work as a social relation, employment discrimination is not the result of faceless markets, but of human actions. The glass-ceiling barriers faced by women might be invisible, but they occur because certain employees are denied promotions by real people. In 2008, a New York sheet metal workers union received a multimillion-dollar fine for using its job referral system to discriminate against African American and Hispanic workers. In the Netherlands, highly educated Muslim immigrants report that "language difficulties" is frequently the stated reason for not being offered a job, but against a backdrop of anti-immigrant cultural discourse, speaking with an accent might symbolize deeper negative images of immigrants. Black nurses in Britain are concentrated in the least desirable areas of nursing because they are channeled into these areas at the time of hiring, excluded from training opportunities that provide the credentials for upward mobility, and generally seen by whites as "appropriate" for such positions. In the Indonesian manufacturing sector, women are limited to low-pay, light-assembly jobs on a similar basis. In a multinational Korean company studied by one researcher, important work projects were assigned to native Korean workers and recent Korean immigrants on the assumption that others do not have the work ethic to stay late; such practices were explicitly seen in ethnic terms and created important distinctions between ethnic groups. In China, mutual hostility between the majority Han ethnic group and the minority Muslim Uighur ethnic group limits the employment opportunities of the Uighur.[33]

Research also demonstrates that the strength of workers' social networks varies by gender, race, and ethnicity. Women and African Americans, for example, have similarly sized networks compared to white men but are less likely to have high-status individuals in their networks. Even in the absence of intentional discrimination, these network differences can have real effects, such as providing those in weak social networks with limited access to good jobs. A similar phenomenon can be found in countries like China and Singapore, where *guanxi* relationships provide access to jobs.[34] The result appears to be vicious cycle: intentional forms of discrimination and differential levels of formal resources (e.g., education) lead to informal stratification through unequal levels of social capital or *guanxi,* which in turn further reinforces patterns of formal stratification. Employment discrimination against women and members of racial and ethnic minority groups therefore works in complex ways. For women, much of this discrimination can be traced back to pervasive gendered norms of women's work as caring.

Remedying Employment Discrimination

Considering different conceptualizations of work provides important contrasts for trying to understand how to remedy employment discrimination on the basis of gender, race, ethnicity, and other socially constructed identities. If work is an economic transaction in perfectly competitive markets (chapter 3), then discrimination on any basis except economic value should not exist, because discriminatory organizations that overpay majority workers or refuse to hire productive minority workers will be driven out of business by nondiscriminatory organizations. If there is imperfect information about worker quality, then organizations might generalize on the basis of demographic characteristics (for example, by assuming that parents of young children will be absent more frequently); this is called statistical discrimination. The human resource management perspective is similar in that discrimination is seen as rooted in ignorance. From these perspectives, the existence of employment-related discrimination is seen as a type of market failure or managerial failure stemming from imperfect competition or poor information.[35] The favored public policies are therefore skill enhancement, so that disadvantaged workers can compete better and add more value to their organizations, and nondiscrimination laws that promote formal equality—that is, laws that promote colorblind or gender-blind equal opportunity processes, not outcomes, for everyone, not just the traditionally disadvantaged.

In the corporate sphere, the drive for equality has turned into a corporate-led diversity movement in which diversity is embraced not as a route toward social justice but as a potential source of competitive advantage in which diverse employees will better serve a diverse customer base. Managing diversity is therefore an important component of contemporary human resource management and starkly reveals an important premise of the human resource management conceptualization of work—that is, the unitarist assumption that the right human resource management policies can align employee and employer interests (in this case, diversity and profitability) (chapter 6). From a social justice perspective, however, corporate diversity programs are at best of limited value and at worst a public relations ploy. By justifying diversity programs on the basis of competitive advantage, such programs become subjected to the vagaries of executives' perceptions of which employees, if any, are a source of competitive advantage. Formal corporate policies can also be undermined by informal discriminatory practices and norms within the organization.[36]

When work is conceptualized as occupational citizenship (chapter 4), occupational segregation and pay discrimination are seen as the result of unequal bargaining power. Women and minorities, for example, might earn less than white men because they lack the bargaining power to win higher pay. Integration, not just diversity or nondiscrimination, is therefore important. The preferred policy solutions consequently involve institutional changes to break down barriers between segments of the labor market and the promotion of labor union representation to enhance workers' bargaining power.[37]

When work is seen as a hierarchical social relation (chapter 7), then deep-seated, socially constructed norms and power differences can create and perpetuate discrimination by gender, race, and ethnicity. That this perspective sees work as embedded in societal institutions further reinforces the structural barriers faced by minorities, such as poor social networks and unequal educational opportunities. Redressing inequalities rooted in gender, race, and ethnicity therefore require deep structural reforms that move beyond skill-enhancement, nondiscrimination laws that are limited to upholding formal equality, or corporate diversity programs that are pursued in the name of organizational performance. Rather, from Marxist, radical feminist, and other critical perspectives, genuine equality and inclusion require redefining social norms and shifting power imbalances by proactively opening up good-paying jobs to traditionally disadvantaged workers. One could further argue that if the nonsocial relations conceptualizations of work are working perfectly in practice, then gender, race, and ethnicity would be non-issues. But in critical scholarship, gender, race, and ethnicity are embraced as sources of identity and mobilization. To some, these sources of mobilization are now becoming more important than identities rooted in occupation, industry, and employer, and this change will have significant effects on labor unions and other work-related institutions that are organized around these traditional dimensions.[38]

Separate Spheres or Blurred Boundaries?

Work is frequently equated to paid employment. Unpaid household work is relegated to a separate sphere of private reproduction distinct from the public realm of economic production. A host of conceptual dualities emerge from this approach to thinking about work, including production/reproduction, public/private, commodity/noncommodity, production/consumption, paid/unpaid, labor/leisure, labor/love, market/domestic, and work/family. These dualities are highly gendered, and women's social roles are traditionally associated with the second half of each of these dualities (reproduction, private, consumption, unpaid, etc.). Women's work, in particular, is seen as caring for others—a reproductive, not productive, activity done out of love. Caring is widespread as a household-based, unpaid responsibility of women, and the paid caring occupations such as child care workers, housekeepers, nurses, and teachers are heavily feminized and relatively low paid. Outside of the caring occupations, gendered discourse rooted in perceived differences between men and women perpetuates the sexual division of labor and occupational segregation.[39]

Feminist scholarship emphasizes the socially, not biologically, constructed nature of gender and therefore of "women's work." Caring is women's work not because of maternal instincts, physical weaknesses, or cognitive limitations, but because of norms that are culturally constructed and reproduced. Caring might frequently involve elements of love, but it is also real work that requires physical and emotional effort and that generates economic and social value, even when unpaid. Caring is therefore an important conceptualization of work that not only emphasizes the inclusion of unpaid, domestic activities in a full understanding of work but also highlights the socially contingent nature of what is considered work.

A careful consideration of work as caring also forces us to confront the mythical nature of the production/reproduction and related conceptual dualities. Feminist scholarship highlights the problems with these dichotomies. On a practical level, they are inaccurate because of blurred boundaries—care work, for example, can easily be commoditized by relying on the market rather than the household to provide caring services. On a social level, these dichotomies marginalize and devalue certain forms of work (typically "women's work") while privileging other forms (typically "men's work"). And on a conceptual level, the dichotomies fail to recognize the interconnected nature of a society's full breadth of work activities. The idealized male breadwinner, for example, cannot devote himself exclusively to paid employment without someone to prepare his meals and otherwise care for him; the idealized housewife cannot remove herself from the public sphere of paid employment without a male breadwinner. The tremendous contemporary concern among academics, policymakers, human resources professionals, and, of course, workers with how to design family-friendly policies and achieve work-family balance graphically illustrates the problems with sharp conceptual distinctions between the public and private or other allegedly separate spheres.[40]

The feminist sociologist Miriam Glucksmann has therefore developed a "total social organization of labor" conceptual framework that emphasizes the interconnections and blurred boundaries, not separate spheres, of the diverse forms of work undertaken by a society. This framework allows the integration of our thinking about work across the processes of production, exchange, and consumption, and also across the various domains of paid and unpaid work. Alternatively, the feminist economist Julie Nelson argues that economics should be the study of provisioning rather than optimal choice and exchange.[41] This could better integrate the allegedly separate spheres of production and reproduction while valuing nonmaterial as well as material sources of human well-being. In both approaches, work as caring is accorded an importance equal to market-based forms of work.

CHAPTER 9

Work as Identity

> I don't like work—no man does—but I like what is in
> the work, the chance to find yourself.
>
> —Joseph Conrad (1857–1924)

In some cultures, a new acquaintance's occupa-
tion and employer is one of the first topics of conversation. That this is frequently phrased as "What do you do?" underscores the tight linkage between
work and identity in these cultures, a linkage that looms large in the main
character's thoughts in an American novel:

> *What do you do?* Huh? *What do you do?* What do I do? *Yes, what do you do?*
> Well, I breathe I eat I drink I dream I sleep I see. . . . *No, no, what do you* do?
> *Your* job. That was the first and only question they asked . . . in all New
> York, the only remnant of any toddler's curiosity inside the city's adult-
> children, their eyes all wrapped in the same gauze of ambition. And if that
> was the only question, then that was the only subject. No one asked Mary
> if she was patriotic, no one asked Jack if he was a heretic, no one asked
> Sam if he had a loving heart. *What do you do?* Huh? *Whatdoyoudo?* That
> was all they needed to know, for that was the existential truth.[1]

As satirized in this passage, one's identity should not be reduced to equal *only*
one's work; but important theories in psychology, sociology, and philosophy
formalize what many experience—work can be a significant *part* of one's
identity.

Scholars, in fact, have developed questions that capture the importance of
work to individuals and thereby measure an individual's "work centrality."

In one international study, for example, individuals were asked to allocate 100 points to indicate the relative importance of five life activities: work, leisure, community, religion, and family. In the United States, family ranked first, with an average of 34 points, followed by work (25 points), leisure (18 points), religion (14 points), and community (9 points). In Japan, work was the highest-ranked activity (36 points), while in Britain, work and leisure were rated to be of equal importance. While work centrality varies across countries, time, and an individual's life cycle, one international group of researchers believes that "work centrality for the individual human organism is a fundamental concept which is nearly universal within industrial societies." To wit, even individuals who win a multimillion-dollar lottery prize are unlikely to quit working.[2] But how does work link to identity?

Identity can be defined in many ways, but they are all ultimately concerned with ways of thinking about the questions "Who am I?" and "Who are you?" Before the rise of individualism in Western thought, these questions were perhaps not that different, because "Who am I?" was answered by others, not yourself. "For most of history men have *been* what they *did*," as work "provided a self-identification for the individual that was stable, consistent, and so recognized both by others and by himself." Work firmly located people in the social structure, whether as teachers and priests at the top of the Hindu caste system, craftsmen in the middle of the Japanese Edo-era social hierarchy, or serfs at the bottom of the European feudal social order. Identity was then determined by the intertwined dimensions of social rank, occupation, and family status; and with limited social mobility, that was the end of the matter.[3]

A unique sense of the self—"Who am I?"—is a product of modern Western thought. Individuals thus become active agents in their own self-identification, and identity comes to be seen as "the part of the self that emerges when we name ourselves."[4] This complicates the relationship between identity and work by creating the potential for conflicts between one's desired self and the identity created by one's work. This also potentially weakens the relationship between identity and work by increasing the importance of personality traits, values, and other elements of a perceived true inner self. With that in mind, the perspective that motivates my discussion in this chapter is that work can be important for identity, not that work is more or less important than other aspects of one's identity, and certainly not that work is or should be the sole determinant of identity.

In this chapter I address those aspects of work that can serve as identity, not every area where work and identity intersect. Gender, race, and ethnicity, in particular, are important identities in the world of work but do not constitute work *as* identity and are therefore discussed in chapter 8. Additionally, it is important not to overgeneralize a work–identity perspective such that it incorrectly encompasses all the ways in which work involves psychological needs. Human needs for autonomy, for example, can be an important work motivator (chapter 6), and lousy work can damage one's self-esteem. But for work to be conceptualized as identity requires that work be seen as something that helps you make sense of who you are and where you stand in the social structure. Psychologist Marie Jahoda, for example, argued that work helps individuals "make some sense out of their existence" by structuring their days, engaging in collective purposes, clarifying their personal identity, and providing regular activity.[5] From this perspective, work is not just a source of economic or psychological utility—it is a source of psychological and social meaning.

Who Am I? Attributes, Categories, and Roles

Individuals create identities to help understand who they are by increasing their comprehension of where they fit into the broader world. Identity creation can occur in several ways and thereby can result in identities with multiple dimensions. The personal identity dimension focuses on stable and consistent attributes and traits that an individual sees as making him or herself unique. While personality receives a lot of attention by psychologists in this regard, personal identity can also contain biographical information, including descriptors related to one's work.[6] I might (partly) define myself as the author of this book.

In addition to looking inward, individuals can further construct their identities by categorizing themselves into various groups. In social identity theory, then, one's social identity is "that part of an individual's self-concept which derives from his knowledge of his membership of a social group (or groups) together with the value and emotional significance attached to that membership." Self-categorization theory similarly posits that one's social identity consists of "self-categories that define the individual in terms of his or her shared similarities with members of certain social categories in contrast to other social categories."[7] These categories and groups can be diverse—such as nationality, ethnicity, religion, socio-economic status, or hobbies and other interests—and therefore can include occupation, employer, and other work-related dimensions. In this respect, I might categorize myself as a University of Minnesota professor or a social scientist and derive some meaning about myself from what these groups represent to me.

Social identity theory and self-categorization theory are closely related and are frequently grouped together under the label "social identity approach."[8] As described in the next section, both theories were developed to better understand group behavior. Nevertheless, these are psychological theories of identity that are rooted in individuals' cognitive evaluations of who they are and what is important to them. In sociological terms, this is not a social approach—in spite of the social identity label—because the cognitive evaluations are largely unchallenged by social institutions such as social norms, conventions, rules, and procedures. In other words, in the social identity approach, I am free to name myself.

Complementing this cognitive approach are sociological theories of identity that focus on the construction of identities through social interactions. In this way of thinking, we come to understand who we are through our interactions with others. For starters, it is theorized that we try to understand ourselves by creating role identities—"the character and the role that an individual devises for himself as an occupant of a particular social position." However, because the expectations for these roles are shaped by society, these aspects of one's identity are negotiated through performances of these roles within the social structure. From this perspective, I can only fully understand my identity as a professor by considering the social standing of professors, the social expectations of a professor's roles, and others' evaluation of my fulfillment of these roles. In these sociological approaches, then, "individuals apprehend and actively incorporate the evaluations, expectations, and behaviors of other people into their self-understandings" such that (at least part of) one's identity is truly social in nature.[9]

Identity, therefore, can be seen as the result of ongoing cognitive and social processes that incorporate personal attributes, group categories, and social roles. All these perspectives see identity as multidimensional—you might label yourself with various attributes, identify with multiple groups, and have numerous social roles. Much of the research on identity analyzes when and how each of these identities comes to the fore and is salient, but this is beyond the purpose of this chapter, which is to explore the implications of seeing work as (part of) identity. Admittedly, contemporary identity scholars typically do not place work at the center of their theorizing, but the importance of work for individuals' daily lives implies that work is important for identity, and that identity is important for work.[10]

Grouping Ourselves at Work

Social identity theory and social categorization theory were developed to understand intergroup and intragroup action, respectively. To the extent that the rational, utility-maximizing approaches in economics (chapter 5) and the cognitive, personality, and individual differences approaches in psychology (chapter 6) are focused on *individual* goals and behaviors, even within the context of work teams and other groups, these theories of social identity and self-categorization provide a richer method for understanding group identities and behavior in the workplace.[11]

First, consider social identity theory. Social identity theory starts with the premise that individuals seek a positive concept of themselves (self-esteem). To the extent that someone categorizes him or herself as a member of a group—what psychologists call a social identity—then the pursuit of a positive self-concept causes that individual "to create, maintain, or enhance the positively valued distinctiveness" of his or her own groups (in-groups) compared with other groups (out-groups).[12] In other words, the individual engages in self-enhancement by magnifying the differences between those groups the individual identifies with and those he or she does not, emphasizing the positive aspects of the in-groups and the negative aspects of the out-groups, and acting to maintain these differences.

Social identity theory therefore provides a theory of discrimination that can be applied to as many aspects of work as there are groupings with which workers identify—gender, race, ethnicity, education, occupation, organization, work team, seniority, and the like. Besides the obvious discriminatory practices that can result, this can also undermine organizational diversity initiatives. Social identity theory similarly provides a theory of intergroup conflict. For example, Hispanic employees might choose to speak Spanish in an American workplace because of an in-group social identity attachment and consequently suffer prejudicial treatment by whites as an out-group. As a second example, intergroup rivalries and conflicts that are present during corporate mergers can be interpreted through the lens of social identity theory.[13] Note carefully that social identity theory sees these behaviors as rooted in the pursuit of self-esteem through positive in-group identities—not based on competition for resources as in other theories of discrimination and conflict—and applying this theory of discrimination to work-related issues requires conceptualizing work as part of one's identity.

Self-categorization theory extends social identity theory by digging deeper into the cognitive process that underlies the categorization process. Specifically, the process of categorizing individuals into groups is seen as one of depersonalizing group members by thinking of them as stereotypes of the in-group or out-group characteristics in order to make sense of a complex world and better predict how individuals (including oneself) will or should act. This means that once individuals are replaced (cognitively) by stereotypes, then the group ceases to be a collection of individuals and instead becomes a singular collective entity with shared perceptions, values, norms, and therefore behaviors. In other words, the process of self-categorization makes true group behavior possible. This has a number of useful implications for understanding aspects of work and organizations.[14]

Consider a work team that reaches a decision by weighing a limited range of options. From the perspective of a team as a collection of individuals, this looks like dysfunctional groupthink in which individuals are afraid to share contrary views. From the perspective of self-categorization theory, however, a consensual decision-making process in a work team with a high level of shared social identity does not stem from the suppression of alternative views but instead reflects a high degree of shared perceptions, cohesiveness, and mutual support. Or consider the question of substandard team productivity. A social identity approach shifts attention away from traditional concerns such as group composition, free-riding, and inappropriate incentives and instead highlights the importance of creating a true sense of shared social identity in fostering high-performance teams. Moreover, the social identity approach also reveals that "aside from what groups actually *do*, the *appraisal* of productivity and performance is itself a highly contestable act grounded in a particular social perspective" because individuals are creating their own social identities and might not agree on the defining characteristics of the group.[15]

Last, the ability of self-categorization theory to produce a singular collective entity means that organizational or corporate identity can be a meaningful concept.[16] Employees who derive sufficient self-esteem from being associated with their employer are predicted to adopt this association as part of their social identity, and through self-categorization the employees (and others) will create stereotypical attributes of this organization. These stereotypical attributes can be seen as an organizational identity, and based on self-categorization theory, they become the basis for action and decision making. Seeing work as identity through the social identity approach therefore means that the identity of one's employer can theoretically become part of that individual's own self-concept, and the individual will act in ways that benefit this organization because it enhances the individual's self-esteem. More generally, the social identity approach provides a basis for various elements of our work to be internalized as part of who we think we are.

Understanding Our Work Selves through Social Interactions

In addition to creating work-related identities for ourselves by categorizing ourselves into groups, we can create self-understanding, and therefore identities, through our interactions with others. These interactions should be seen as not only including direct relationships with other individuals, but also more generally as including experiences with social understandings and norms:

> First, identities are formed as actors put together their reflectively constructed self images with culturally supplied stories about themselves and their place in social worlds. Second, these identities operate by linking the individual to both local, directly experienced social settings, and to societal, symbolically mediated ones.

In this way, our identity cannot be separated from what others think of us and our work, nor from how we see our work fitting into the broader, social world. This might not be a purely modern phenomenon—archaeologists have found that ancient "craftworkers signal who they are with every choice made in production, their compatriots raised under similar circumstances readily, if implicitly, decoding their messages." In modern societies with complex conceptions of identity, interactionist theorists see us as constantly presenting ourselves in different roles and renegotiating how we see ourselves and how society sees us.[17]

From this perspective, the social roles attached to occupations and careers are a major source of our self-presentation and identity during our adult years. Except for the sexist language that should not be seen as excluding women, noted sociologist Everett Hughes's observation from 1971 remains relevant today: "A man's work is one of the things by which he is judged, and certainly one of the more significant things by which he judges himself." How we see ourselves in these roles is closely intertwined with how others see us. For example, one study shows how professional American club musicians distinguish between what they see as being a jazz musician (playing what they want) and being a commercial musician (playing what the customer wants). These socially constructed meanings form the basis for how they see each other, and individual musicians have to therefore consider how they present themselves, because this presentation affects their identity. To "go commercial," a musician must "make a radical change in his self-conception; he must learn to think of himself in a new way, to regard himself as a different kind of person."[18]

This interactionist perspective also predicts that individuals actively manage their identity through perceptions of their work:

> It happens over and over that the people who practice an occupation attempt to revise the conceptions which their various publics have of

the occupation and the people in it. In doing so, they also attempt to revise their own conception of themselves and of their work. . . . Even in the lowest occupations people [develop] collective pretensions to give their work, and consequently themselves, value in the eyes of each other and of outsiders.

To enhance views of their work, custodians, for example, in interviews about their work, emphasize the autonomy, responsibility, ability to see the tangible results of their work, and relations with their customers. Workers might also demand higher pay to increase the status of their work in their own eyes and in the eyes of others. In the words of one worker, "Pay is a status symbol as well as a means of existence, so 'not getting the rate for the job' is a blow to a man's pride as well as his pocket." But if others do not legitimize these attempts at work redefinition, and if higher pay is not attainable, the social interactionist perspective theorizes that the individual worker will have difficulty deriving the desired enhanced meaning. An alternative, then, is for workers in low-status jobs to distance their work from their identity and instead rely on alternative social roles, such as being a parent or spouse, to carve out a desirable location in the social structure.[19]

The connection between occupation and social standing is made explicit through measures of occupational prestige, which have been analyzed for many countries. For example, an analysis of contemporary British data using a statistical procedure that analyzes the occupations of friends reveals a continuing status hierarchy with professional occupations at top and service and manual occupations at the bottom. As such, there appears to be a consensus among sociologists that "in modern societies occupation is one of the most salient characteristics to which status attaches," and therefore to which identity attaches. Occupation can also be a major determinant of one's lifestyle, including consumption patterns, leisure interests, and values, and occupation is therefore a major unit of analysis in the sociology of work.[20]

Like occupations, careers are also important for status and identity:

Careers have everything to do with identity and with the location of people within a social hierarchy; they provide not only a way of knowing one's self, but also a way of knowing about other people and where one stands in the broader society, for workers in all kinds of jobs.

But where does this leave the twenty-first-century worker? In the postwar period, the classic vision of a career consisted of William Whyte's "organization man" working his way up the corporate ladder by remaining loyal and dedicated to a single organization. Today, it is common to believe that the ideal of an organizational career has been replaced by boundaryless careers or employee free-agents because expectations of stable employment have disappeared in the era of globalization and organizational flexibility. If stable careers provide individuals with the continuity and predictability needed to self-reflexively understand who they are, how can individuals form a meaningful identity in a tumultuous world characterized by constant change and ambiguous, risky, boundaryless careers?[21]

In thinking about this important question, it is important not to overstate the extent to which the organizational career ideal was ever a reality for many workers, and therefore the extent to which it has eroded. Nevertheless, it is hard to ignore the pervasiveness of the popular discourse on the new contingent and flexible employment relationship. That this discourse has real effects is demonstrated by research showing that Australian managers now portray themselves in market-oriented narratives, and that this new narrative provides the basis for reflectively adopting identities of "strategic actors making choices in a social world constituted by market-like interactions." Whether this is seen as being freed from the stifling bureaucracy of organization man or as being cast adrift in a risky, anchorless world likely depends on the psychological, monetary, or social resources of the individual. The increased blurring of organizational boundaries through strategic alliances, partnerships, and the use of contingent workers such as temps and contract employees can also mean that individuals working side by side but "belonging" to different organizations experience difficulties constructing meaningful identities.[22] All these cases reflect the importance of seeing work as identity conditioned by the social context.

A different aspect of identity that comes out of "interacting" with the general social fabric is an identity of being a contributing member of society. In a number of cultures, society confirms this identity only when you work. For individuals, then, a sense of self-respect and therefore positive self-identity might depend on working. Those who are unable or unwilling to work might suffer from a poor sense of self. Being able to work as a contributing member of society is therefore an important objective of services for adolescents with developmental disabilities, substance abusers, and offenders in correctional facilities. Whether one is seen as a contributing member of society also determines whether one is entitled to income support. The replacement of welfare with workfare in the United States and Great Britain in the 1990s and the Western European emphasis on active labor market policies to get individuals back into the labor force underscore the power of socially determined identities that are equated to working.[23] The importance of paid work for obtaining social affirmation of one's positive self-identity also magnifies the concerns with the marginalization of unpaid caring work that is frequently seen as "women's work" (chapter 8).

Class Consciousness

Work can also be seen as the source of class identity and class consciousness. The typical layperson probably associates "class" with broad income categories, as in "middle class," or with lifestyle. But to sociologists, class is about "the rights and powers people have over productive assets" such that "what you have determines what you get" and "what you have determines what you have to do to get what you get." Class does not reflect inequality— class relations *cause* inequality. Marxist theory emphasizes two antagonistic classes: those who own the means of production (capitalists) and those who do not (the working class). Max Weber identified four semi-antagonistic social classes (a privileged propertied and educated class, professionals, small proprietors, and the working class) defined by similar life chances as captured by a shared "probability of procuring goods, gaining a position in life, and finding inner satisfactions." Other theories divide up classes based on varying gradations of occupations, though at some point fine gradations stop being classes.[24]

In all these conceptions of class, from the "big class" approaches of Marx and Weber to the microclass approaches, work is of central importance. In Marxist class theory, class identity stems from whether or not one has to work for others for a living. In the occupational approaches, class identity is formed whenever there is shared occupational identity. In neo-Weberian class analysis, work is important but not solely determinative of class identity because life chances are seen as differing across classes as the result of differences in marketable assets (e.g., property, educational credentials) and practices that limit social mobility (e.g., norms against marrying outside one's class).[25]

Class identities become salient through class consciousness:

> Class happens when some men, as a result of common experiences (inherited or shared), feel and articulate the identity of their interests as between themselves, and as against other men whose interests are different from (and usually opposed to) theirs. . . . Class-consciousness is the way in which these experiences are handled in cultural terms: embodied in traditions, value-systems, ideas, and institutional forms.

If antagonistic class relations are objective (that is, they necessarily result from a structural feature of society such as ownership of the means of production) rather than subjective (that is, they exist only if individuals perceive them to exist), then a lack of class consciousness can be seen as false consciousness. False consciousness is a failure to see one's true interests and therefore to submit to a disadvantaged position.[26]

But do workers have class consciousness? The empirical evidence is controversial and subject to multiple interpretations. If you force individuals to identify themselves as part of a class, they will. But open-ended questions about one's identity are less likely to generate responses related to class, except perhaps in Britain, and even in that case the responses are not overwhelmingly class-oriented. An Australian study, for example, concluded that "salience of class for identity is almost minimal." A lack of class identity can also be observed in behavior. For example, a case study of a European Works Council in which British and Dutch worker representatives fought for jobs in their own countries instead of aligning against the company to preserve jobs can be interpreted as showing the importance of national over class identity.[27]

That individuals do not explicitly express class consciousness as part of their self-identity, however, does not necessarily mean that class relations are not important for the workplace and society. Class is significantly related to attitudes toward work, income inequality, and gender equality. Thinking about class in terms of relative power over terms and conditions of employment rather than income levels provides a useful mechanism for understanding debates over globalization and other contemporary issues. And as was discussed in chapter 7, seeing class relations as reflecting antagonistic, socially rooted interests in the employment relationship provides an important perspective for analyzing conflict and consent in the workplace.[28] Unless class is reduced to occupation, however, it does not appear to be widely linked to subjective views of who we think we are.

Humankind Identity—Work as Who We All Are?

Thinking about work as identity allows us to consider how work relates to what makes humans distinctly human. In other words, is work part of our identity not only as individuals or classes, but as a species? The question of what makes us distinctly human is a question of what distinguishes us from other animals. For Greek and Roman philosophers, work was seen as necessary for survival and thus was not viewed as distinguishing people from animals. Rather, these philosophers believed that the ability to shape the human community through contemplation and persuasion ("politics") made humans special.[29] So as described in chapter 1, work was not revered, and in this view it is not part of our species identity.

In contrast, work was seen as distinctly human in some important areas of nineteenth- and twentieth-century German philosophy. Georg Hegel reasoned that animals fulfill their instinctual needs by consuming nature without delay, whereas human work is creation for later consumption. Natural objects manipulated for our own uses take on a human form (philosophically). Unlike animals, we therefore come to understand ourselves as human beings through our work, as described here by the contemporary philosopher Sean Sayers:

> Through this process we establish a relation to the natural world and to our own natural desires that is mediated through work. We objectify ourselves in our product, and come to recognize our powers and abilities, embodied in the world. We develop as reflective, self-conscious beings.

In other words, through work we become an objective reality to ourselves and others; or as Hegel put it, "I have done something, I have externalized myself."[30]

This conception of work as a fundamental element of being human is echoed in the later existentialist philosophy of Martin Heidegger: human existence is achieved through work because "as someone who works man is transported into the publicness of existence." In other words, humans do not exist because they are physical objects, but exist when they reveal themselves through using tools and working with others with a sense of purpose and through the accompanying feelings about themselves. Work is "an expression of authenticity"—something that makes humans human. Sigmund Freud also wrote that work is our strongest link to reality: "Laying stress upon the importance of work has a greater effect than any other technique of living in the direction of binding the individual more closely to reality."[31]

But the Hegelian view of the centrality of work for humanness was most famously advanced by Karl Marx. Marx started with Hegel's idea that "Conscious life-activity directly distinguishes man from animal life-activity" and argued that it is work ("practical activity") that generates this human consciousness:

> In creating an objective world by his practical activity, in working-up inorganic nature, man proves himself a conscious species being, i.e., as a being that treats the species as its own essential being, or that treats itself as a species-being. Admittedly animals also produce. They build themselves nests, dwellings, like the bees, beavers, ants, etc. But an animal only produces what it immediately needs for itself or its

young. . . . while man produces even when he is free from physical need and only truly produces in freedom therefrom. . . . It is just in the working-up of the objective world, therefore, that man first really proves himself to be a species being. This production is his active species life. Through and because of this production, nature appears as his work and his reality.

Or in more contemporary language,

Working is in our bones, in the very tissues of our being. . . . Human beings reach out, gather the materials of nature, and fashion them into objects of one kind or another. We collect an armful of wood, pick up a piece of flint, extract a stone from a quarry—or, for that matter, capture a sight or a sound that happens to move us. The true character of humankind is reflected in the objects we produce as a result of that process: a campfire, an axe, a cathedral, a sonnet.[32]

Work, then, is thought of as critical for human fulfillment in the deepest way possible. This is not to say that work is the only thing that defines humanness or the only source of fulfillment, and it is not to deny that work can be painful or stressful, but it is a powerful statement of the importance of work to humans as a species.

While this may seem like esoteric philosophy, there are very practical applications. This perspective forms the foundation for Marx's call for the overthrow of capitalism because under capitalism work is reduced to effort or exertion bought and sold as a commodity in a marketplace. Humans therefore become alienated from the very essence of their humanness (chapter 3). This should not be confused with an individual's subjective sense of job dissatisfaction; for Marx, alienation is an objective loss of human identity that affects all workers in capitalism. Some contemporary scholars and activists, therefore, skeptically see human resource management as rhetoric that is unable to change the fundamental nature of modern employment. Similarly, improvements via collective bargaining or government legislation are seen as only partial solutions to problems of low pay and lousy working conditions because they fail to change the fundamental, alienating nature of work under capitalism.[33]

Apart from the connection to alienation or the overthrow of capitalism, these philosophical views can be seen as the basis for a more general view that work has fundamental meaning. For example, Catholic social thought presents the importance of work to humans in terms strikingly similar to those presented by Marx:

> Work is one of the characteristics that distinguish man from the rest of creatures, whose activity for sustaining their lives cannot be called work. Only man is capable of work, and only man works, at the same time by work occupying his existence on earth. Thus work bears a particular mark of man and of humanity, the mark of a person operating within a community of persons. And this mark decides its interior characteristics; in a sense it constitutes its very nature.

This belief in the importance of work for humanness, in turn, provides the foundation for the world's major religions and secular human rights advocates to call for decent working conditions and labor standards. From this perspective, work is not something to be taken lightly or for granted. Rather, its deep importance for the quality of individual lives and the societies in which we live must be considered. Beyond calls for reform, this deep importance motivates numerous academic works, such as sociologist Randy Hodson's analysis of dignity at work, my emphasis on equity and voice in the employment relationship, Harry Braverman's concern with de-skilling, and economist Francis Green's analysis of job quality in today's affluent economy.[34]

The Postmodern Identity Worker

Postmodern thought provides another important perspective on identity. Postmodernism can be seen as an intellectual shift away from the modern, positivist focus on searching for objective truths and understandings, toward a focus on how individuals come to understand things and develop meanings. From the perspective largely attributed to Michel Foucault, meaning comes from talking, reading, observing, experiencing, and other forms of discourse. Knowledge is therefore subjective rather than objective and is seen as fluid and fragile, not static, as individuals strive to (re)make sense of things based on a constant stream of discursive experiences. Applying this perspective to the self means that your understanding of yourself—your identity—is a fluid and fragile understanding based on discourse.[35]

To see work as postmodern identity is to see individuals as employees embedded in organizations full of discourse—meetings, social gatherings, formal and informal feedback, performance appraisal systems, promotional ladders, training programs, motivational posters, campaigns to create organizational culture, and the like—that constantly (re)shape their understandings of themselves. A major task of human resource management is to manage these understandings in ways that promote organizational commitment, loyalty, and identity with the organization. As such, the individual becomes "an identity worker" who continually incorporates "new managerial discourses into

narratives of self-identity." Under the assumptions of the unitarist employment relationship with shared employee-employer interests (chapter 6), a self-
identity that largely internalizes the organization's identity is perhaps not
problematic. But like other critical scholars, postmodernists see the employment relationship as characterized by antagonistic employee-employer interests (chapter 7). Managerial discourse to shape workers' identities is therefore
seen as a form of normative control—an exercise of organizational power to
obtain and control worker effort through internalizing the norms and values
of the organization.[36]

In fact, in Foucauldian postmodernism, discourse always involves power.
Power is seen as the ability "to structure the possible field of action of others." By shaping meanings, discourse limits the possible courses of action and
is therefore an exercise in power. For example, identifying an employee as
a manager draws on the employee's understanding of what it means to be
a manager—responsible, loyal, results oriented—and shapes that employee's
choice of actions. Acting in a manner consistent with these understandings
confirms, to him or herself, the employee's (fragile) identity as a competent
manager and "has the unintended effect of reproducing the conditions of
[his or her] own subordination" by reinforcing the limited choices of action
as seen by the employee. The employee thus becomes "self-disciplining."
From this perspective, identity at work is not about individuals finding their
true selves, but is about discourse and power that serve organizational interests by intentionally shaping the subjective, fluid identities of workers.[37]

Work and the Desired Self

Identity can be theorized from various perspectives, but a general commonality is a vision of an individual trying to establish a positive, multidimensional self-identity that is partly self-determined and partly determined by
social dynamics and that is frequently being renegotiated as new experiences
and interactions arise. Work, then, can be seen as providing the basis for at
least part of a person's identity in various ways—from being the source of
unique personal attributes to being the source of group affinities; from helping you and others in understanding your social roles and place in the social
structure to understanding what it means to be human. This has deep implications for understanding work. To get Mexican men to work in a tortilla
factory requires reconstituting this work as "men's work" by emphasizing
it as hard labor involving the use of machinery. Otherwise, tortilla making is considered "women's work" and is a threat to the desired masculine
identity. To prevent the development of worker solidarity in the workplace

that might threaten managerial power, some managers intentionally manipulate group-based identities—for example, by using college students to break strikes, by hiring African American workers into predominantly white occupations, or by mixing documented and undocumented immigrant workers.[38] The power of identity therefore makes workers complicit in perpetuating a divided workforce because their positive in-group identities magnify their prejudices toward their co-workers who are members of other groups.

The importance of identity for the quality of life at both an individual and species level also means that the intersection of work and identity is where the best and the worst aspects of work come to the fore. When work is individually fulfilling, socially prestigious, or consistent with the highest purposes of humans, then work creates a positive identity. But this is a double-edged sword—if work is part of a person's identity, then lousy work can create unhealthy identities. In fact, seeing work as identity can compound problematic aspects of the employment relationship. If work partly defines who you are, then gender and racial discrimination, for example, are a problem not just of economic stratification, but also of degradation of the self.[39]

The nature of work, especially in industrialized, capitalist economies and modern bureaucratic organizations, has therefore troubled sociologists and philosophers since at least the nineteenth century. This is reflected in Marx's critique of capitalism's alienation of workers from their work, Georg Simmel's concern with the division of labor's alienation of workers from their work, Émile Durkheim's unease with the division of labor's erosion of the collective conscience and social cohesion, Max Weber's hesitations about the stifling nature of bureaucracies, and Hannah Arendt's lamentation of the modern triumph of laboring to consume and survive over working to create. While not necessarily couched in the language of identity by these authors, these concerns can be interpreted as misgivings over the loss of human and individual identity. In this vein, sociologist Peter Berger explicitly links the specialization and frequent obsolescence of jobs to a crisis of identity:

> Precisely because work has been for so long a fundamental human category, any particular work has been not only a means of a livelihood but also a source of self-identification. . . . This is no longer the case with most work in industrial society. To say "I am a railroad fireman" may be a source of pride, but the pride is as precarious as the occupational title. To say "I am an electroencephalographic technician"

means nothing to most people to whom it is said. . . . Fragmented and ever-changing work thus tends to become divorced from those social relationships and events from which the individual derives his self-identification, and *ipso facto* begins to appear to him as problematic if not downright meaningless.

As noted earlier in this chapter, the turbulence of the twenty-first-century employment relationship has renewed interest in these same concerns.[40] In these ways, we should question whether contemporary forms of work make it difficult for individuals to create their desired positive self-identities.

One potential area of difficulty is rooted in the authentic or true self—one's belief about who one really is. Not all scholars necessarily believe that we have one true self, and even if we do, we might frequently act in ways contrary to our authentic selves in order to manage the impressions that others have of us. But if the authentic self is important for humans, then work can be particularly problematic. Marx's concern with alienation, for example, is rooted in seeing work under capitalism as denying workers their authentic self as creative workers. As another example, the increased importance of the service sector in many industrialized countries has brought together the psychological and sociological approaches to work-related identities in a shared concern with emotional labor. Whether the worker is a flight attendant, police officer, customer service agent, or fast-food cashier, an essential element of service work is personal interaction with customers or members of the public in conformance with the employer's expectations for service with a smile (or not), courteousness, professionalism, and other positive (or negative) emotional displays. The term "emotional labor" was coined by sociologist Arlie Hochschild to capture the psychological effort involved in producing "a publicly observable facial and bodily display" and to recognize that this can be hard work:

> A young businessman said to a flight attendant, "Why aren't you smiling?" She put her tray back on the food cart, looked him in the eye, and said, "I'll tell you what. You smile first, then I'll smile." The businessman smiled at her. "Good," she replied. "Now freeze and hold that for fifteen hours."[41]

A major element of emotional labor is the emotional dissonance that comes from suppressing one's true feelings and emotions—for example, being courteous to a rude customer, appearing to be upbeat when exhausted, or, in the case of a bill collector, showing a lack of sympathy when feeling sympathetic.

Therein lies the potential problem. In noted sociologist Erving Goffman's terms, emotional labor requires presenting oneself to others in certain ways and acting out specific roles—that is, projecting a certain identity—but this projected work identity can conflict with one's true sense of who one is and produce an inauthenticity reminiscent of Marx's alienation. To the extent that social norms direct women to caring roles, women might be expected to suffer more from emotional labor demands than men. Empirical research reveals that emotional labor is indeed related to feelings of inauthenticity, but under the right circumstances emotional labor can also be rewarding and enhance one's authentic self.[42]

This idea that there can be conflicts between work-imposed identities and perceptions of authentic selves has been extended to a number of areas. Service workers lose a sense of personal identity when they are forced to present themselves in certain ways, such as wearing ugly uniforms or following corporate scripts in interacting with customers. In some call centers in India, customer service agents who handle calls from the United States are required to suppress their national identity and present themselves as American; as described by one agent, "I am two individuals—"Jeff" at work and "Gaurav" in my social life. Jeff is artificial. It is an artificial soul. It's not me. In this room is Jeff now, but Gaurav is enjoying life outside." Organizational change or the restructuring of jobs can also engender resistance because they undermine work-related identities that workers have established for themselves through self-categorization and social interaction.[43]

Embedded in these concerns with conflicts between work selves and authentic selves, however, is an assumption that the authentic self is situated in the individual. But this is a belief specific to Western individualism. In contrast, Asian cultures see the self as more of a collective entity defined by interdependence rather than independence. Emotions are seen as a product of social expectations, not individual feelings. Managing these emotions is considered a form of self-control, not being phony. It is important for workers to manage their emotions in these cultures—perhaps even more important than in Western cultures—but as emotions are seen as following social scripts, emotional labor does not create a problematic issue of (in)authentic identity.[44]

In sum, scholars from diverse perspectives conceptualize work as a source of meaning for individuals on various levels, regardless of whether we have authentic modern selves or highly fluid and fragile postmodern selves. The innate human drive for a positive identity underlies all these perspectives, though the mechanisms by which work becomes (part of) one's identity are seen in very different ways, from a cognitive process of self-categorization or a social process of interactionist self-presentation to a species-level under-standing of humanness. Unfortunately, work does not always create a positive identity; yet work as identity is an important conceptualization of work. The effects of work on identity should not be ignored by practitioners and poli-cymakers, and those interested in a deep understanding of work should use this conceptualization to further recognize the complex interests individuals have in work and the employment relationship.[45]

CHAPTER 10

Work as Service

> All men were created to busy themselves with labor for the common good.
>
> —John Calvin (1509–64)

Before the decisive British naval victory at the Battle of Trafalgar in 1805, Admiral Horatio Nelson famously signaled one last message to the rest of his fleet: "England expects that every man will do his duty." In his 1961 inauguration speech, President John F. Kennedy called on Americans to "ask not what your country can do for you—ask what you can do for your country." Hindu scripture instructs individuals to "strive constantly to serve the welfare of the world; by devotion to selfless work one attains the supreme goal in life," while Islam teaches that "the best of men are those who are useful to others." For centuries, children in East Asia have learned the twenty-four exemplars of filial piety through stories like the one about the poor farmer Dong Yong who sells himself into servitude to pay for a proper burial for his father. To fulfill these expectations requires work, whether on behalf of God, humanity, or one's country, community, or family, that goes beyond serving individual needs. In this way, work can be seen as service.

Conceptualizing work as service can be interpreted in two ways. From religious, patriotic, and humanitarian perspectives, serving others is seen as a truly beneficial way of improving the world, or one's country, community, or family that also (ideally) benefits the individual. From a critical perspective, in contrast, an ideology or ethos of service can be interpreted as a method of social control that serves elite interests. Religious preaching on serving God

through hard work, for example, might be a discursive method for glorify-
ing inhumane forms of work and perpetuating hierarchical social structures,
similar to other forms of normative control that arise when work is seen as
a hierarchical social relation (chapter 7). In this way, biblical passages such as
this one have been used to justify slavery and can be seen as ordering workers
of all kinds to obey their bosses:

> Slaves, obey your earthly masters in everything; and do it, not only
> when their eye is on you and to win their favor, but with sincerity of
> heart and reverence for the Lord. Whatever you do, work at it with all
> your heart, as working for the Lord, not for men, since you know that
> you will receive an inheritance from the Lord as a reward. It is the Lord
> Christ you are serving.

To a Christian believer, however, this passage glorifies even the lowliest work
as serving God.[1] Such debates will not be resolved here, but these divergent
perspectives are an important reminder about the complexities of conceptualizing work.

To the extent that someone besides the worker is an important beneficiary
of the work, work as service might also be seen as similar to work as caring
for others (chapter 8). Beyond this commonality, however, work as caring
for others is a highly gendered concept and therefore merits its own treatment distinct from work as service. Moreover, caring work is often focused
on one-to-one personal relationships—a parent caring for a child, a nurse
for a patient, a teacher for a student—while work as service includes broader
activities such as serving one's community or country.

Serving the Kingdom of God

Many people likely go to their church, synagogue, mosque, or other house
of worship to forget about the burdens of their work. And if the practice
of Christianity in the United States is any guide, their local priest, minister,
rabbi, imam, or other worship leader frequently obliges by omitting themes
of work from worship services and other activities.[2] In other words, work
is popularly seen as a secular activity, not a religious or spiritual one. But a
number of religious leaders and scholars have conceptualized work from
various theological perspectives that provide provocative ways for thinking
about work.

Dating back to the first millennium of the Christian church, work has
been seen as a way to serve God's kingdom by preventing idleness (leading
to sin), providing for one's family, and generating surpluses for charitable

giving. In the Bible, Paul instructs that "If anyone does not provide for his relatives, and especially for his immediate family, he has denied the faith and is worse than an unbeliever" and that "He who has been stealing must steal no longer, but must work, doing something useful with his own hands, that he may have something to share with those in need." Saint Benedict's monastic rules (circa 500 CE) required monks to work, often strenuously, as well as engage in prayer and other spiritual activities. This manual work not only protected against idleness and taught self-discipline but also provided sustenance for the monastery and the needy. In this way, Benedict "placed the practical life of the *opus manuum* [work of the hands] within a spiritual context created by the needs of the *opus Dei* [work of God]."[3]

In this early period, then, work was seen as serving God indirectly—it was not valued as inherently rewarding or spiritual, but for the ways it supported God's kingdom. As summarized by the famous Roman Catholic theologian Thomas Aquinas in the thirteenth century, "Manual labor is directed to four things. First and principally it is to obtain food. . . . Secondly, it is directed to the avoidance of idleness, from which many evils arise. . . . Thirdly, it is directed to the restraining of concupiscence. . . . Fourthly, it is directed to almsgiving."[4]

Three centuries later, however, Martin Luther challenged the exclusive control of the pope, bishops, priests, and other church officials over religious affairs by rejecting the privileged nature of their spiritual work: "All Christians are truly of the 'spiritual estate,' and there is among them no difference at all but that of office. . . . We are all one body, yet every member has its own work, whereby it serves every other, all because we have one baptism, one Gospel, one faith." Luther therefore not only sparked the Protestant Reformation but also "placed a crown on the sweaty forehead of labor":

> Within the limits of [one's] own profession, whatever that may be, as long as it is legitimate, Luther held that work is a form of serving God. There is just one best way to serve God—to do most perfectly the work of one's profession. With this idea Luther swept away all distinction between religious piety and activity in the world, all question of superiority of one to the other. So long as work is done in a spirit of obedience to God and of love for one's neighbor, every variety of labor has equal spiritual dignity, each is the service of God on earth.

Luther, and John Calvin after him, thus enhanced the status of daily work by believing that everyone's occupation (excepting sinful occupations) represented a calling. The idea of work as a calling will be explored in the next section; the key element for the present discussion is that Luther and Calvin saw work as a direct, not just indirect or subordinate, way to serve God. In the words of Luther from *A Treatise on Good Works*, written in 1520,

> So a Christian who lives in this confidence toward God, knows all things, can do all things, undertakes all things that are to be done, and does everything cheerfully and freely; not that he may gather many merits and good works, but because it is a pleasure for him to please God thereby, and he serves God purely for nothing, content that his service pleases God.

These early Christian and Reformation-era perspectives on ways in which work serves God and his kingdom continue to be echoed today. Christian spiritual consultants Doug Sherman and William Hendricks, for example, preach that our "work contributes to God's work" by serving people (either directly or indirectly via jobs that provide useful products), providing for ourselves and our families, and earning money to give to charity.[5]

Beyond these long-standing approaches, today's Christian theology of work is frequently complemented by a conceptualization of work as an act of co-creation with God. According to Christian theologian Miroslav Volf, "In both Protestant and Roman Catholic traditions there is agreement today that the deepest meaning of human work lies in the cooperation of men and women with God." This perspective typically draws on the biblical creation story in Genesis in which humans are created in the image of God to subdue the earth and till the Garden of Eden. In working, then, humans are carrying out God's ongoing creative activity. In a 1981 papal encyclical on work, Pope John Paul II emphasized this co-creativity:

> Awareness that man's work is a participation in God's activity ought to permeate . . . even the most ordinary everyday activities. For, while providing the substance of life for themselves and their families, men and women are performing their activities in a way which appropriately benefits society. They can justly consider that by their labor they are unfolding the Creator's work, consulting the advantages of their brothers and sisters, and contributing by their personal industry to the realization in history of the divine plan.

Since the Hebrew and Christian Bibles both include the book of Genesis, work in Judaism can be interpreted similarly. In the words of one Jewish commentator,

> [There is an] underlying similarity between the labourer's toil and service rendered to God. It affirms that every human being, in his or her

actions in the world, that is, through work, participates in the glorifica-
tion of God the Creator. . . . Action in the world becomes an act of
partnership with God.[6]

Seeing work as co-creation with God is a provocative conceptualization. It gives work a "profound religious significance" and creates a personal relationship between worker and God. Consequently, adherents to
co-creationism believe that we should care deeply about the conditions
under which humans toil. By emphasizing work as a creative act, the co-
creation perspective allows individuals to use free will and reason when
working in a dynamic environment, but this free choice also means that
individuals need to be vigilant about making good choices. South African
Catholic theologian Edith Raidt argues that the co-creation conceptualization "uplifts work and the working person into the friendship with the
Creator, and it brings to the fore an almost forgotten reality, i.e. that work
was part of the happiness of paradise, and that according to God's plan it
should be a source of happiness even today." For theologian Matthew Fox,
co-creationism means that "our work is a thank-you for being participants
in work—the cosmos's work, our species' work, our own work, God's work."
This conceptualization, however, is not without its critics. Some of them
question whether this undermines the supremacy of God by portraying
humans as co-Gods, while others argue that work is granted too high a
status at the expense of other life activities.[7]

As with other religions, conceptualizations of work in Islam are subject
to multiple interpretations and debate. There seems to be agreement that
Muslims are expected to work to support themselves and their families, but
opinions differ over the centrality of work for one's life and for serving God,
and therefore over how hard individuals are expected to work. Pakistani
labor leader Khalil-ur-Rehman asserts that

> Islam regards this world as the place of action for Muslims. Hence
> through his work a Muslim not only serves himself but the entire
> Muslim society. Thereby he becomes entitled to a reward not only in
> this world, but in the Hereafter as well.

From some perspectives, then, work in Islam is at least partly conceptualized as service. Theologians from various Hindu sects also embrace
a vision of work as service.[8] Christian views on work as service might
therefore be distinguished by their dogmatic roots, but setting aside doc-
trinal differences, work as service appears to be a more widespread religious conceptualization.

Similar notions can be found among lay worshippers. Labor educator Robert Bruno interviewed working-class Christian, Jewish, and Muslim believers about the relationship between their work and their faiths and found that "putting formal doctrine aside (something most workers emphatically claimed no real understanding of), there was little significant religious difference in how working-class believers lived out their faith." The underlying commonality was a love of God that translated into "meeting human need and acting for the benefit of others." As one custodian told Bruno,

> I think that God puts us in different positions and different work to help people out. I think that it's a service. The work serves a purpose, someone, and a need. It's like being a missionary. . . . Anytime you can serve someone or in [my] case if you look at the school, I am doing this so that kids can learn without having to worry about trash on the floor or sitting with vandalism on the wall, so yes it's godly work.[9]

Work as a Calling

In various places, the Bible calls individuals to be Christians by believing in and serving God. In medieval Christian thought, most people were not seen as fulfilling this call through their work, but by living a Christian life; only by becoming a priest, monk, or other religious worker could one have an occupational calling or vocation that served God through one's daily work. When Martin Luther translated biblical verses such as "Let each one remain in the same calling in which he was called" from the original Greek into German in the early sixteenth century, he used the German word for "occupation" for "calling." Luther therefore ushered in a drastically new perspective in which all individuals are called by God to their occupations and "hence every legitimate calling has exactly the same worth in the sight of God." This provides the foundation for today's idea that a calling is something that God summons us to do by providing special gifts or talents: "something that fits how we were made, so that doing it will enable us to glorify God, serve others, and be most richly ourselves." Luther, however, retained traditional beliefs regarding a lack of social mobility and believed that one should serve God by doing one's work well, not by rising above one's natural station in life.[10]

Another influential participant in the Protestant Reformation, John Calvin, echoed Luther's view of work as a calling: God "has appointed duties for every man in his particular way of life. . . . It is enough if we know that the Lord's calling is in everything the beginning and foundation of well-doing." Additionally, in Calvinist theology, individuals are predestined by God for

salvation or damnation. Fulfilling one's calling in the service of God was not
believed to determine one's salvation, but was thought to reveal one's prede-
termined destination. Calvinist believers were therefore motivated to work
diligently in their homes, fields, workshops, and businesses in order to be
reassured that they were among the chosen. But this work was seen as serving
God, not individual needs or wants. By the start of the eighteenth century,
however, Puritanism had morphed the Lutheran and Calvinist views of callings into a justification for the secular pursuit of profit and self-interest:

> The late Puritans approached the concept of the calling in such a fash-
> ion as to give increased autonomy to man's natural desires and abilities,
> and increased sanctification to the accumulations of the worldly voca-
> tion. . . . Finally, the late Puritans came to think of Christian liberty
> more and more in terms of the ability of the individual to determine
> his own destiny in the economic realm, in terms of the freedom of
> mobility in the world, rather than a freedom from bondage to self and
> sin which enabled the individual to serve God and neighbor.[11]

This Puritan view of work as a calling provided the foundation for Max
Weber's famous argument that the Protestant work ethic spawned a unique
"spirit of capitalism" that contributed to the development of Western capitalism. Weber argued that, blessed by this view of work spanning the sixteenth to the eighteenth centuries,

> a specifically bourgeois economic ethic had grown up. With the con-
> sciousness of standing in the fullness of God's grace and being visibly
> blessed by Him, the bourgeois business man, as long as he remained
> within the bounds of formal correctness, as long as his moral conduct
> was spotless and the use to which he put his wealth was not objection-
> able, could follow his pecuniary interests as he would and feel that
> he was fulfilling a duty in doing so. The power of religious asceti-
> cism provided him in addition with sober, conscientious, and unusually
> industrious workmen, who clung to their work as to a life purpose
> willed by God.

The extent to which the Protestant work ethic actually *caused* the Industrial
Revolution and the spread of capitalism has been extensively debated and is
frequently challenged. Nevertheless, measuring and uncovering the importance of work ethics or work values continues to be a thriving area of interest,
even if these work ethics have lost their religious foundations and are now
typically seen as national or cultural in nature.[12]

The reduction of the previously religious conceptualization of work as a calling/vocation to a secular justification for selfishness and wealth accumulation is troubling for some Christian theologians. Having largely abandoned the idea that work is a calling from God, Protestant faiths are criticized for drawing a sharp line between religious practices, which typically happen in church on the weekend, and everyday work, which occurs the rest of the week.[13] This is seen as reducing the relevance of religion to people's lives, impairing the ability of the church to help individuals be Christian workers, and leaving a moral vacuum in the economic arena.

To try to expand its moral influence over work and business, the Roman Catholic Church, starting with the Second Vatican Council in the early 1960s, adopted the previously Protestant view that allows for nonreligious work to be a vocation—that is, "a calling to work in an industrious manner in the world . . . to perfect oneself and to work toward the common good as part of one's responsibilities to God and to others." The Second Vatican Council further reinforced the Catholic belief that working enhances one's holiness and chances of salvation:

Those who engage in labor—and frequently it is of a heavy nature—should better themselves by their human labors. They should be of aid to their fellow citizens. They should raise all of society, and even creation itself, to a better mode of existence. Indeed, they should imitate by their lively charity, in their joyous hope and by their voluntary sharing of each others' burdens, the very Christ who plied His hands with carpenter's tools and Who in union with His Father, is continually working for the salvation of all men. In this, then, their daily work they should climb to the heights of holiness and apostolic activity.

From a contemporary Protestant perspective, Volf also argues for a new and improved embracing of work as a religious calling:

When God calls people to become children of God, the Spirit gives them callings, talents, and "enablings" (charisms) so that they can do God's will in the Christian fellowship and in the world of God's eschatological new creation. All Christians have several gifts of the [Holy] Spirit. Since most of these gifts can be exercised only through work, work must be considered a central aspect of Christian living.[14]

Moreover, the Protestant belief, traced back to Luther, that salvation stems from faith alone is criticized by some because it "disallow[s] a rightful honor and meaning that work should have." To enhance the religious importance of work, it is then argued, requires making work "count," as captured in this poem by the thirteenth-century Muslim philosopher Rumi:

> On Resurrection Day God will say, "What did you do with the strength and energy
>
> your food gave you on earth? How did you use your eyes? What did you make with
>
> your five senses while they were dimming and playing out? I gave you hands and feet
>
> as tools for preparing the ground for planting. Did you, in the health I gave,
>
> do the plowing? . . ."

At the same time, advocates for seeing work as a calling try to guard against making a calling too important, such that work becomes all-consuming or that all work is justified regardless of how lousy the working conditions. Others reject altogether the idea that work is a calling. Theologian Jacques Ellul argued that after the fall of humans in the Garden of Eden,

> work becomes painful and compulsory in the attempt to survive. . . . It does not represent a service to God. It is an imperative of survival, and the Bible remains realist enough not to superimpose upon this necessity a superfluous spiritual decoration. Moreover, the Bible is not essentially concerned with this situation of work. It is the common and distressing lot of everyone, but it is not particularly important.

A diversity of perspectives of work as a calling can therefore be identified.[15] Work as a calling is an important, albeit not unitary, conceptualization of work.

Working for the Household

In the countries of East Asia, including China, Taiwan, Japan, Korea, Vietnam, and Singapore, work has traditionally been centered on the multigenerational household, not the individual or the individual's immediate family. This long-standing view of work reflects the importance of the Confucian tradition in these countries. Confucianism is a Chinese ethical philosophy that stems from the work of Confucius (Kong Fuzi) in the fifth century BCE and many disciples afterward to revitalize ancient Chinese ideals and rituals.[16] While Confucianism has been mixed with various indigenous traditions and reinterpreted in various ways over the centuries, it continues to provide a foundation for contemporary East Asian culture.

The teachings of Confucius date from a turbulent period in Chinese feudal history, so Confucianism emphasizes social harmony rooted in respect for social hierarchies. Harmony is based on the pursuit of the virtue *ren*— "goodness, humaneness, benevolence, human-heartedness, and humanity"— within prescribed hierarchical relationships, such as parent-child. In contrast to Western liberal individualism structured around autonomous individuals, then, Confucian thought sees a person as "a relational being, socially situated and defined within an interactive context" of relationships that are governed by strict norms of appropriate relationship roles. The family, not the individual, is the primary social unit, and filial piety—"the subordination of the will and welfare of each individual to the will and welfare of his or her real or classificatory parents"—is a cardinal virtue. The importance of the family relationship is further reflected by the fact that the Confucian model of good government is an extension of the ideals of the parent-child relationship based on care, guidance, obedience, and loyalty.[17]

Given the centrality of the family in Confucian thought, work is seen as serving the multigenerational family and the common good, not the individual. In China, then, work has been household-based for centuries. In fact, the failure of collective agriculture under Mao after the Communist Party came to power in 1949 was arguably partly due to the ways in which collectivization clashed with these centuries-old norms of household-based work. Seeing work as serving the household is not limited to agrarian labor and also applies to household production, family-run businesses, and outside work in which the earnings are turned over to the household. The increasing influence of Western individualism in East Asia in recent years likely means that the following claim from 1985 should be qualified somewhat, but it demonstrates the lasting power of household-based work ideals: "In no Chinese society do individuals work primarily for individual benefit. The group, of course, that has been the intended beneficiary of [hard work] throughout most of Chinese history has been the *jia,* or economic family." Similar household or family-based conceptualizations of work are apparent in other East Asian countries. For example, in Japan, kinship might be defined differently than in China, but it is nevertheless true that "subordinating one's individual desires to that of the household enterprise takes on the character of moral virtue" regardless of whether the household enterprise is a farm or a family-run business.[18]

As the East Asian countries have industrialized, Confucian values have also carried over into the employment relationship for wage and salary workers. The Japanese ideal of lifetime employment in which employees are recruited by a company and expected to stay with that company for their working life can be seen as a reflection of Confucian importance of familial reciprocity and loyalty, even if this ideal is a reality for only a minority of the workforce:

> By recruiting someone, the company assumes the obligation of a family to take care of him for his entire career. This means that the company must be prepared to make sacrifices for its employees. . . . The company's commitment to its employees in terms of job security is reciprocated by a higher degree of commitment from its employees. . . . With this exchange of commitments, the Japanese company becomes an extension of an employee's own family.

With industrialization in Korea starting in the 1960s,

> Confucian values, such as respect for authority and elders, loyalty, and the importance of education and diligence, which are traditional values aimed at maintaining social order, harmony in the family or self-cultivation, were transferred to new structures and groupings of the industrial setting: communal or family loyalty was transformed into company loyalty; diligence for self-cultivation was changed to working hard for one's workplace, and domestic paternalism was adapted to modern industrial conditions.[19]

In other words, working for the family became working for the corporate family. Taking this idea to an extreme, some workers even commit suicide to restore honor to a company they have disgraced, just as some might try to restore honor to their family.

Lastly, a Confucian work ethic emphasizing hard work, loyalty, self-discipline, and self-improvement has been hypothesized to underlie the economic success of Japan, Korea, Taiwan, Hong Kong, and Singapore. This is reminiscent of Weber's famous thesis that the Protestant work ethic created a spirit of capitalism, and also contains a bit of irony, as Weber argued that Confucianism hindered economic development by preserving the status quo, inhibiting risk-taking, and presenting other restraints. Critics of the claimed importance of the Confucian work ethic today argue that employers and states selectively use Confucian rhetoric to manipulatively serve their own modernization agendas by actively constructing a docile, hardworking labor force and disguising the true nature of corporate authority over labor.[20]

Family-centered societies are not limited to Confucian cultures. For example, the extended family is the primary social unit of the Native American Cheyenne. A Cheyenne extended family group can include in-laws, married adult children and their children, and others, and can therefore be quite large. These families are commonly organized as "a cooperative work group, with some members working for wages, some taking care of the children, and others undertaking domestic work both for themselves and for those who work for wages." The cooperative nature of the family and the importance of familial rather than individual identity are revealed by the practice of sending a sibling or a cousin to work as a temporary replacement when a worker has to be absent from a job—to the frustration of some employers, "since from their individualistic perspective, they have employed one person for a job, not a family."[21]

Volunteering and Working for the Community and the Nation

Archaeological evidence suggests that until the end of the last ice age ten thousand years ago, early hunter-gatherer humans lived in small, intimate bands. Work was aided by increasingly specialized stone tools, and the fruits of this physically demanding effort—food and shelter—were extensively shared within the band. Fast forward to early modern England in the fifteenth century and "labor was viewed as a common resource to which the community had rights, and laborers and artificers had legal obligations to make that resource available to community members on terms and conditions the community prescribed." A variety of local and national statutes therefore restricted workers from looking for work outside their towns and required them to complete their work before leaving a job. And then in 1630, John Winthrop instructed the Puritan colonists who were settling New England that in order to survive,

> we must be knit together in this work as one man. We must entertain each other in brotherly affection, we must be willing to abridge ourselves of our superfluities, for the supply of others' necessities. We must uphold a familiar commerce together in all meekness, gentleness, patience and liberality. We must delight in each other, make others' conditions our own, rejoice together, mourn together, labor and suffer together, always having before our eyes our commission and community in the work, our community as members of the same body.

These examples underscore that it takes work for human communities to sustain themselves, and therefore work can be seen as an important method for serving the community.[22]

Today, a popular way of serving a community is through volunteering. While volunteering is typically unpaid (or minimally paid), it should nevertheless be seen as work—it involves effort, it produces benefits for the volunteer and others, and it is structured by the same factors that shape paid work, such as labor market opportunities, individual motivation, social norms, and gender. Volunteering can take many forms. It is commonly seen as an altruistic or philanthropic way of helping others who are less fortunate than ourselves. When volunteering is formalized through an institution-alized, intensive commitment, it can instead be seen as civic service: "an organized period of substantial engagement and contribution to the local, national, or world community, recognized and valued by society, with mini-mal monetary compensation to the participant." In some cases, civic service is mandatory for youths or provides an alternative to mandatory military service. Other forms of community building should also not be overlooked, such as participating in friendly societies, labor unions, business associations, social organizations, and governmental entities (e.g., a local school board), or even by forms of informal work that make you a good neighbor, like cutting someone's lawn or watching a neighbor's child.[23]

There are diverse reasons why individuals pursue or are encouraged to pursue volunteer work, civic service, and community building. Helping oth-ers who are impoverished frequently stems from humanitarian concerns motivated by religious and/or ethical principles. In a very different vein, the classical republicanism school of thought in political philosophy emphasizes civic virtue in order to hold a community or a nation together. For the eighteenth-century American founders, for example,

> the Revolutionary ideal lay, not in the pursuit of private matters, but in the shared public life of civic duty, in the subordination of individual interests to the *res publica*. . . . To the first American generation, the political community was a single organic whole, binding each of its members into a single civic body of shared interests that transcended individual concerns. Natural leaders were expected to rise up among the people; others would . . . contribute their own talents to the com-mon good.

From this perspective, which continues today, civic service is seen as "simul-taneously changing politically indifferent citizens into virtuous ones and transforming society into more intimate, private communities of actively engaged citizens." This can be achieved by formal civic service (as in national service programs) as well as by local participation in community organiza-tions and other informal activities that contribute to the life of a community. Serving others is also advocated as a way of repaying one's debt to society. This perspective contrasts with the Lockean liberal tradition in which individuals own their own work, and instead believes that "to the extent that people are mutually involved in the production of each others' existence, the products of their respective labours are due to all." Lastly, volunteering and service are important for the rewards they provide to the volunteer, both intrinsically (e.g., enjoyment of the nature of the work and seeing others helped) and extrinsically (e.g., enhanced human capital, social networks, and civic skills).[24]

Conceptualizing work as service to one's community or country is not limited to unpaid volunteering and civic service. Military service is frequently seen as patriotic service for one's country. Work more generally can also be seen in this way. English mercantilist economists in the late seventeenth century imbued work with a nationalistic duty to serve the country's economic interests and believed that it was a worker's "duty to perform the amount and kind of work which the purposes of the nation require." Before the rise of wage work in America, "Revolutionary [era] republicanism portrayed work as the production by free citizens of useful goods for the benefit of the community." With the spread of wage work in Korea, the South Korean government tried to spur rapid economic development from the 1960s to the 1980s by making

> industrial labor into a national campaign by associating the concept of work with that of ethnic nationalism or *minjokjuui*. Work . . . was regarded as a social obligation, patriotic duty and moral duty, replete with the notion that the more each individual works, the better off everyone is, including the company, and more importantly, the country. In addition, the motive force for participation in labor was not identified as self-interest, but rather as a contribution to the state's nation-building.[25]

Under communism, the thought of work as serving the community is definitional—the *Oxford English Dictionary*, for example, defines communism as "a theory which advocates a state of society in which there should be no private ownership, all property being vested in the community and labour organized for the common benefit of all members." As explained in a speech by Lenin in 1920, communist labor

> is labour performed gratis for the benefit of society, labour performed not as a definite duty, not for the purpose of obtaining a right to certain products, not according to previously established and legally fixed quotas, but voluntary labour, irrespective of quotas; it is labour performed without expectation of reward, without reward as a condition, labour

performed because it has become a habit to work for the common good, and because of a conscious realisation (that has become a habit) of the necessity of working for the common good—labour as the requirement of a healthy organism.

A similar view of work was part of the ideology of Nazi Germany, but also imbued with racist superiority. According to the Nazi Party, "For the greatest portion of his life each productive man stands at his work post; his bearing at work is built upon the recognition that his life's work is not a commodity that can be freely disposed of but rather that his life must uphold the duty to his people and to his family that is constituted by his blood."[26] And so while work as service on behalf of one's community and country can be seen as good, bad, or ugly, it is undeniably a conceptualization of work that is found across diverse cultures, eras, and political systems.

The Tension between Service and Individualism

Whether in the form of serving the Holy Lord or the feudal lord, work as service was a dominant conceptualization of work before the rise of Western individualism. Multiple factors gave rise to the ascendancy of the individual in Western thought starting in the 1500s.[27] Religious schisms such as the Protestant Reformation and the English Reformation created multiple models for how to live one's life and thereby opened up the possibility of choosing what path to follow. Protestantism, and especially Puritanism, strengthened earlier developments toward individual salvation and increasingly made religious activity more individual and less hierarchical. Economic changes and the breakdown of the feudal order enhanced social mobility. One's place in society and standard of living increasingly depended on individual achievement, not a preordained social assignment. The eventual emergence of a secular rather than Christian social order furthered individuals' desires for personal, nonreligious fulfillment in the present life rather than religious salvation in the afterlife. And challenging the hierarchical authority of the church and various monarchies created a movement for individual liberties.

The importance of the individual in modern Western thought yields conceptualizations of work as an activity that serves the individual rather than someone else. First, work can be seen as a source of individual freedom (chapter 2) and a freely traded commodity (chapter 3). And then work becomes seen as various forms of free activity distinguished by differing views on the nature of our self-interest—especially, the consumption of goods and leisure (chapter 5), personal fulfillment (chapter 6), or a positive self-identity (chapter 9). To the extent that the rise of individualism has freed workers from the shackles of slavery, feudalism, and authoritarian political systems, these shifts can be evaluated as positive developments. But one can also question whether individualism has gone too far.

Economist Stephen Marglin shows how the concept of individual self-interest went "from vice to virtue in a century," especially due to the influential writings of John Locke and Adam Smith between the 1680s and the 1770s. Society thereby became seen as a collection of self-interested, atomistic individuals (or nuclear families) who focus on their own consumption and wealth. In this way, economic markets trumped and undermined the importance of community:

> Commodification may make for greater efficiency, but every time a good or service is turned into something that is bought and sold, the result is to substitute impersonal market relationships for personal relationships of reciprocity and the like. Eventually economic ties wither altogether, and the community is put at risk.

These trends have also been criticized from a religious perspective, as captured by Miroslav Volf's scornful observation that the contemporary worshipping of hard work "has little to do either with worship of God or with God's demands on human life; it has much to do with 'worship' of self and human demands on the self" and thereby degrades humans' relations with God and with each other.[28]

The shift from seeing work as service to serving the individual is therefore not without cost, and the contemporary calls to serve God, to volunteer in the community, to create national service programs, and to see traditional forms of paid work in broader community-oriented terms can be seen as attempts to temper overly individualistic and selfish conceptualizations of work in the modern, Western world. In the words of a Hindu spiritual leader,

> Service, therefore, is about people's relationships with each other, God, time, nature and the world around them. A significant role of work will always be to generate a financial reward, but this needs to be seen as only a means to the end of a better quality of life for the individual and his or her family, not an end in itself. To add the dimension of service into work will put people at the heart of work, and fill it with a meaning and purpose that it often seems to lack.[29]

Conceptualizing work as service therefore has been and remains an important element of understanding the totality of work, albeit in the presence of long-standing tensions between community and individual.

Conclusion: Work Matters

Labour is Life.

—Thomas Carlyle (1795–1881)

Work is frequently invisible.[1] Everything we use, right down to the paper and ink for this book, is made and transported by people we rarely see or know and who work under conditions we rarely think about. Employees are typically invisible in business education and in corporate governance. Issues related to work or labor standards are seldom at the top of many countries' political agendas, and in the international arena, the World Trade Organization has explicitly said that labor standards are not its concern. In academia, work-related research is typically not viewed as being on the vanguard of contemporary scholarship and is therefore largely invisible to many scholars. The popularity of disciplinary subfields in economics, history, political science, psychology, and sociology that study work has declined, and the one discipline devoted to work—industrial relations—is fading away. But work should not be invisible. Work matters.

Not only practically, but also intellectually. Recall the range of historical figures and intellectual giants whose ideas have been important in the previous ten chapters—such as sociologists Max Weber and Émile Durkheim, economists Adam Smith, Karl Marx, W. Stanley Jevons, Sidney and Beatrice Webb, and John R. Commons, political scientist John Locke, psychologists Sigmund Freud and Abraham Maslow, philosophers Confucius, Aristotle, Georg Hegel, Hannah Arendt, and Michel Foucault, theologians such as Saint Thomas Aquinas, Martin Luther, and John Calvin, management experts such as Frederick Winslow Taylor and Mary Parker Follett, feminists such as Charlotte Perkins Gilman, and many others. The result of centuries of theorizing and observation is a set of disciplinary conceptualizations of work that together provide powerful lenses for analyzing work. But the specialized nature of today's scholarship focuses on narrow aspects of work through each discipline's preferred lens. Work is seen as disutilty *or* personal fulfillment *or* a social relation. We need to appreciate not only the importance of these different conceptualizations, but the limitations of being overly focused. With a singular thought of work we are left with a fragmentary understanding of a highly complex yet critical aspect of the human experience, and a correspondingly incomplete basis for evaluating actual forms of work and designing private and public policies on work. The resolution to these limitations, and the key to a deep understanding of work, is to recognize multiple conceptualizations of work.

Work as Fundamentally Important

At the highest level, argued Karl Marx and some others, work is *the* fundamental characteristic of being human because it distinguishes us from animals (chapter 9). While it is dangerous to elevate work to such an exalted position, because work will never be able to fulfill all our human needs, we need also to guard against relegating work to the margins of how we think about the human experience. Work defines who we are, individually and collectively. Not completely, but in important ways. Whether in unpaid household work, paid employment, or the many other forms that work can take, when we work we experience our biological, psychological, economic, and social selves. We sweat, we think, we care, we create. Work is how we earn a living, build a material world, develop (or lose) our self-esteem and social identity, interact with others least like ourselves, and experience society's power imbalances. Work, therefore, is a fully human activity.

The importance of work is reinforced by its effects on our mental health. Individuals with high levels of self-identity in their work experience occupational devotion. In such instances, work yields such a large degree of self-fulfillment, achievement, success, and reward that it might seem more like leisure than work. Psychological well-being, self-esteem, and the perceived ability to control one's success are affected by one's job security as well as the structural features of jobs, such as complexity, routinization, and opportunities for self-direction. The problems that accompany the absence of work further illustrate work's importance. In the words of the legal scholar Kenneth Karst:

- If stable, adequately paid work is a source of independence, its absence means dependence on others.
- If stable, adequately paid work is an avenue to personal achievement, its absence signifies failure.
- If stable, adequately paid work offers advancement up the socio-economic ladder, its absence means that one's social station is either fixed or in decline.
- If stable, adequately paid work provides family security, its absence means insecurity.
- If stable, adequately paid work elicits the esteem of others, its absence means shame.

A large body of evidence also shows that unemployment significantly reduces mental health. In these ways, problems of underemployment and unemployment are more than simply problems of a lack of income and instead strike at the heart of the human condition so sharply that some concerned individuals advocate for legislating a guaranteed right to decent work. Others call for new values to govern employment and labor law and for new norms in which business leaders would see layoffs as a policy of last resort rather than as a normal operating procedure.[2] These issues are particularly important in the wake of the global financial crisis in 2008 that increased unemployment globally by an estimated thirty-four million individuals, so that at the beginning of 2010 over two hundred million individuals were without work. But the rich importance of work also means that simply having any job is not enough.

As described in more detail in the introductory chapter, work also shapes the world we live in. Work is created by, and creates, social structures, culture, and inequalities. Human history and social evolution cannot be divorced from changes in the nature of work. The fundamental societal changes that were generated by the Neolithic Revolution's shift from hunting-gathering to agriculture and the Industrial Revolution's further shift to industrial production represent profound changes in how people work and therefore how they relate to each other. Feudalism, colonialism, capitalism, communism, and other social systems are similarly defined by how work is structured—who does what, who has the power to determine who does what, who gets what, and who has the power to determine who gets what. Social change invariably disrupts established work patterns and replaces them with new patterns—in effect, "all revolutions . . . are in a sense about the division of labor."[3]

Work continues to determine the kind of society we embrace and strive for. Are we a collection of consumers who work only to be able to live outside of work? Is aggregate economic growth the sole yardstick for measuring the effectiveness and meaning of our work? As noted by political scientist Russell Muirhead, markets are powerful for achieving high levels of productivity, but this reduces working to earning paychecks, and paychecks "do not offer a very profound reason for an individual to do this sort of work rather than that. They say nothing about why a person should find work meaningful or fulfilling, or about why it is an appropriate expression of one's identity." Should work be driven by more than the market? Should work be embraced as an integral human activity such that we are a collection of workers, not just consumers, who value broader yardsticks than economic efficiency for evaluating the nature of work? Should efficiency trump employee equity and voice—as is the case in today's neoliberal market ideology—or do we strive for a balance or some other set of priorities?[4]

Similar questions can be asked about caregiving and spiritual life. Is unpaid caring for others "real" work worthy of respect, or is it a marginal activity that fails to produce tangible economic benefits? Is the increasingly commoditized nature of care a sign of increasing professionalization, or of a weakening of the collective commitment to care for the young and the elderly? Is work seen as a secular activity sharply distinct from religious activities? Or can religious believers do God's work through their daily work activities? Whatever we choose as answers to these questions—whether through intentional discussion or through an unquestioned acceptance of trends that appear to be beyond our control—how we experience work is inseparable from how we experience life.

How a society defines work also reflects and reveals how that society implicitly defines human nature. To see work as freedom is to define humans as compelled to master nature and create things. To embrace work as disutility is to specify human nature as rational, self-interested, atomistic, and largely materialistic. Emphasizing the personal fulfillment element of work casts humans as seeking inner satisfaction, while a perspective that recognizes work as service shifts our deepest intentions outward toward others and perhaps toward a higher spiritual purpose. And to see work as a social relation is to characterize human nature as fundamentally concerned with how we relate to others, and perhaps as driven to dominate others. The meaning of work in a particular society is therefore an inherent part of the deeper cultural fabric.

Conceptualizations Matter

Owing to the fundamental importance of work, my objective in this book is to provide a foundation for a deep understanding of work through ten conceptualizations of work. These conceptualizations represent a critical synthesis of academic theories of work from across the social and behavioral sciences and important philosophical traditions. An explicit appreciation of the various conceptualizations of work can promote cross-disciplinary understanding and dialogue. Scholars of work from different disciplines typically only see work through the conceptualizations of their own disciplines. Even a seemingly simple concept like a job is therefore understood differently. When work is seen as personal fulfillment (chapter 6), jobs are seen as bundles of tasks designed to promote intrinsic rewards and motivation. If work is disutility (chapter 5), jobs are seen as crafted to promote monitoring and the revelation of how much effort workers have expended. If work is an antagonistic social relation (chapter 7), jobs are seen as shaped by power dynamics between employers and employees.

Or consider technological change. Economists will generally analyze how technological change affects the relative supply and demand of skills and any incentive effects brought on by technological change. Psychologists will be most interested in how technological change affects employee attitudes, stress, and satisfaction. Sociologists will see technological change as an intentional act—not something that just occurs—that reflects the dynamics of social relations between various groups, and will analyze how workers accommodate and resist technological change, and might highlight structural or discursive elements. Feminist scholars will question the gendered nature of technological change, and industrial relations scholars will concentrate on whether any institutional interventions are needed to protect workers' rights. The focal points of these disciplinary approaches all stem from how work is conceptualized in each discipline. This example is, of course, an oversimplification, but it highlights how ideas about work shape scholarly research agendas, and therefore demonstrates the need to explicitly appreciate the conceptualizations of work developed in the preceding chapters.

By making these conceptualizations explicit, we are better positioned not only to appreciate their contributions toward understanding the full breadth of human work, but also to see the importance of these conceptualizations for how work is understood, experienced, and analyzed. Some examples of this were presented in earlier chapters—such as how we evaluate human resource management (chapter 6), diversity initiatives (chapter 8), or minimum wage laws and labor unions (chapter 4). Legal scholar Ellen Dannin shows how American judges have effectively rewritten U.S. labor law not because of some antiunion bias, but because they implicitly see employment through a distinct lens.[5] Specifically, judges conceptualize work as a freely exchanged commodity and therefore have trouble seeing how workers who were fired for trying to organize a labor union should enjoy any special protections—protections that are written into labor law based on seeing work as occupational citizenship. Labor advocates often push for reforms that strengthen labor law through legislative action, but unless the underlying conceptualization of work implicitly embraced by judges changes, such reforms are likely to be muted by judicial interpretation, because conceptualizations matter.

How one conceptualizes work in the modern business organization can also have important effects. Why do companies lay off workers rather than cut wages during recessions? Because business leaders believe that wage reductions will harm productivity through reduced employee morale and increased employee turnover. This reflects the influence of mainstream economic thought on business education. By conceptualizing work as disutility, business leaders believe that workers are motivated by money, so a wage reduction is seen as reducing effort and as causing employees to look for more money elsewhere. This can result in a self-fulfilling prophecy: given all the attention on performance-based pay, employees probably come to believe that they are supposed to need higher pay to be motivated. And yet research shows that monetary incentives can crowd out intrinsic motivators. Or why do managers monitor employees? By thinking of work as disutility, managers feel compelled to tightly monitor employees to prevent shirking. But this signals to employees that they are not trusted, and can thereby create the very behavior it was intended to counteract.[6] The multiple ways of thinking about work developed in this book, however, imply that the governance challenges for business leaders are significantly more complex than simply monitoring and controlling employees. Not only do organizational leaders need to find ways to respect the deep importance of work for individuals, but they must also confront the possibility that different employees will think of work differently and therefore be motivated differently. A better understanding of the fundamental conceptualizations of work is an important foundation for tackling these challenges.

Conceptualizations also matter for how we evaluate working conditions. If work is seen as a freely exchanged commodity, then workers are free to quit jobs that are perceived as lousy, so working conditions are not a societal concern. This conceptualization of work underlies the perception among many policymakers that global labor standards are unnecessary. If work is disutility, then work is always lousy—what is important is the compensation. If work is a source of personal fulfillment, then poor working conditions are seen as detrimental to productivity because of reduced job satisfaction. When work is seen as a source of self-identity, then lousy working conditions are of broader concern to the extent that they undermine one's identity, but these concerns can also be tempered by a belief that individuals are able to craft a positive identity in adverse situations by focusing on selected attributes. When work is conceptualized as a social relation, poor working conditions are generally seen as a reflection of employer power, but are also subject to worker resistance and renegotiation. If hard work is the result of a god's curse then there is little scope for questioning the quality of one's working conditions; but if work is seen as a co-creative activity with God, then undignified working conditions are of great concern. If work is thought of as occupational citizenship, then working conditions should at least meet some societal threshold consistent with treating labor as a human citizen, not just a commodity. And if work is characterized by multiple conceptualizations, then dignified working conditions and citizenship rights should attach to diverse forms of paid and unpaid work, not just full-time, paid employment.[7]

On a broader level, how work is conceptualized affects who and what is valued and where resources are devoted. When work is conceptualized as a curse of the lowly and the enslaved, as in ancient Greece and Rome, technological progress is slower because the highly educated choose other pursuits and there are limited ways for spreading and popularizing technological advances. When work is viewed as an expression of human creativity, society is more tolerant of diverse lifestyles and provides greater support to artistic and cultural institutions. When work is seen as a way to achieve independence from the natural world by mastering it, natural resources are extracted rather than sustained. When industrialized cultures see work as a commodity, paid employment is privileged over caring for and serving others, and "women's work" and volunteering are marginalized. In the United States, then, unpaid housework and child care are not deemed worthy of earning credits toward Social Security coverage and only fulfill the work requirements for receiving welfare in limited circumstances; volunteers are excluded from legal protections against discrimination, sexual harassment, and other abuses.[8]

To reiterate, conceptualizations matter. The conceptualizations of work do not simply describe alternative perspectives on work; rather, they actively structure our understandings of and our experiences with work by providing frames of references, norms, values, and attitudes toward work that actors translate into specific practices. Researchers study particular aspects of work, workers expect certain things out of their work, business leaders implement particular employment practices, workers' rights advocates push for specific protections, policymakers enact employment regulations of a certain kind, judges interpret employment and labor laws in particular ways, and social approval and economic resources accrue to some individuals but not others—all because of how people think about work. And when questions abound regarding the contemporary state of work—particularly global unemployment, widespread job insecurity, significant work-family conflict, and communities hollowed out by layoffs—the dominant conceptualizations of work must be scrutinized. In the words of industrial relations scholar Peter Ackers, "Nothing is more central to the reconstitution of community and civil society than rethinking work, which consumes so much of our daylight hours, confers income and status, and shapes life-changes in so many ways."[9]

The Thought of Work?

With multiple conceptualizations of work, it is tempting to ask which conceptualization is right or which one is best. As just shown, conceptualizations matter. So the specific conceptualizations of work embraced by a particular society should be subject to critical examination and debate. By crafting a comprehensive integration of the diverse conceptualizations of work, I hope *The Thought of Work* provides a rich foundation for this type of critical discourse. To be clear, I do not intend this book to universalize how work is experienced by specific individuals in specific cultures. There are clearly "place-specific particularities of work" that create unique cultural logics of work.[10] The ten conceptualizations presented here provide the basis for understanding these cultural logics, not for homogenizing them.

In contrast to Frederick Winslow Taylor's belief in the one best way of accomplishing work, there is no one best conceptualization of work. Work is too multifaceted to be reduced to a single manner of thinking. Writing this book has been work that has provided personal fulfillment but has also conflicted with family responsibilities, my children's soccer games, and leisure activities—and the time spent reading as research for this book might even be considered leisure by some. Crafting *The Thought of Work* has been a source of individual creativity, independence, and, by being part of my job as a professor, income, and hopefully it will serve a broader community through the sharing of ideas. Occasionally, writing this book seemed more like a chore, if not a curse, as I labored over some areas that did not evolve as smoothly as wished. And it has been at many times a solitary effort, but also a collective activity as I have benefited from the writings of my predecessors and the advice and encouragement of my contemporaries. Hopefully the end result will satisfy the social norms for academic work, but however it is received, it will, in some small way, reproduce those norms.

The *thought* of work is therefore richly textured. In practice, maybe we experience necessity, dread, fulfillment, or a range of other emotions at the thought of work—perhaps all within a single day. Theorists of work might conceive of financial, psychic, or social rewards and controls. In all cases, work is too important to take for granted, but too dynamic to be universalized as good or bad, and too complex to be reduced to a single conceptualization. Rather, we need to analyze the ways in which the various conceptualizations are complementary, and from this multidisciplinary approach create richer understandings of work that reflect its true breadth and deep importance.

These richer understandings, in turn, can provide the basis for reevaluating how society thinks about work and therefore what forms of work are valued or devalued, what defines acceptable employer practices or working conditions, whether there is a need for institutional safeguards, and which workers are able to craft a positive, healthy identity from their work. Work is too important for individuals and society to be dismissed as a curse, treated as a just another commodity or economic resource, or viewed solely as a source of income. The need for environment sustainability means that we need to rethink how Western civilization considers work as the domination and mastery of nature. And the need for greater social inclusion of typically marginalized groups demands a wider embrace of work that goes beyond paid employment. In sum, we need to *think* about work as a fully human activity that is complex and fundamentally important not only to better understand work, but also to value and structure work in ways that embrace its deep significance.

NOTES

Author's note: To keep the number of notes manageable, references are cited by paragraph rather than by sentence. Wherever necessary, the notes contain brief annotations linking one or more sources to the relevant sentence(s) or idea(s) in the text. Please note that the annotations do not necessarily capture a source's content; rather, they point to a subject or a phrase in the text in order to connect the text and the sources. The order of the citations in each note follows the order of the cited ideas in each paragraph.

Introduction

1. Work when individuals undertake same tasks: Robert W. Drago, *Striking a Balance: Work, Family, Life* (Boston: Dollars and Sense, 2007). Packaging tasks: William Bridges, *JobShift: How to Prosper in a Workplace without Jobs* (Reading, MA: Addison-Wesley, 1994).

2. Symbolic value: Anthony P. Cohen, "The Whalsay Croft: Traditional Work and Customary Identity in Modern Times," in Sandra Wallman, ed., *Social Anthropology of Work* (London: Academic Press, 1979): 249–67. Work v. labor: Hannah Arendt, *The Human Condition* (Chicago: University of Chicago Press, 1958); Guy Standing, *Work after Globalization: Building Occupational Citizenship* (Cheltenham, Gloucestershire, UK: Edward Elgar, 2009).

3. Cultural norms define: Sabine Gürtler, "The Ethical Dimension of Work: A Feminist Perspective," trans. Andrew F. Smith, *Hypatia* 20 (Spring 2005): 119–34. China: Gail E. Henderson et al., "Re-Drawing Boundaries of Work: Views on the Meaning of Work (*Gongzuo*)," in Barbara Entwisle and Gail E. Henderson, eds., *Re-Drawing Boundaries: Work, Households, and Gender in China* (Berkeley: University of California Press, 2000): 33–50. Turkey: Jenny B. White, *Money Makes Us Relatives: Women's Labor in Urban Turkey* (Austin: University of Texas Press, 1994).

4. Miriam A. Glucksmann, "Why 'Work'? Gender and the 'Total Social Organization of Labour,'" *Gender, Work, and Organization* 2 (April 1995): 63–75 at 69. Production of something of value: E. Kevin Kelloway, Daniel G. Gallagher, and Julian Barling, "Work, Employment, and the Individual," in Bruce E. Kaufman, ed., *Theoretical Perspectives on Work and the Employment Relationship* (Champaign, IL: Industrial Relations Research Association, 2004): 105–31.

5. Nebulous borders: Herbert Applebaum, *The Concept of Work: Ancient, Medieval, and Modern* (Albany: State University of New York Press, 1992); John T. Haworth and A. J. Veal, eds., *Work and Leisure* (London: Routledge, 2004); David Kaplan, "The Darker Side of the 'Original Affluent Society,'" *Journal of Anthropological Research* 56 (Autumn 2000): 301–24. Caregivers: Kathy Peiss, *Cheap Amusements: Working Women*

NOTES TO PAGES 4–6

and Leisure in Turn-of-the-Century New York (Philadelphia: Temple University Press, 1986). Fulfilling careers: Robert A. Stebbins, *Between Work and Leisure: The Common Ground of Two Separate Worlds* (New Brunswick, NJ: Transaction Publishers, 2004). Regulating nonwork activities: Terry Morehead Dworkin, "It's My Life—Leave Me Alone: Off-the-Job Employee Associational Privacy Rights," *American Business Law Journal* 35 (Fall 1997): 47–99.

6. Always a central feature: Richard Donkin, *Blood, Sweat, and Tears: The Evolution of Work* (New York: Texere, 2001). Early tools, also village labor force: Peter Bogucki, *The Origins of Human Society* (Malden, MA: Blackwell, 1999); Richard G. Klein, *The Human Career: Human Biological and Cultural Origins,* 2nd ed. (Chicago: University of Chicago Press, 1999). Storing hunter-gatherer: Alain Testart, "The Significance of Food Storage among Hunter-Gatherers: Residence Patterns, Population Densities, and Social Inequalities," *Current Anthropology* 23 (October 1982): 523–30.

7. Emergence of craft specialization: Robert K. Evans, "Early Craft Specialization: An Example from the Balkan Chalcolithic," in Charles L. Redman et al., eds., *Social Archaeology: Beyond Subsistence and Dating* (New York: Academic Press, 1978): 113–29. Pottery: Gil J. Stein, "Producers, Patrons, and Prestige: Craft Specialists and Emergent Elites in Mesopotamia from 5500–3100 B.C.," in Bernard Wailes, ed., *Craft Specialization and Social Evolution: In Memory of V. Gordon Childe* (Philadelphia: University of Pennsylvania Museum of Archaeology and Anthropology, 1996): 25–38. Standard professions list: Hans J. Nissen, "The Archaic Texts from Uruk," *World Archaeology* 17 (February 1986): 317–34. Part-time v. full-time specialists: Bernard Wailes, ed., *Craft Specialization and Social Evolution: In Memory of V. Gordon Childe* (Philadelphia: University of Pennsylvania Museum of Archaeology and Anthropology, 1996). Plato: P. D. Anthony, *The Ideology of Work* (London: Tavistock, 1977).

8. Surplus food: Bogucki, *The Origins of Human Society.* Complex societies: V. Gordon Childe, *The Prehistory of European Society* (Harmondsworth, UK: Penguin, 1958).

9. Pyramids: Christopher J. Eyre, "Work and the Organization of Work in the Old Kingdom," in Marvin A. Powell, ed., *Labor in the Ancient Near East* (New Haven, CT: Ancient Oriental Society, 1987): 5–47; Zahi Hawass, "Tombs of the Pyramid Builders," *Archaeology* 50 (January/February 1997): 39–43. Mesopotamia: Hartmut Waetzoldt, "Compensation of Craft Workers and Officials in the Ur III Period," in Marvin A. Powell, ed., *Labor in the Ancient Near East* (New Haven, CT: Ancient Oriental Society, 1987): 117–41. Tang dynasty: Charles Benn, *Daily Life in Traditional China: The Tang Dynasty* (Westport, CT: Greenwood Press, 2002). Inca Empire: Michael A. Malpass, *Daily Life in the Inca Empire* (Westport, CT: Greenwood Press, 1996).

10. Indus: Rita P. Wright, "Contexts of Specialization: V. Gordon Childe and Social Evolution," in Bernard Wailes, ed., *Craft Specialization and Social Evolution: In Memory of V. Gordon Childe* (Philadelphia: University of Pennsylvania Museum of Archaeology and Anthropology, 1996): 123–32. Pre-urban villages: Bogucki, *The Origins of Human Society.* Viking era: Christopher Dyer, *Making a Living in the Middle Ages: The People of Britain, 850–1520* (New Haven, CT: Yale University Press, 2002); Julian D. Richards, *Viking Age England* (Stroud, Gloucestershire, UK: Tempus, 2004).

11. Three classes: Georges Duby, *The Three Orders: Feudal Society Imagined,* trans. Arthur Goldhammer (Chicago: University of Chicago Press, 1980); Jacques Le Goff,

Time, Work and Culture in the Middle Ages, trans. Arthur Goldhammer (Chicago: University of Chicago Press, 1980). Quote: Applebaum, *The Concept of Work,* 236. Elizabethan era: Dyer, *Making a Living in the Middle Ages;* Keith Wrightson, *Earthly Necessities: Economic Lives in Early Modern Britain* (New Haven, CT: Yale University Press, 2000).

12. Putting-out system: Sheilagh C. Ogilvie and Markus Cerman, eds., *European Proto-Industrialization* (Cambridge: Cambridge University Press, 1996); E. P. Thompson, *The Making of the English Working Class* (London: Gollancz, 1963). Women at work: Applebaum, *The Concept of Work;* R. E. Pahl, *Divisions of Labour* (Oxford: Basil Blackwell, 1984); Wrightson, *Earthly Necessities.* Task variety: Joel Mokyr, "Editor's Introduction: The New Economic History and the Industrial Revolution," in Joel Mokyr, ed., *The British Industrial Revolution: An Economic Perspective,* 2nd ed. (Boulder, CO: Westview Press, 1999): 1–127. Colonial America: Stephen Innes, *Labor in a New Land: Economy and Society in Seventeenth-Century Springfield* (Princeton: Princeton University Press, 1983).

13. Sexual division of labor: George P. Murdock and Caterina Provost, "Factors in the Division of Labor by Sex: A Cross-Cultural Analysis," *Ethnology* 12 (April 1973): 203–25. Slavery: Orlando Patterson, *Slavery and Social Death: A Comparative Study* (Cambridge, MA: Harvard University Press, 1982); M. L. Bush, ed., *Serfdom and Slavery: Studies in Legal Bondage* (London: Addison Wesley Longman, 1996).

14. Fourteenth-century business: Edwin S. Hunt and James M. Murray, *A History of Business in Medieval Europe, 1200–1550* (Cambridge: Cambridge University Press, 1999). Brewers: Richard W. Unger, *Beer in the Middle Ages and the Renaissance* (Philadelphia: University of Pennsylvania Press, 2004). Silver mines: Susan C. Karant-Nunn, "From Adventurers to Drones: The Saxon Silver Miners as an Early Proletariat," in Thomas Max Safley and Leonard N. Rosenband, eds., *The Workplace before the Factory: Artisans and Proletarians, 1500–1800* (Ithaca, NY: Cornell University Press, 1993): 73–99. Britain: Joel Mokyr, "The Rise and Fall of the Factory System: Technology, Firms, and Households since the Industrial Revolution," *Carnegie-Rochester Conference Series on Public Policy* 55 (December 2001): 1–45; Sidney Pollard, *The Genesis of Modern Management: A Study of the Industrial Revolution in Great Britain* (Cambridge, MA: Harvard University Press, 1965).

15. Organizational aspect of industrial revolution: Mokyr, "Editor's Introduction"; Peter N. Stearns, *The Industrial Revolution in World History,* 3rd ed. (Boulder, CO: Westview Press, 2007); G. N. von Tunzelmann, "Technological and Organizational Change in Industry during the Early Industrial Revolution," in Patrick K. O'Brien and Roland Quinault, eds., *The Industrial Revolution and British Society* (Cambridge: Cambridge University Press, 1993): 254–82. Employer control: Harry Braverman, *Labor and Monopoly Capital: The Degradation of Work in the Twentieth Century* (New York: Monthly Review Press, 1974); Pollard, *The Genesis of Modern Management;* Charles Perrow, *Organizing America: Wealth, Power, and the Origins of Corporate Capitalism* (Princeton, NJ: Princeton University Press, 2002). Widespread growth: Stearns, *The Industrial Revolution in World History.*

16. Loss of control: Braverman, *Labor and Monopoly Capital;* Thompson, *The Making of the English Working Class.* Quote: Bridges, *JobShift,* viii. Unpaid caring work: Jeanne Boydston, *Home and Work: Housework, Wages, and the Ideology of Labor in the Early Republic* (New York: Oxford University Press, 1990). New supervisory

occupations: Pollard, *The Genesis of Modern Management*. Colonization: Stearns, *The Industrial Revolution in World History*. Indigenous peoples: Martha C. Knack and Alice Littlefield, "Native American Labor: Retrieving History, Rethinking Theory," in Alice Littlefield and Martha C. Knack, eds., *Native Americans and Wage Labor: Ethnohistorical Perspectives* (Norman: University of Oklahoma Press, 1996): 3–44.

17. Manufacturing division of labor: Karl Marx, *Economic and Philosophic Manuscripts of 1844* (1844), trans. Martin Milligan (Amherst, NY: Prometheus Books, 1988); Braverman, *Labor and Monopoly Capital*. Cigar-makers: Ronald Mendel, *"A Broad and Ennobling Spirit": Workers and Their Unions in Late Gilded Age New York and Brooklyn, 1886–1898* (Westport, CT: Praeger, 2003). Taylorism: Robert Kanigel, *The One Best Way: Frederick Winslow Taylor and the Enigma of Efficiency* (New York, Penguin, 1997); Braverman, *Labor and Monopoly Capital*.

18. Spread of industrialization: Stearns, *The Industrial Revolution in World History*. Flexible specialization: Michael J. Piore and Charles F. Sabel, *The Second Industrial Divide: Possibilities for Prosperity* (New York: Basic Books, 1984). Employee empowerment: Barry Bluestone and Irving Bluestone, *Negotiating the Future: A Labor Perspective on American Business* (New York: Basic Books, 1992); Eileen Appelbaum and Rosemary Batt, *The New American Workplace: Transforming Work Systems in the United States* (Ithaca, NY: Cornell University Press, 1994). Service sector: Stephen A. Herzenberg, John A. Alic, and Howard Wial, *New Rules for a New Economy: Employment and Opportunity in Postindustrial America* (Ithaca, NY: Cornell University Press, 1998). Creative sector: Richard Florida, *The Rise of the Creative Class: And How It's Transforming Work, Leisure, Community, and Everyday Life* (New York: Basic Books, 2002). Globalization: Kim Moody, *Workers in a Lean World: Unions in the International Economy* (London: Verso, 1997).

19. Recent immigrants: Immanuel Ness, *Immigrants, Unions, and the New U.S. Labor Market* (Philadelphia: Temple University Press, 2005). Female manufacturing workers: Teri L. Caraway, *Assembling Women: The Feminization of Global Manufacturing* (Ithaca, NY: Cornell University Press, 2007). Quote: Kevin Bales, *Disposable People: New Slavery in the Global Economy*, rev. ed. (Berkeley: University of California Press, 2004), 26.

20. David Ricardo, *On the Principles of Political Economy and Taxation* (1821) (London: G. Bell, 1919). Luddites: Malcolm I. Thomis, *The Luddites: Machine-Breaking in Regency England* (Hamden, CT: Archon Books, 1970). Utopian writers, also Rifkin prediction: Jeremy Rifkin, *The End of Work: The Decline of the Global Labor Force and the Dawn of the Post-Market Era* (New York: Putnam Books, 1995).

21. Compare: Marshall Sahlins, *Stone Age Economics* (Chicago: Aldine-Atherton, 1972); Kaplan, "The Darker Side of the 'Original Affluent Society.'"

22. Creation of written language: Nissen, "The Archaic Texts from Uruk." Literature, art, and culture: Tim Barringer, *Men at Work: Art and Labour in Victorian Britain* (New Haven, CT: Yale University Press, 2005); Nicholas Coles and Janet Zandy, eds., *American Working-Class Literature: An Anthology* (New York: Oxford University Press, 2006); Helen Molesworth, ed., *Work Ethic* (University Park: Penn State University Press, 2003). Time: E. P. Thompson, "Time, Work-Discipline, and Industrial Capitalism," *Past and Present* 38 (December 1967): 56–97. Human-made world: Arendt, *The Human Condition*. Agricultural, scientific, and industrial revolutions: Clifford D. Conner, *A People's History of Science: Miners, Midwives, and 'Low Mechanicks'* (New

NOTES TO PAGES 12–20

York: Nation Books, 2005). Martin Luther: Adriano Tilgher, *Work: What It Has Meant to Men through the Ages,* trans. Dorothy Canfield Fisher (London: George Harrap, 1931); Applebaum, *The Concept of Work.* True equality: Nancy MacLean, *Freedom Is Not Enough: The Opening of the American Workplace* (Cambridge, MA: Harvard University Press, 2006).

23. Alienation: Marx, *Economic and Philosophic Manuscripts of 1844.* Profound theorist of work: George Ritzer, *Classical Sociological Theory* (New York: McGraw-Hill, 1992).

24. Benchmark for affluence: Kaplan, "The Darker Side of the 'Original Affluent Society.'" Juliet B. Schor, *The Overworked American: The Unexpected Decline of Leisure* (New York: Basic Books, 1991). Pietro Basso, *Modern Times, Ancient Hours: Working Lives in the Twenty-first Century,* trans. Giacomo Donis (London: Verso, 2003).

25. Steven L. Kuhn and Mary C. Stiner, "What's a Mother to Do? The Division of Labor among Neandertals and Modern Humans in Eurasia," *Current Anthropology* 47 (December 2006): 953–80 at 959.

26. Important milestone: Kuhn and Stiner, "What's a Mother to Do?" Complex societies: Bogucki, *The Origins of Human Society*; T. Douglas Price and Gary M. Feinman, eds., *Foundations of Social Inequality* (New York: Plenum, 1995); Childe, *The Prehistory of European Society;* Wailes, *Craft Specialization and Social Evolution.*

27. Purchasing nonessential goods: Peter N. Stearns, *Consumerism in World History: The Global Transformation of Desire* (London: Routledge, 2001). Quote: Rick Fantasia and Kim Voss, *Hard Work: Remaking the American Labor Movement* (Berkeley: University of California Press, 2004), 27.

28. Ethical issues and work: John W. Budd and James G. Scoville, eds., *The Ethics of Human Resources and Industrial Relations* (Champaign, IL: Labor and Employment Relations Association, 2005).

29. New economy narrative: Kevin Doogan, *New Capitalism? The Transformation of Work* (Cambridge: Polity, 2009); Standing, *Work after Globalization.*

30. Work locates us: Diane Watson, "Individuals and Institutions: The Case of Work and Employment," in Margaret Wetherell, ed., *Identities, Groups, and Social Issues* (London: Sage, 1996): 239–82.

1. Work as a Curse

1. Sigmund Freud, *Civilization and Its Discontents,* trans. Joan Riviere (London: Hogarth Press, 1930), 34.

2. Biblical verses: Genesis 1:1, 2:15, 3:17, and 3:19. Some theological interpretations, compare: Doug Sherman and William Hendricks, *Your Work Matters to God* (Colorado Springs, CO: NavPress, 1987); Jacques Ellul, "Work and Calling," trans. James S. Albritton, in James Y. Holloway and Will D. Campbell, eds., *Callings!* (New York: Paulist Press, 1974): 18–44.

3. Hesiod: Frederick J. Teggart, "The Argument of Hesiod's *Works and Days,*" *Journal of the History of Ideas* 8 (January 1947): 45–77. Virgil: Bonnie A. Catto, "Lucretian *Labor* and Vergil's *Labor Improbus,*" *Classical Journal* 81 (April–May 1986): 305–18. Quote: Janet Lembke, *Virgil's Georgics: A New Verse Translation* (New Haven, CT: Yale University Press, 2005), 7, lines 125–28.

4. Monastic rules: George Ovitt, *The Restoration of Perfection: Labor and Technology in Medieval Culture* (New Brunswick, NJ: Rutgers University Press, 1987); Birgit van den Hoven, *Work in Ancient and Medieval Thought: Ancient Philosophers, Medieval Monks and Theologians and Their Concept of Work, Occupations and Technology* (Amsterdam: J. C. Gieben, 1996). Penitential activity: Jacques Le Goff, *Time, Work and Culture in the Middle Ages,* trans. Arthur Goldhammer (Chicago: University of Chicago Press, 1980). First quote: Pope Leo XIII, *Rerum Novarum* (1891), § 17. Second quote: Pope John Paul II, *Laborem Exercens* (1981), § 27.

5. Biblical verses: 2 Thessalonians 3:10; Proverbs 21:25. Benedictine monastic rules quote: Abbot Parry, trans., *The Rule of Saint Benedict* (Leominster, Herefordshire, UK: Gracewing, 1990), 77. Calvin quote: Paul Bernstein, *American Work Values: Their Origin and Development* (Albany: State University of New York Press, 1997), 56. Protestant work ethic: Max Weber, *Protestant Work Ethic and the Spirit of Capitalism* (1904), trans. Talcott Parsons (London: Allen & Unwin, 1976). Islam: Khalil-ur-Rehman, *The Concept of Labour in Islam,* trans. K. Naziri (Karachi: Arif Publications, 1995); Darwish A. Yousef, "The Islamic Work Ethic as a Mediator of the Relationship between Locus of Control, Role Conflict, and Role Ambiguity—A Study in an Islamic Country Setting," *Journal of Managerial Psychology* 15 (2000): 283–98. Buddhist quote: Susan Mann, "Work and Household in Chinese Culture: Historical Perspectives," in Barbara Entwisle and Gail E. Henderson, eds., *Re-Drawing Boundaries: Work, Households, and Gender in China* (Berkeley: University of California Press, 2000): 15–32 at 22.

6. Biblical verses: Genesis 3:17–19; Genesis 2:15. Affirmation quote: Miroslav Volf, *Work in the Spirit: Toward a Theology of Work* (New York: Oxford University Press, 1991), 168. Also and compare: Sherman and Hendricks, *Your Work Matters to God*; Ellul, "Work and Calling"; Jacques Ellul, "From the Bible to a History of Non-Work," trans. David Lovekin, *Cross Currents* 35 (Spring 1985): 43–48. Independence, charity, and serving God: Ovitt, *The Restoration of Perfection*; Herbert Applebaum, *The Concept of Work: Ancient, Medieval, and Modern* (Albany: State University of New York Press, 1992). Islam: Khalil-ur-Rehman, *The Concept of Labour in Islam*; Yousef, "The Islamic Work Ethic." Papal encyclical quote: Pope John Paul II, *Laborem Exercens* (1981), § 9. Ambiguous reality quote: Volf, *Work in the Spirit,* 168.

7. Quotes: Anna Feldman Leibovich, *The Russian Concept of Work: Suffering, Drama, and Tradition in Pre- and Post-Revolutionary Russia* (Westport, CT: Praeger, 1995), 28 and 135.

8. Absence from worship: Sherman and Hendricks, *Your Work Matters to God*; Armand Larive, *After Sunday: A Theology of Work* (New York: Continuum, 2004). Quote: Robert Anthony Bruno, *Justified by Work: Identity and the Meaning of Faith in Chicago's Working-Class Churches* (Columbus: Ohio State University Press, 2008), 14.

9. Proper v. improper work: P. D. Anthony, *The Ideology of Work* (London: Tavistock, 1977). Quote: Claude Mossé, *The Ancient World at Work,* trans. Janet Lloyd (London: Chatto & Windus, 1969), 28. Flourishing: Hannah Arendt, *The Human Condition* (Chicago: University of Chicago Press, 1958); Applebaum, *The Concept of Work*.

10. Aristotle, *The Nicomachean Ethics,* trans. William D. Ross (Oxford: Oxford University Press, 1980). Quote: Anthony, *The Ideology of Work,* 17. Sparta: Applebaum, *The Concept of Work*.

11. Cicero: Applebaum, *The Concept of Work*; Van den Hoven, *Work in Ancient and Medieval Thought*. Castes: Louis Dumont, *Homo Hierarchicus: The Caste System and Its Implications,* trans. Basia Gulati (Chicago: University of Chicago Press, 1980). Untouchables: Rosa Maria Perez, *Kings and Untouchables: A Study of the Caste System in Western India* (New Delhi: Chronicle Books, 2004). Dirty work stigmas: Shirley K. Drew, Melanie Mills, and Bob Gassaway, eds., *Dirty Work: The Social Construction of Taint* (Waco, TX: Baylor University Press, 2007). Human body: Carol Wolkowitz, *Bodies at Work* (London: Sage, 2006). Villain: Richard Donkin, *Blood, Sweat, and Tears: The Evolution of Work* (New York: Texere, 2001).

12. Ancient artisans: Applebaum, *The Concept of Work*; Alison Burford, *Craftsmen in Greek and Roman Society* (Ithaca, NY: Cornell University Press, 1972). Slaves: Orlando Patterson, *Slavery and Social Death: A Comparative Study* (Cambridge, MA: Harvard University Press, 1982). Dirty work: Blake E. Ashforth and Glen E. Kreiner, "'How Can You Do It?' Dirty Work and the Challenge of Constructing a Positive Identity," *Academy of Management Review* 24 (July 1999): 413–34.

13. Indian creation story: Brian K. Smith, *Classifying the Universe: The Ancient Indian Varna System and the Origins of Caste* (New York: Oxford University Press, 1994). European colonialism: J. M. Blaut, *The Colonizer's Model of the World: Geographical Diffusionism and Eurocentric History* (New York: Guilford Press, 1993). Bell curve, compare: Richard J. Herrnstein and Charles Murray, *The Bell Curve: Intelligence and Class Structure in American Life* (New York: Free Press, 1994); Russell Jacoby and Naomi Glauberman, eds., *The Bell Curve Debate: History, Documents, Opinions* (New York: Times Books, 1995).

14. Aristotle: Peter Garnsey, *Ideas of Slavery from Aristotle to Augustine* (Cambridge: Cambridge University Press, 1996). Echoed across time and culture, also social death: Patterson, *Slavery and Social Death*. Quotes: William Harper, "Harper's Memoir on Slavery," in *The Pro-Slavery Argument, as Maintained by the Most Distinguished Writers of the Southern States* (Philadelphia: Lippincott, Grambo, 1853): 1–98 at 14 and 19. Southern beliefs: David Brion Davis, *Inhuman Bondage: The Rise and Fall of Slavery in the New World* (New York: Oxford University Press, 2006). Biblical curse: Genesis 9:25; Stephen R. Haynes, *Noah's Curse: The Biblical Justification of American Slavery* (New York: Oxford University Press, 2002).

15. Poems and sayings: Keith Thomas, ed., *The Oxford Book of Work* (Oxford: Oxford University Press, 1999). Quote: quoted in A. W. Coats, "Changing Attitudes to Labour in the Mid-Eighteenth Century," *Economic History Review* 11 (1958): 35–51 at 46. Work requirements: Ivar Lødemal and Heather Trickey, eds., *An Offer You Can't Refuse: Workfare in International Perspective* (Bristol, UK: Policy Press, 2001).

16. Lack of social mobility: Adriano Tilgher, *Work: What It Has Meant to Men through the Ages,* trans. Dorothy Canfield Fisher (London: George Harrap, 1931). Trespass quote: Paul Ransome, *The Work Paradigm: A Theoretical Investigation of Concepts of Work* (Aldershot, Hampshire, UK: Avebury, 1996), 107. Thomas Aquinas: quoted in Dino Bigongiari, *The Political Ideas of St. Thomas Aquinas* (New York: Hafner Press, 1953), ix and 160. Medieval belief quotes: Applebaum, *The Concept of Work,* 63 and 252.

17. Russell Muirhead, *Just Work* (Cambridge, MA: Harvard University Press, 2004), 2 and 4, emphasis in original.

18. Muirhead, *Just Work*.

2. Work as Freedom

1. First quote: Genesis 3:17–19. Second and third quotes: M.-D. Chenu, *Nature, Man, and Society in the Twelfth Century: Essays on New Theological Perspectives in the Latin West* (1957), trans. Jerome Taylor and Lester K. Little (Toronto: University of Toronto Press, 1997), 44 and 45. Marx quote: Karl Marx, *Capital: A Critique of Political Economy* (1867), trans. Samuel Moore and Edward Aveling (New York: Modern Library, 1936), 201. Impose culture quote: Sandra Wallman, "Introduction," in Sandra Wallman, ed., *Social Anthropology of Work* (London: Academic Press, 1979): 1–24 at 1.

2. First quote: Joel Mokyr, *The Lever of Riches: Technological Creativity and Economic Progress* (New York: Oxford University Press, 1990), viii. Other quotes: Richard Florida, *The Rise of the Creative Class: And How It's Transforming Work, Leisure, Community, and Everyday Life* (New York: Basic Books, 2002), 8 and 10.

3. Long contrasted: David A. Spencer, *The Political Economy of Work* (London: Routledge, 2009). Quote: Hannah Arendt, *The Human Condition* (Chicago: University of Chicago Press, 1958), 144.

4. French sociologists: Catherine Paradeise, "French Sociology of Work and Labor: From Shop Floor to Labor Markets to Networked Careers," *Organization Studies* 24 (May 2003): 633–53.

5. Quote and male dominance: Maria Mies, *Patriarchy and Accumulation on a World Scale: Women in the International Division of Labour* (London: Zed Books, 1986), 56–57, emphases in original. Civilized man: J. M. Blaut, *The Colonizer's Model of the World: Geographical Diffusionism and Eurocentric History* (New York: Guilford Press, 1993); Cole Harris, "How Did Colonialism Dispossess? Comments from an Edge of Empire," *Annals of the Association of American Geographers* 94 (March 2004): 165–82.

6. Qualities of personhood: Tim Ingold, "Hunting and Gathering as Ways of Perceiving the Environment," in Roy Ellen and Katsuyoshi Fukui, eds., *Redefining Nature: Ecology, Culture and Domestication* (Oxford: Berg, 1996): 117–55. Quote: Colleen M. O'Neill, *Working the Navajo Way: Labor and Culture in the Twentieth Century* (Lawrence: University Press of Kansas, 2005), 40. Barbara Alice Mann, *Iroquoian Women: The Gantowisas* (New York: Peter Lang, 2000). Lack of distinct word for work: Louis-Jacques Dorais, *Quaqtaq: Modernity and Identity in an Inuit Community* (Toronto: University of Toronto Press, 1997); Herbert Applebaum, *The Concept of Work: Ancient, Medieval, and Modern* (Albany: State University of New York Press, 1992).

7. Guard against: Anne-Christine Hornborg, *Mi'kmaq Landscapes: From Animism to Sacred Ecology* (Aldershot, Hampshire, UK: Ashgate, 2008). Quote on participation in the natural environment: Erich Fromm, *Escape from Freedom* (1941) (New York: Macmillan, 1994), 260.

8. John Locke, *Two Treatises of Government* (1690) (Cambridge: Cambridge University Press, 1960).

9. Quote: Locke, *Two Treatises of Government,* 305–6, emphases in original. Hallmark: James W. Ely, *The Guardian of Every Other Right: A Constitutional History of Property Rights* (New York: Oxford University Press, 1998).

10. Economic liberalism: C. B. Macpherson, *The Political Theory of Possessive Individualism: Hobbes to Locke* (London: Oxford University Press, 1962); Alan Fox, *Beyond Contract: Work, Power and Trust Relations* (London: Faber and Faber, 1974). Quote:

Adam Smith, *An Inquiry into the Nature and Causes of the Wealth of Nations* (1776) (New York: Bantam Books, 2003), 168.

11. Quote: Edmund S. Morgan, *The Puritan Family: Religion and Domestic Relations in Seventeenth-Century New England* (New York: Harper & Row, 1966), 19. New imagined social order: Robert J. Steinfeld, *The Invention of Free Labor: The Employment Relation in English and American Law and Culture, 1350–1870* (Chapel Hill: University of North Carolina Press, 1991).

12. Legal obligations of servants: Steinfeld, *The Invention of Free Labor;* Simon Deakin and Frank Wilkinson, *The Law of the Labour Market: Industrialization, Employment, and Legal Evolution* (Oxford: Oxford University Press, 2005). Quote: Fox, *Beyond Contract,* 185.

13. Master-servant: Steinfeld, *The Invention of Free Labor;* Deakin and Wilkinson, *The Law of the Labour Market.* Work-book system: Bruno Veneziani, "The Evolution of the Contract of Employment," in Bob Hepple, ed., *The Making of Labour Law in Europe: A Comparative Study of Nine Countries up to 1945* (London: Mansell, 1986): 31–72.

14. Steinfeld, *The Invention of Free Labor.*

15. Quote: Harvey Fowler, *Official Report of the Debates and Proceedings in the State Convention, Assembled May 4th, 1853, to Revise and Amend the Constitution of the Commonwealth of Massachusetts, Volume 1* (Boston: White and Potter, 1853), 550. Invalidating state laws: William E. Forbath, "The Ambiguities of Free Labor: Labor and the Law in the Gilded Age," *Wisconsin Law Review* 1985 (July/August 1985): 767–817. Necessary for optimal allocation: Richard A. Epstein, *Simple Rules for a Complex World* (Cambridge, MA: Harvard University Press, 1995).

16. Still debated: Richard A. Bales, "Explaining the Spread of At-Will Employment as an Inter-Jurisdictional Race-to-the-Bottom of Employment Standards," *Tennessee Law Review* 75 (Spring 2008): 453–71. Quote: Steinfeld, *The Invention of Free Labor,* 157.

17. Henry Sumner Maine, *Ancient Law: Its Connection with the Early History of Society, and Its Relation to Modern Ideas* (New York: Charles Scribner, 1864), 165 and 163, emphasis in original.

18. Incomplete shift: Deakin and Wilkinson, *The Law of the Labour Market.* Extension of master-servant principles: Christopher L. Tomlins, *Law, Labor, and Ideology in the Early American Republic* (Cambridge: Cambridge University Press, 1993).

19. Capitalist countries: Beth Ahlering and Simon Deakin, "Labor Regulation, Corporate Governance, and Legal Origin: A Case of Institutional Complementarity?" *Law and Society Review* 41 (December 2007): 865–908. Britain: Deakin and Wilkinson, *The Law of the Labour Market.* Europe: Veneziani, "The Evolution of the Contract of Employment." Japan: Kazuo Sugeno, *Japanese Employment and Labor Law,* trans. Leo Kantowitz (Durham, NC: Carolina Academic Press, 2002).

20. Unfair dismissal protections: Hoyt N. Wheeler and Jacques Rojot, eds., *Workplace Justice: Employment Obligations in International Perspective* (Columbia: University of South Carolina Press, 1992). Welfare states: Gøsta Esping-Andersen, *The Three Worlds of Welfare Capitalism* (Princeton, NJ: Princeton University Press, 1990). Loyalty duty: Benjamin Aaron, "Employees' Duty of Loyalty: Introduction and Overview," *Comparative Labor Law and Policy Journal* 20 (Winter 1999): 143–53; Reinhold Fahlbeck, "Employee Loyalty in Sweden," *Comparative Labor Law and Policy Journal*

20 (Winter 1999): 297–319; Matthew W. Finkin, "Disloyalty! Does *Jefferson Standard* Stalk *Still?*" *Berkeley Journal of Employment and Labor Law* 28 (2007): 541–68. Criticized by detractors: Veneziani, "The Evolution of the Contract of Employment."

21. Maximize freedom: Richard A. Epstein, "In Defense of the Contract at Will," *University of Chicago Law Review* 51 (Fall 1984): 947–82. Contract law should not apply: Ellen Dannin, *Taking Back the Workers' Law: How to Fight the Assault on Labor Rights* (Ithaca, NY: Cornell University Press, 2006); Alain Supiot, "The Dogmatic Foundations of the Market," *Industrial Law Journal* 29 (September 2000): 321–46; Veneziani, "The Evolution of the Contract of Employment."

22. First quote: Tom Brass, "Some Observations on Unfree Labour, Capitalist Restructuring, and Deproletarianization," in Tom Brass and Marcel van der Linden, eds., *Free and Unfree Labour: The Debate Continues* (Bern: Peter Lang, 1997): 57–75 at 58. Second quote: Frederick Cooper, "Conditions Analogous to Slavery: Imperialism and Free Labor Ideology in Africa," in Frederick Cooper, Thomas C. Holt, and Rebecca J. Holt, *Beyond Slavery: Explorations of Race, Labor, and Citizenship in Postemancipation Societies* (Chapel Hill: University of North Carolina Press, 2000): 107–49 at 108.

23. Various forms: Tom Brass and Marcel van der Linden, eds., *Free and Unfree Labour: The Debate Continues* (Bern: Peter Lang, 1997); Kevin Bales, *Disposable People: New Slavery in the Global Economy*, rev. ed. (Berkeley: University of California Press, 2004). Continuum of possibilities: Robert J. Steinfeld and Stanley L. Engerman, "Labor—Free or Coerced? A Historical Reassessment of Differences and Similarities," in Tom Brass and Marcel van der Linden, eds., *Free and Unfree Labour: The Debate Continues* (Bern: Peter Lang, 1997): 107–26. Wage workers: Brass, "Some Observations on Unfree Labour, Capitalist Restructuring, and Deproletarianization"; Gertrude Ezorsky, *Freedom in the Workplace?* (Ithaca, NY: Cornell University Press, 2007).

24. Satanic mills: Joel Mokyr, "The Rise and Fall of the Factory System: Technology, Firms, and Households since the Industrial Revolution," *Carnegie-Rochester Conference Series on Public Policy* 55 (December 2001): 1–45. Measuring time: E. P. Thompson, "Time, Work-Discipline, and Industrial Capitalism," *Past and Present* 38 (December 1967): 56–97.

25. First quote: Judith N. Shklar, *American Citizenship: The Quest for Inclusion* (Cambridge, MA: Harvard University Press, 1991), 64. Second quote: Kenneth L. Karst, "The Coming Crisis of Work in Constitutional Perspective," *Cornell Law Review* 82 (March 1997): 523–70 at 538.

26. Wage slavery: Josiah Bartlett Lambert, *"If the Workers Took a Notion": The Right to Strike and American Political Development* (Ithaca, NY: Cornell University Press, 2005); Clayton Sinyai, *Schools of Democracy: A Political History of the American Labor Movement* (Ithaca, NY: Cornell University Press, 2006). Quote: John G. Nicolay and John Hay, eds., *The Complete Works of Abraham Lincoln, Volume 5* (New York: Francis D. Tandy Company, 1905), 249–50. Homestead Act: Jack Beatty, *Age of Betrayal: The Triumph of Money in America, 1865–1900* (New York: Knopf, 2007).

27. U.S. craft unions: Sinyai, *Schools of Democracy.* British artisans: John Rule, "The Property of Skill in the Period of Manufacture," in Patrick Joyce, ed., *The Historical Meanings of Work* (Cambridge: Cambridge University Press, 1987): 99–118.

28. Quote: Alice Kessler-Harris, *In Pursuit of Equity: Women, Men, and the Quest for Economic Citizenship in 20th-Century America* (New York: Oxford University Press,

2001), 31. Nonwhite men: Evelyn Nakano Glenn, *Unequal Freedom: How Race and Gender Shaped American Citizenship and Labor* (Cambridge, MA: Harvard University Press, 2002).

29. First quote: Bruce Barry, *Speechless: The Erosion of Free Expression in the American Workplace* (San Francisco: Berrett-Koehler, 2007), 16. Coercive power: Rafael Gely and Leonard Bierman, "Social Isolation and American Workers: Employee Blogging and Legal Reform," *Harvard Journal of Law and Technology* 20 (Spring 2007): 288–331; Lewis Maltby, *Can They Do That? Retaking Our Fundamental Rights in the Workplace* (New York: Portfolio, 2009). Second quote: Lewis Maltby, "Office Politics: Civic Speech Shouldn't Get Employees Fired," *Legal Times* (August 29, 2005). Company e-mail systems: BIPAC, "Prosperity Project and Prosperity Fund Report" (Washington, DC: Business Industry Political Action Committee, 2006).

30. Carole Pateman, *Participation and Democratic Theory* (London: Cambridge University Press, 1970). Freedom to structure work: Stephen M. Bainbridge, "Corporate Decision Making and the Moral Rights of Employees: Participatory Management and Natural Law," *Villanova Law Review* 43 (1998): 741–828.

31. Shame of dependence: Richard Sennett, *Respect in a World of Inequality: The Formation of Character in a World of Inequality* (New York: Norton, 2003). Adulthood transition: Jeffrey Jensen Arnett, "Emerging Adulthood: A Theory of Development from the Late Teens through the Twenties," *American Psychologist* 55 (May 2000): 469–80. Bad marriages: Robert Schoen et al., "Women's Employment, Marital Happiness, and Divorce," *Social Forces* 81 (December 2002): 643–62. Post-divorce independence: Nehami Baum, Giora Rahav, and Dan Sharon, "Changes in the Self-Concepts of Divorced Women," *Journal of Divorce and Remarriage* 43 (2005): 47–67.

32. Acceptance of Locke quote: Tim Ingold, *The Appropriation of Nature: Essays on Human Ecology and Social Relations* (Iowa City: University of Iowa Press, 1987), 227.

33. Early Christian theology and secularization of labor: George Ovitt, *The Restoration of Perfection: Labor and Technology in Medieval Culture* (New Brunswick, NJ: Rutgers University Press, 1987). Quote: Arendt, *The Human Condition*, 101. Unfree labor: Brass and van der Linden, *Free and Unfree Labour*; Bales, *Disposable People*.

3. Work as a Commodity

1. Mesopotamia: Robert Francis Harper, *Assyrian and Babylonian Literature: Selected Translations* (New York: D. Appleton, 1901). Separate sphere: Herbert Applebaum, *The Concept of Work: Ancient, Medieval, and Modern* (Albany: State University of New York Press, 1992). Distinctively conceptualized: Karl Marx, *Capital: A Critique of Political Economy* (1867), trans. Samuel Moore and Edward Aveling (New York: Modern Library, 1936); Richard Biernacki, *The Fabrication of Labor: Germany and Britain, 1640–1914* (Berkeley: University of California Press, 1995).

2. Early British economists: Biernacki, *The Fabrication of Labor.* Quote: Robert J. Steinfeld, *The Invention of Free Labor: The Employment Relation in English and American Law and Culture, 1350–1870* (Chapel Hill: University of North Carolina Press, 1991), 92.

3. Adam Smith, *An Inquiry into the Nature and Causes of the Wealth of Nations* (1776) (New York: Bantam Books, 2003), 19.

4. Marx, *Capital*.

5. First quote: John Locke, *Two Treatises of Government* (1690) (Cambridge: Cambridge University Press, 1960), 315. Second quote: Ronald L. Meek, *Studies in the Labour Theory of Value,* 2nd ed. (London: Lawrence & Wishart, 1973), 20.

6. First quote: Meek, *Studies in the Labour Theory of Value,* 39, emphases in original. Second quote: David Ricardo, *On the Principles of Political Economy and Taxation* (1821) (London: G. Bell, 1919), 5.

7. Socialist writers: Meek, *Studies in the Labour Theory of Value.* Conservative economist example: Nassau William Senior, *An Outline of the Science of Political Economy* (1836) (New York: Farrar & Rinehart, 1939).

8. Marx, *Capital*.

9. Meek, *Studies in the Labour Theory of Value.*

10. Neoclassical economics: Gary S. Becker, *The Economic Approach to Behavior* (Chicago: University of Chicago Press, 1976). Labor becomes a commodity: Bruce E. Kaufman, "The Social Welfare Objectives and Ethical Principles of Industrial Relations," in John W. Budd and James G. Scoville, eds., *The Ethics of Human Resources and Industrial Relations* (Champaign, IL: Labor and Employment Relations Association, 2005): 23–59; Donald Stabile, *Work and Welfare: The Social Costs of Labor in the History of Economic Thought* (Westport, CT: Greenwood Press, 1996). Quote: George J. Borjas, "Earnings Determination: A Survey of the Neoclassical Approach," in Garth L. Mangum and Peter Philips, eds., *Three Worlds of Labor Economics* (Armonk, NY: M. E. Sharpe, 1988): 21–50 at 21.

11. Labor demand: Daniel S. Hamermesh, *Labor Demand* (Princeton, NJ: Princeton University Press, 1993). Globalization: Matthew J. Slaughter, "International Trade and Labor-Demand Elasticities," *Journal of International Economics* 54 (June 2001): 27–56. New information technologies: Frank Levy and Richard J. Murnane, *The New Division of Labor: How Computers Are Creating the Next Job Market* (New York: Russell Sage Foundation, 2004).

12. Quote: John R. Hicks, *The Theory of Wages,* 2nd ed. (London: Macmillan, 1963), 1. Also: Arthur L. Perry, *Elements of Political Economy* (New York: Scribner Armstrong, 1875).

13. Harm the economy: Bruce E. Kaufman, "What Do Unions Do? Insights from Economic Theory," in James T. Bennett and Bruce E. Kaufman, eds., *What Do Unions Do? A Twenty-Year Perspective* (New Brunswick, NJ: Transaction Publishers, 2007): 12–45. Best protection: Perry, *Elements of Political Economy*; Milton Friedman and Rose Friedman, *Free to Choose: A Personal Statement* (New York: Harcourt Brace Jovanovich, 1980).

14. Neoliberal ideology: David Harvey, *A Brief History of Neoliberalism* (Oxford: Oxford University Press, 2005). Prosperity: Dell P. Champlin and Janet T. Knoedler, "Wages in the Public Interest: Insights from Thorstein Veblen and J. M. Clark," *Journal of Economic Issues* 36 (December 2002): 877–91.

15. Biernacki, *The Fabrication of Labor,* 12. Also: Richard Biernacki, "Labor as an Imagined Commodity," *Politics and Society* 29 (June 2001): 173–206.

16. Biernacki, *The Fabrication of Labor.* Biernacki, "Labor as an Imagined Commodity."

17. Marx, *Capital,* 81.

18. First quote: Marx, *Capital,* 95. Second quote: Karl Marx, *A Contribution to the Critique of Political Economy* (1859), trans. S. W. Ryazanskaya (London: Lawrence & Wishart, 1971), 34.

19. Alienation: István Mészáros, *Marx's Theory of Alienation,* 4th ed. (London: Merlin Press, 1975); Bertell Ollman, *Alienation: Marx's Conception of Man in Capitalist Society,* 2nd ed. (Cambridge: Cambridge University Press, 1976); Sean Sayers, "Why Work? Marx and Human Nature," *Science and Society* 69 (October 2005): 606–16; Barry L. Padgett, *Marx and Alienation in Contemporary Society* (New York: Continuum, 2007). First quote: Karl Marx, *Wage-Labour and Capital* (1847), trans. Frederick Engels (New York: International Publishers, 1933), 19. Second quote: Friedrich Schiller, "Letters on the Aesthetic Education of Man" (1801), trans. Elizabeth M. Wilkinson and L. A. Willoughby, in Walter Hinderer and Daniel O. Dahlstrom, eds., *Essays* (New York: Continuum, 1993): 86–178 at 100.

20. Karl Marx, *Economic and Philosophic Manuscripts of 1844* (1844), trans. Martin Milligan (Amherst, NY: Prometheus Books, 1988). Ollman, *Alienation.*

21. Objective feature: Paul Edwards and Judy Wajcman, *The Politics of Working Life* (Oxford: Oxford University Press, 2005). First quote: Marx, *Economic and Philosophic Manuscripts of 1844,* 74. Second quote: Ollman, *Alienation,* 131.

22. Humans to animals: Marx, *Economic and Philosophic Manuscripts of 1844.* Modern curse: Harry Braverman, "The Degradation of Work in the Twentieth Century," *Monthly Review* 34 (May 1982): 1–13. German scholarship: Joan Campbell, *Joy in Work, German Work: The National Debate, 1800–1945* (Princeton, NJ: Princeton University Press, 1989).

23. Karl Polanyi, *The Great Transformation* (New York: Rinehart, 1944), 71 and 72.

24. British enclosure: Marx, *Capital*; E. P. Thompson, *The Making of the English Working Class* (London: Gollancz, 1963); Michael Perelman, *The Invention of Capitalism: Classical Political Economy and the Secret History of Primitive Accumulation* (Durham, NC: Duke University Press, 2000). Quotes: Martha C. Knack and Alice Littlefield, "Native American Labor: Retrieving History, Rethinking Theory," in Alice Littlefield and Martha C. Knack, eds., *Native Americans and Wage Labor: Ethnohistorical Perspectives* (Norman: University of Oklahoma Press, 1996): 3–44 at 15 and 42. Also: John H. Moore, "The Myth of the Lazy Indian: Native American Contributions to the U.S. Economy," *Nature, Society, and Thought* 2 (April 1989): 195–215. Spanish colonialism: Ann Zulawski, *They Eat from Their Labor: Work and Social Change in Colonial Bolivia* (Pittsburgh: University of Pittsburgh Press, 1995). Setswana language: John L. Comaroff and Jean Comaroff, "The Madman and the Migrant: Work and Labor in the Historical Consciousness of a South African People," *American Ethnologist* 14 (May 1987): 191–209.

25. White women: Evelyn Nakano Glenn, *Unequal Freedom: How Race and Gender Shaped American Citizenship and Labor* (Cambridge, MA: Harvard University Press, 2002). Unproductive housewife: Nancy Folbre, "The Unproductive Housewife: Her Evolution in Nineteenth-Century Economic Thought," *Signs* 16 (Spring 1991): 463–84.

26. First quote: Smith, *An Inquiry into the Nature and Causes of the Wealth of Nations,* 422. Second quote: Wally Seccombe, "Domestic Labour and the Working-Class Household," in Bonnie Fox, ed., *Hidden in the Household: Women's Domestic*

Labour under Capitalism (Toronto: Women's Press, 1980): 25–99 at 83. Feminist economics: Marianne A. Ferber and Julie A. Nelson, eds., *Beyond Economic Man: Feminist Theory and Economics* (Chicago: University of Chicago Press, 1993); Drucilla K. Barker and Susan F. Feiner, *Liberating Economics: Feminist Perspectives on Families, Work, and Globalization* (Ann Arbor: University of Michigan Press, 2004). Third quote: Katharine Silbaugh, "Turning Labor into Love: Housework and the Law," *Northwestern University Law Review* 91 (Fall 1996): 1–86 at 4. Patriarchal system: Maria Mies, *Patriarchy and Accumulation on a World Scale: Women in the International Division of Labour* (London: Zed Books, 1986).

27. Euro-American views: Patricia C. Albers, "From Legend to Land to Labor," in Alice Littlefield and Martha C. Knack, eds., *Native Americans and Wage Labor: Ethnohistorical Perspectives* (Norman: University of Oklahoma Press, 1996): 245–73. Quote: Stevan Harrell, "The Changing Meanings of Work in China," in Barbara Entwisle and Gail E. Henderson, eds., *Re-Drawing Boundaries: Work, Households, and Gender in China* (Berkeley: University of California Press, 2000): 67–76 at 74.

28. Value-free economics: Lowell Gallaway and Richard Vedder, "Ideas versus Ideology: The Origins of Modern Labor Economics," *Journal of Labor Research* 24 (Fall 2003): 643–68. Normative principles: Stephen A. Marglin, *The Dismal Science: How Thinking Like an Economist Undermines Community* (Cambridge, MA: Harvard University Press, 2008); Peter D. McClelland, *The American Search for Justice* (Cambridge, MA: Basil Blackwell, 1990). Widely criticized: John W. Budd and James G. Scoville, "Moral Philosophy, Business Ethics, and the Employment Relationship," in John W. Budd and James G. Scoville, eds., *The Ethics of Human Resources and Industrial Relations* (Champaign, IL: Labor and Employment Relations Association, 2005): 1–21; John Wright, *The Ethics of Economic Rationalism* (Sydney: University of New South Wales Press, 2003).

4. Work as Occupational Citizenship

1. John W. Budd, *Employment with a Human Face: Balancing Efficiency, Equity, and Voice* (Ithaca, NY: Cornell University Press, 2004).

2. Industrial citizenship: T. H. Marshall, *Citizenship and Social Class, and Other Essays* (Cambridge: Cambridge University Press, 1950); J. M. Barbalet, *Citizenship: Rights, Struggle and Class Inequality* (Minneapolis: University of Minnesota Press, 1988). Contemporary treatments: Judy Fudge, "After Industrial Citizenship: Market Citizenship or Citizenship at Work?" *Relations Industrielles / Industrial Relations* 60 (Fall 2005): 631–53; Colin Crouch, "The Globalized Economy: An End to the Age of Industrial Citizenship?" in Ton Wilthagen, ed., *Advancing Theory in Labour Law and Industrial Relations in a Global Context* (Amsterdam: North-Holland, 1998): 151–64; Guy Standing, *Work after Globalization: Building Occupational Citizenship* (Cheltenham, Gloucestershire, UK: Edward Elgar, 2009). Similar definition as here: Crouch, "The Globalized Economy."

3. Human rights: Michael A. Santoro, *Profits and Principles: Global Capitalism and Human Rights in China* (Ithaca, NY: Cornell University Press, 2000); James A. Gross, *A Shameful Business: The Case for Human Rights in the American Workplace* (Ithaca, NY: Cornell University Press, 2010); Hoyt N. Wheeler, "Globalization and Business Ethics in Employment Relations," in John W. Budd and James G. Scoville,

eds., *The Ethics of Human Resources and Industrial Relations* (Champaign, IL: Labor and Employment Relations Association, 2005): 115–40. First quote: Michael J. Perry, *The Idea of Human Rights: Four Inquiries* (New York: Oxford University Press, 1998), 13. Also: Paul Gordon Lauren, *The Evolution of International Human Rights: Visions Seen* (Philadelphia: University of Pennsylvania Press, 1998); Jerome J. Shestack, "The Philosophic Foundations of Human Rights," *Human Rights Quarterly* 20 (May 1998): 201–34. Citizenship v. human rights: Guy Mundlak, "Industrial Citizenship, Social Citizenship, Corporate Citizenship: I Just Want My Wages," *Theoretical Inquiries in Law* 8 (July 2007): 719–48. Second quote: Thomas A. Kochan, Harry C. Katz, and Robert B. McKersie, *The Transformation of American Industrial Relations* (New York: Basic Books, 1986), 22–23.

 4. Quote: Lauren, *The Evolution of International Human Rights,* 5. Theological roots: David J. Schnall, *By the Sweat of Your Brow: Reflections on Work and the Workplace in Classic Jewish Thought* (New York: Yeshiva University Press, 2001); Armand Larive, *After Sunday: A Theology of Work* (New York: Continuum, 2004); Dominique Peccoud, ed., *Philosophical and Spiritual Perspectives on Decent Work* (Geneva: International Labour Office, 2004).

 5. First quote: Bruce E. Kaufman, "The Social Welfare Objectives and Ethical Principles of Industrial Relations," in John W. Budd and James G. Scoville, eds., *The Ethics of Human Resources and Industrial Relations* (Champaign, IL: Labor and Employment Relations Association, 2005): 23–59 at 37. Second quote: Immanuel Kant, *Groundwork of the Metaphysics of Morals* (1785), trans. H. J. Patton (London: Hutchinson, 1969), 96. Pope John Paul II, *Laborem Exercens* (1981), § 6. Pope Leo XIII, *Rerum Novarum* (1891), § 31.

 6. Friedrich Engels, *The Condition of the Working Class in England in 1844* (1845), trans. Florence Kelley Wischnewetzky (London: G. Allen & Unwin, 1892). Henry Mayhew, *London Labour and the London Poor: A Cyclopaedia of the Condition and Earnings of Those That Will Work, Those That Cannot Work, and Those That Will Not Work* (London: Griffin, Bohn and Co., 1861). Modern exposés: Barbara Ehrenreich, *Nickel and Dimed: On (Not) Getting By in America* (New York: Henry Holt, 2001); Katharine Mumford and Anne Power, *East Enders: Family and Community in East London* (Bristol, UK: Policy Press, 2003); Dan Zuberi, *Differences That Matter: Social Policy and the Working Poor in the United States and Canada* (Ithaca, NY: Cornell University Press, 2006); Alexandra Harney, *The China Price: The True Cost of Chinese Competitive Advantage* (New York: Penguin, 2008).

 7. Early academic efforts: Bruce E. Kaufman, *The Global Evolution of Industrial Relations: Events, Ideas, and the IIRA* (Geneva: International Labour Office, 2004); Kaufman, "The Social Welfare Objectives and Ethical Principles of Industrial Relations." First quote: John R. Commons, *Myself* (New York: Macmillan, 1934), 143. Second quote: Richard T. Ely, *The Labor Movement in America* (New York: Thomas Y. Crowell, 1886), 3. Founding of industrial relations: Kaufman, *The Global Evolution of Industrial Relations.* Modern approaches: Budd, *Employment with a Human Face;* Dell P. Champlin and Janet T. Knoedler, eds., *The Institutionalist Tradition in Labor Economics* (Armonk, NY: M. E. Sharpe, 2004). Feminist and social economists: Julie A. Nelson, "The Study of Choice or the Study of Provisioning? Gender and the Definition of Economics," in Marianne A. Ferber and Julie A. Nelson, eds., *Beyond Economic Man: Feminist Theory and Economics* (Chicago: Chicago University Press, 1993): 23–36;

Deborah M. Figart and Ellen Mutari, "Work: Its Social Meanings and Role in Provisioning," in John B. Davis and Wilfred Dolfsma, eds., *The Elgar Companion to Social Economics* (Cheltenham, Gloucestershire, UK: Edward Elgar, 2008): 287–301.

8. First quote: J. A. Estey, *The Labor Problem* (New York: McGraw-Hill, 1928), 1. Second quote: Sidney Webb and Beatrice Webb, *Industrial Democracy* (London: Longmans, Green, and Co., 1902), 821. Third quote: John R. Commons, *Industrial Goodwill* (New York: McGraw-Hill, 1919), 33. Endure today: Barbalet, *Citizenship*; Fudge, "After Industrial Citizenship."

9. First quote: Webb and Webb, *Industrial Democracy,* 589. Second quote: Kaufman, *The Global Evolution of Industrial Relations,* 206. Decent work: International Labour Office, *Decent Work* (Geneva, 1999).

10. Human rights advocates: Santoro, *Profits and Principles*; Wheeler, "Globalization and Business Ethics in Employment Relations." Criticizing government: Gross, *A Shameful Business*; Lance Compa, *Unfair Advantage: Workers' Freedom of Association in the United States under International Human Rights Standards* (Ithaca, NY: Cornell University Press, 2004); Roy J. Adams, *Labour Left Out: Canada's Failure to Protect and Promote Collective Bargaining as a Human Right* (Ottawa: Canadian Centre for Policy Alternatives, 2006). Not without problems: Richard P. McIntyre, *Are Worker Rights Human Rights?* (Ann Arbor: University of Michigan Press, 2008).

11. Arthur L. Perry, *Elements of Political Economy* (New York: Scribner Armstrong, 1875), 160.

12. Reject perfect competition: Bruce E. Kaufman, ed., *How Labor Markets Work: Reflections on Theory and Practice by John Dunlop, Clark Kerr, Richard Lester, and Lloyd Reynolds* (Lexington, MA: Lexington Books, 1988); Bruce E. Kaufman, "Labor Markets and Employment Regulation: The View of the 'Old' Institutionalists," in Bruce E. Kaufman, ed., *Government Regulation of the Employment Relationship* (Madison, WI: Industrial Relations Research Association, 1997): 11–55. Quote: Alan Manning, *Monopsony in Motion: Imperfect Competition in Labor Markets* (Princeton, NJ: Princeton University Press, 2003), 4.

13. Range of indeterminacy: Richard A. Lester, "A Range Theory of Wage Differentials," *Industrial and Labor Relations Review* 5 (July 1952): 483–500. Bargained exchange: John W. Budd, Rafael Gomez, and Noah M. Meltz, "Why a Balance Is Best: The Pluralist Industrial Relations Paradigm of Balancing Competing Interests," in Bruce E. Kaufman, ed., *Theoretical Perspectives on Work and the Employment Relationship* (Champaign, IL: Industrial Relations Research Association, 2004): 195–227. Quote: Adam Smith, *An Inquiry into the Nature and Causes of the Wealth of Nations* (1776) (New York: Bantam Books, 2003), 94.

14. Greater bargaining power: Kaufman, "Labor Markets and Employment Regulation." Pluralist industrial relations thought: Bruce E. Kaufman, *The Origins and Evolution of the Field of Industrial Relations in the United States* (Ithaca, NY: Cornell University Press, 1993); Budd, Gomez, and Meltz, "Why a Balance is Best"; Stephen F. Befort and John W. Budd, *Invisible Hands, Invisible Objectives: Bringing Workplace Law and Public Policy into Focus* (Stanford, CA: Stanford University Press, 2009).

15. Labor market segmentation: Michael J. Piore, "Notes for a Theory of Labor Market Stratification," in Richard C. Edwards, Michael Reich, and David M. Gordon, eds., *Labor Market Segmentation* (Lexington, MA: D.C. Heath, 1975): 125–50; Jerry Gray and Richard Chapman, "The Significance of Segmentation for Institu-

tionalist Theory and Public Policy," in Dell P. Champlin and Janet T. Knoedler, eds., *The Institutionalist Tradition in Labor Economics* (Armonk, NY: M. E. Sharpe, 2004): 117–30; Clark Kerr, "The Balkanization of Labor Markets," in E. Wight Bakke et al., *Labor Mobility and Economic Opportunity* (Cambridge, MA: Technology Press of MIT, 1954): 92–110. Internal labor markets: Peter B. Doeringer and Michael J. Piore, *Internal Labor Markets and Manpower Analysis* (Lexington, MA: D.C. Heath, 1971); Paul Osterman and M. Diane Burton, "Ports and Ladders: The Nature and Relevance of Internal Labor Markets in a Changing World," in Stephen Ackroyd et al., eds., *The Oxford Handbook of Work and Organization* (Oxford: Oxford University Press, 2005): 425–45. Overeducation: Séamus McGuinness, "Overeducation in the Labour Market," *Journal of Economic Surveys* 20 (July 2006): 387–418. Cycle of poverty: Ehrenreich, *Nickel and Dimed;* Beth Shulman, *The Betrayal of Work: How Low-Wage Jobs Fail 30 Million Americans and Their Families* (New York: New Press, 2003). Contingent employees: Peter Cappelli and David Neumark, "External Churning and Internal Flexibility: Evidence on the Functional Flexibility and Core-Periphery Hypotheses," *Industrial Relations* 43 (January 2004): 148–82. Developing economies: Gary S. Fields, "A Guide to Multisector Labor Market Models," Social Protection Discussion Paper Series, no. 505 (Washington, DC: World Bank, 2005).

16. Paul Ryan, "Segmentation, Duality, and the Internal Labour Market," in Frank Wilkinson, ed., *The Dynamics of Labour Market Segmentation* (London: Academic Press, 1981): 3–20.

17. Innate needs: Marshall Sashkin, "Participative Management Is an Ethical Imperative," *Organizational Dynamics* 12 (Spring 1984): 5–22; Edward L. Deci and Richard M. Ryan, *Intrinsic Motivation and Self-Determination in Human Behavior* (New York: Plenum Press, 1985). Citizens in democracies: Carole Pateman, *Participation and Democratic Theory* (London: Cambridge University Press, 1970). Quote: T. B. Bottomore, *Elites and Society* (London: C. A. Watts, 1964), 115. Also: Paul Brest, "Further beyond the Republican Revival: Toward Radical Republicanism," *Yale Law Journal* 97 (July 1988): 1623–31. Needs manifest as employee voice: Budd, *Employment with a Human Face.* Numerous surveys: Richard B. Freeman and Joel Rogers, *What Workers Want* (Ithaca, NY: Cornell University Press, 2006); Richard B. Freeman, Peter Boxall, and Peter Haynes, eds., *What Workers Say: Employee Voice in the Anglo-American World* (Ithaca, NY: Cornell University Press, 2007). Inclusive perspective: Tony Dundon et al., "The Meanings and Purpose of Employee Voice," *International Journal of Human Resource Management* 15 (September 2004): 1149–70; Befort and Budd, *Invisible Hands, Invisible Objectives.*

18. Albert O. Hirschman, *Exit, Voice, and Loyalty: Responses to Decline in Firms, Organizations, and States* (Cambridge, MA: Harvard University Press, 1970). Quote: Richard J. Hackman and Greg. R. Oldham, *Work Redesign* (Reading, MA: Addison-Wesley, 1980), 79. Not solely determined: Befort and Budd, *Invisible Hands, Invisible Objectives.*

19. Rules of the workplace: John T. Dunlop, *Industrial Relations Systems* (New York: Henry Holt, 1958); H. A. Clegg, *The System of Industrial Relations in Great Britain* (Oxford: Basil Blackwell, 1970). Industrial governments: John R. Commons, *Industrial Government* (New York: Macmillan, 1921). Industrial democracy: Milton Derber, *The American Idea of Industrial Democracy, 1865–1965* (Urbana: University of Illinois Press, 1970). Pluralist analogue: H. A. Clegg, "Pluralism in Industrial Relations," *British Journal of Industrial Relations* 13 (November 1975): 309–16.

20. Webb and Webb, *Industrial Democracy.* Unions for legitimacy: Patricia A. Greenfield and Robert J. Pleasure, "Representatives of Their Own Choosing: Finding Workers' Voice in the Legitimacy and Power of Their Unions," in Bruce E. Kaufman and Morris M. Kleiner, eds., *Employee Representation: Alternatives and Future Directions* (Madison, WI: Industrial Relations Research Association, 1993): 169–96. Long history: Clayton Sinyai, *Schools of Democracy: A Political History of the American Labor Movement* (Ithaca, NY: Cornell University Press, 2006).

21. Notable examples: Bruce E. Kaufman, "Accomplishments and Shortcomings of Nonunion Employee Representation in the Pre-Wagner Act Years: A Reassessment," in Bruce E. Kaufman and Daphne Gottlieb Taras, eds., *Nonunion Employee Representation: History, Contemporary Practice, and Policy* (Armonk, NY: M. E. Sharpe, 2000): 21–60. Contentious issues: Bruce E. Kaufman and Daphne Gottlieb Taras, eds., *Nonunion Employee Representation: History, Contemporary Practice, and Policy* (Armonk, NY: M. E. Sharpe, 2000); Paul J. Gollan, *Employee Representation in Non-Union Firms* (London: Sage, 2006); Andy Charlwood and Mike Terry, "21st-Century Models of Employee Representation: Structures, Processes and Outcomes," *Industrial Relations Journal* 38 (July 2007): 320–37; Freeman, Boxall, and Haynes, *What Workers Say.*

22. Codetermination: Jean Jenkins and Paul Blyton, "Works Councils," in Paul Blyton et al., eds., *Sage Handbook of Industrial Relations* (London: Sage, 2008): 346–57; John W. Budd and Stefan Zagelmeyer, "Public Policy and Employee Participation," in Adrian Wilkinson et al., eds., *The Oxford Handbook of Participation in Organizations* (Oxford: Oxford University Press, 2010): 476–503. Pluralist academics: Paul Weiler, *Governing the Workplace: The Future of Labor and Employment Law* (Cambridge, MA: Harvard University Press, 1990); Paul J. Gollan, Ray Markey, and Iain Ross, eds., *Works Councils in Australia: Future Prospects and Possibilities* (Sydney: Federation Press, 2002); Befort and Budd, *Invisible Hands, Invisible Objectives.*

23. Jenkins and Blyton, "Works Councils."

24. Multiple frames of reference: John W. Budd and Devasheesh Bhave, "Values, Ideologies, and Frames of Reference in Industrial Relations," in Paul Blyton et al., *Sage Handbook of Industrial Relations* (London: Sage, 2008): 92–112; John W. Budd and Devasheesh Bhave, "The Employment Relationship," in Adrian Wilkinson et al., eds., *Sage Handbook of Human Resource Management* (London: Sage, 2010): 51–70. Pluralist perspective: Budd, Gomez, and Meltz, "Why a Balance Is Best." Inherent conflicts: Kochan, Katz, and McKersie, *The Transformation of American Industrial Relations.*

25. Conflicts should be balanced: Budd, Gomez, and Meltz, "Why a Balance Is Best"; Kochan, Katz, and McKersie, *The Transformation of American Industrial Relations.* Quote: Noah M. Meltz, "Industrial Relations: Balancing Efficiency and Equity," in Jack Barbash and Kate Barbash, eds., *Theories and Concepts in Comparative Industrial Relations* (Columbia: University of South Carolina Press, 1989): 109–13 at 111. Protection of all stakeholders: Webb and Webb, *Industrial Democracy;* Paul Osterman et al., *Working in America: A Blueprint for the New Labor Market* (Cambridge, MA: MIT Press, 2001). Balancing workers' rights and property rights: Budd, *Employment with a Human Face.*

26. Legitimacy of multiple stakeholders: Clegg, "Pluralism in Industrial Relations." Legitimate inequalities: Marshall, *Citizenship and Social Class, and Other Essays*; Barbalet, *Citizenship*; Mundlak, "Industrial Citizenship, Social Citizenship, Corporate Citizenship."

27. Pluralist thought: Budd, *Employment with a Human Face*; Peter Ackers, "Reframing Employment Relations: The Case for Neo-Pluralism," *Industrial Relations Journal* 33 (March 2002): 2–19. Unions as central: Webb and Webb, *Industrial Democracy*; Commons, *Industrial Goodwill*; Weiler, *Governing the Workplace*; Budd, Gomez, and Meltz, "Why a Balance Is Best." Quote: United States Industrial Commission, *Report of the Industrial Commission on the Relations and Conditions of Capital and Labor Employed in Manufactures and General Business, Volume 7* (Washington, DC: Government Printing Office, 1901), 478.

28. Institutionalizing conflict: Kochan, Katz, and McKersie, *The Transformation of American Industrial Relations.* Promoting a balance: Budd, *Employment with a Human Face.* Provide intellectual foundations: Budd and Zagelmeyer, "Public Policy and Employee Participation."

29. Befort and Budd, *Invisible Hands, Invisible Objectives.*

30. Views that are quite different: Budd and Bhave, "The Employment Relationship." Monopoly unions: Richard A. Epstein, "A Common Law for Labor Relations: A Critique of the New Deal Labor Legislation," *Yale Law Journal* 92 (July 1983): 1357–408; Morgan Reynolds, "A New Paradigm: Deregulating Labor Relations," *Journal of Labor Research* 17 (Winter 1996): 121–28.

31. Legitimizing inequality: Alan Fox, *Beyond Contract: Work, Power and Trust Relations* (London: Faber and Faber, 1974). Social movement unionism: Ray M. Tillman and Michael S. Cummings, eds., *The Transformation of U.S. Unions: Voices, Visions, and Strategies from the Grassroots* (Boulder, CO: Lynne Rienner Publishers, 1999); Dan Clawson, *The Next Upsurge: Labor and the New Social Movements* (Ithaca, NY: Cornell University Press, 2003); Rick Fantasia and Kim Voss, *Hard Work: Remaking the American Labor Movement* (Berkeley: University of California Press, 2004). Collective mobilization: John Kelly, *Rethinking Industrial Relations: Mobilization, Collectivism and Long Waves* (London: Routledge, 1998).

32. Variety of national models: Greg J. Bamber, Russell D. Lansbury, and Nick Wailes, eds., *International and Comparative Employment Relations: Globalisation and the Developed Market Economies* (London: Sage, 2010). Northern Europe: Bernhard Ebbinghaus and Jelle Visser, *Trade Unions in Western Europe since 1945* (London: Macmillan, 2000). Market, class, and civil society: Richard Hyman, *Understanding European Trade Unionism: Between Market, Class and Society* (London: Sage, 2001). Varieties of capitalism: Peter A. Hall and David Soskice, *Varieties of Capitalism: The Institutional Foundations of Comparative Advantage* (Oxford: Oxford University Press, 2001). Affecting industrial relations: John Godard, "The New Institutionalism, Capitalist Diversity, and Industrial Relations," in Bruce E. Kaufman, ed., *Theoretical Perspectives on Work and the Employment Relationship* (Champaign, IL: Industrial Relations Research Association, 2004): 229–64; Kerstin Hamann and John Kelly, "Varieties of Capitalism and Industrial Relations," in Paul Blyton et al., eds., *Sage Handbook of Industrial Relations* (London: Sage, 2008): 129–48.

33. Moral foundations: Peccoud, *Philosophical and Spiritual Perspectives on Decent Work.* Quote: Russell Muirhead, *Just Work* (Cambridge, MA: Harvard University Press, 2004), 94. Well-being: David Guest, "Worker Well-Being," in Paul Blyton et al., eds., *Sage Handbook of Industrial Relations* (London: Sage, 2008): 529–47.

34. Job insecurity and intensification: Francis Green, *Demanding Work: The Paradox of Job Quality in the Affluent Economy* (Princeton, NJ: Princeton University Press,

2006); Guest, "Worker Well-Being." Two hundred more hours: Lawrence Mishel, Jared Bernstein, and Sylvia Allegretto, *The State of Working America 2006/2007* (Ithaca, NY: Cornell University Press, 2007). Hollowing out: Maarten Goos and Alan Manning, "Lousy and Lovely Jobs: The Rising Polarization of Work in Britain," *Review of Economics and Statistics* 89 (February 2007): 118–33. Gloves-off economy: Annette Bernhardt et al., eds., *The Gloves-Off Economy: Workplace Standards at the Bottom of America's Labor Market* (Champaign, IL: Industrial Relations Research Association, 2008). Massive deficit: International Labour Office, *Global Employment Trends: January 2010* (Geneva, 2010).

35. Industrial relations relevance: Peter Ackers and Adrian Wilkinson, "Industrial Relations and the Social Sciences," in Paul Blyton et al., eds., *Sage Handbook of Industrial Relations* (London: Sage, 2008): 53–68; Charles J. Whalen, ed., *New Directions in the Study of Work and Employment: Revitalizing Industrial Relations as an Academic Enterprise* (Northampton, MA: Edward Elgar Publishing, 2008). Denied full citizenship: Alice Kessler-Harris, *In Pursuit of Equity: Women, Men, and the Quest for Economic Citizenship in 20th-Century America* (New York: Oxford University Press, 2001). Broader realm: Standing, *Work after Globalization.*

36. Standing, *Work after Globalization.*

5. Work as Disutility

1. Lyrics by Allen Reynolds (1965).

2. Two distinct ways: David I. Green, "Pain-Cost and Opportunity-Cost," *Quarterly Journal of Economics* 8 (January 1894): 218–29; David A. Spencer, *The Political Economy of Work* (London: Routledge, 2009). Quote: W. Stanley Jevons, *The Theory of Political Economy* (London: Macmillan, 1871), 164.

3. Jevons, *The Theory of Political Economy,* 47.

4. Jevons, *The Theory of Political Economy,* 173.

5. Reduction in leisure: Spencer, *The Political Economy of Work.* Labor supply decision: Richard Blundell and Thomas MaCurdy, "Labor Supply: A Review of Alternative Approaches," in Orley Ashenfelter and David Card, eds., *Handbook of Labor Economics, Vol. 3A* (Amsterdam: Elsevier, 1999): 1559–695.

6. Incentives to avoid work: Emmanuel Saez, "Optimal Income Transfer Programs: Intensive versus Extensive Labor Supply Responses," *Quarterly Journal of Economics* 117 (August 2002): 1039–73. Partial income replacement: Peter Fredriksson and Bertil Holmlund, "Improving Incentives in Unemployment Insurance: A Review of Recent Research," *Journal of Economic Surveys* 20 (July 2006): 357–86. Work requirements: Ivar Lødemal and Heather Trickey, eds., *An Offer You Can't Refuse: Workfare in International Perspective* (Bristol, UK: Policy Press, 2001).

7. Spencer, *The Political Economy of Work.*

8. Maximize lifetime earnings: George J. Borjas, "Earnings Determination: A Survey of the Neoclassical Approach," in Garth L. Mangum and Peter Philips, eds., *Three Worlds of Labor Economics* (Armonk, NY: M. E. Sharpe, 1988): 21–50. Huge literature: David Card, "The Causal Effect of Education on Earnings," in Orley Ashenfelter and David Card, eds., *Handbook of Labor Economics, Vol. 3A* (Amsterdam: Elsevier, 1999): 1801–63. Claudia Goldin and Lawrence F. Katz, *The Race between Education and Technology* (Cambridge, MA: Harvard University Press, 2008).

9. Simple competitive model: Gary S. Becker, *Human Capital: A Theoretical and Empirical Analysis, with Special Reference to Education* (New York: Columbia University Press, 1964). More likely to provide training: Daron Acemoglu and Jörn-Steffen Pischke, "The Structure of Wages and Investment in General Training," *Journal of Political Economy* 107 (June 1999): 539–72; Colleen F. Manchester, "Perk or Productivity Tool? Provision of Tuition Reimbursement by Employers," unpublished paper, University of Minnesota (2008). Empirical support: Alison L. Booth and Mark L. Bryan, "Testing Some Predictions of Human Capital Theory: New Training Evidence from Britain," *Review of Economics and Statistics* 87 (May 2005): 391–94; Edwin Leuven, "Returns to Training," in Joop Hartog and Henriëtte Maassen van den Brink, eds., *Human Capital: Advances in Theory and Evidence* (Cambridge: Cambridge University Press, 2007): 38–51.

10. Equalizing differences: Sherwin Rosen, "The Theory of Equalizing Differences," in Orley C. Ashenfelter and Richard Layard, eds., *Handbook of Labor Economics, Vol. 1* (Amsterdam: North-Holland, 1986): 641–92. In the extreme: Alan B. Krueger and David Schkade, "Sorting in the Labor Market: Do Gregarious Workers Flock to Interactive Jobs?" *Journal of Human Resources* 43 (Fall 2008): 859–83. Costly search: Kevin Lang and Sumon Majumdar (2004) "The Pricing of Job Characteristics When Markets Do Not Clear: Theory and Policy Implications," *International Economic Review* 45 (November 2004): 1111–28. Empirical research: W. Kip Viscusi, "The Value of Life: Estimates with Risks by Occupation and Industry," *Economic Inquiry* 42 (January 2004): 29–48; Robert Sandy and Robert F. Elliott, "Long-Term Illness and Wages," *Journal of Human Resources* 40 (Summer 2005): 744–68.

11. Karl Marx, *Capital: A Critique of Political Economy* (1867), trans. Samuel Moore and Edward Aveling (New York: Modern Library, 1936).

12. Paul Milgrom and John Roberts, *Economics, Organization, and Management* (Englewood Cliffs, NJ: Prentice-Hall, 1992).

13. First quote: Edward P. Lazear, *Personnel Economics* (Cambridge, MA: MIT Press, 1995), 14. Dislikes effort quote: Pietro Garibaldi, *Personnel Economics in Imperfect Labour Markets* (Oxford: Oxford University Press, 2006), 84. On-the-job leisure: Spencer, *The Political Economy of Work.*

14. Milgrom and Roberts, *Economics, Organization, and Management.* Lazear, *Personnel Economics.* Garibaldi, *Personnel Economics in Imperfect Labour Markets.*

15. Sell worker a franchise: Lazear, *Personnel Economics.* Commission system: Garibaldi, *Personnel Economics in Imperfect Labour Markets.* Quote: Avner Ben-Ner, J. Michael Montias, and Egon Neuberger, "Basic Issues in Organizations: A Comparative Perspective," *Journal of Comparative Economics* 17 (June 1993): 207–42 at 214.

16. Malnourished workers: Christopher Bliss and Nicholas Stern, "Productivity, Wages and Nutrition: Part 2: Some Observations," *Journal of Development Economics* 5 (December 1978): 363–98. Attract high-quality workers: Andrew Weiss, "Job Queues and Layoffs in Labor Markets with Flexible Wages," *Journal of Political Economy* 88 (June 1980): 526–38. Gift exchange: George A. Akerlof, "Labor Contracts as Partial Gift Exchange," *Quarterly Journal of Economics* 97 (November 1982): 543–69. Threat of financial penalty: Carl Shapiro and Joseph E. Stiglitz, "Equilibrium Unemployment as a Worker Discipline Device," *American Economic Review* 74 (June 1984): 433–44.

17. Elicits additional effort: Edward P. Lazear and Sherwin Rosen, "Rank-Order Tournaments as Optimum Labor Contracts," *Journal of Political Economy* 89 (October 1981): 841–64; Lazear, *Personnel Economics.* Applied to numerous situations: Edward P. Lazear and Paul Oyer, "Personnel Economics," in Robert Gibbons and D. John Roberts, eds., *Handbook of Organizational Economics* (Princeton, NJ: Princeton University Press, forthcoming).

18. Douglas W. Allen, "The British Navy Rules: Monitoring and Incompatible Incentives in the Age of Fighting Sail," *Explorations in Economic History* 39 (2002): 204–31.

19. Better than spot market: James M. Malcomson, "Individual Employment Contracts," in Orley Ashenfelter and David Card, eds., *Handbook of Labor Economics, Vol. 3B* (Amsterdam: Elsevier, 1999): 2291–372. Sufficiently competitive: Lazear, *Personnel Economics;* Garibaldi, *Personnel Economics in Imperfect Labour Markets.*

20. Spencer, *The Political Economy of Work.* Marginal disutility of labor: Alfred Marshall, *Principles of Economics,* 3rd ed. (London: Macmillan, 1895); Lazear and Oyer, "Personnel Economics."

21. Creating a mind-set: Damian Grimshaw and Jill Rubery, "Economics and HRM," in Peter Boxall, John Purcell, and Patrick Wrights, eds., *The Oxford Handbook of Human Resource Management* (Oxford: Oxford University Press, 2007): 68–87. Quote: Frederick Winslow Taylor, *The Principles of Scientific Management* (New York: Harper and Brothers, 1911), 19.

22. Gary S. Becker, *A Treatise on the Family* (Cambridge, MA: Harvard University Press, 1991). Pierre-André Chiappori, "Introducing Household Production in Collective Models of Labor Supply," *Journal of Political Economy* 105 (February 1997): 191–209.

23. Inderjit Singh, Lyn Squire, and John Strauss, eds., *Agricultural Household Models: Extensions, Applications, and Policy* (Baltimore: Johns Hopkins University Press, 1986).

24. Nirvikar Singh, "Theories of Sharecropping," in Pranab Bardhan, ed., *The Economic Theory of Agrarian Institutions* (Oxford: Clarendon Press, 1989): 33–72.

25. New institutional economics: Gregory K. Dow, "The New Institutional Economics and Employment Regulation," in Bruce E. Kaufman, ed., *Government Regulation of the Employment Relationship* (Madison, WI: Industrial Relations Research Association, 1997): 57–90. Smoothing consumption: Paul Beaudry and John DiNardo, "The Effect of Implicit Contracts on the Movement of Wages over the Business Cycle: Evidence from Micro Data," *Journal of Political Economy* 99 (August 1991): 665–88. Diverge from the competitive paradigm: Alan Manning, *Monopsony in Motion: Imperfect Competition in Labor Markets* (Princeton, NJ: Princeton University Press, 2003).

26. On the margin: Lazear and Oyer, "Personnel Economics." Benefits of autonomy: Sharon K. Parker and Toby D. Wall, "Work Design: Learning from the Past and Mapping a New Terrain," in Neil Anderson et al., eds., *Handbook of Industrial, Work, and Organizational Psychology, Volume 1* (London: Sage, 2001): 90–109. Nuanced approach: Francis Green, "Leeway for the Loyal: A Model of Employee Discretion," *British Journal of Industrial Relations* 46 (March 2008): 1–32.

27. Quote, also popularizing the idea: Spencer, *The Political Economy of Work,* 3. Disguised by a perception: John Kenneth Galbraith, *The Affluent Society* (Boston:

Houghton Mifflin, 1958); Alan Fox, *Beyond Contract: Work, Power and Trust Relations* (London: Faber and Faber, 1974).

28. Marxist economics: Samuel Bowles and Herbert Gintis, "Contested Exchange: New Microfoundations for the Political Economy of Capitalism," *Politics and Society* 18 (June 1990): 165–222. Feminist economists: Marianne A. Ferber and Julie A. Nelson, eds., *Beyond Economic Man: Feminist Theory and Economics* (Chicago: University of Chicago Press, 1993). Behavioral economists and others: Avner Ben-Ner and Louis Putterman, "Values and Institutions in Economic Analysis," in Avner Ben-Ner and Louis Putterman, eds., *Economics, Values, and Organization* (Cambridge: Cambridge University Press, 1998): 3–69; Dell P. Champlin and Janet T. Knoedler, eds., *The Institutionalist Tradition in Labor Economics* (Armonk, NY: M. E. Sharpe, 2004); Daniel Kahneman, "A Psychological Perspective on Economics," *American Economic Review* 93 (May 2003): 162–68; A. Allan Schmid, *Conflict and Cooperation: Institutional and Behavioral Economics* (Malden, MA: Blackwell, 2004). Sociologists: Mark Granovetter, "Economic Action and Social Structure: The Problem of Embeddedness," *American Journal of Sociology* 91 (November 1985): 481–510; James N. Baron, "The Employment Relation as a Social Relation," *Journal of the Japanese and International Economies* 2 (December 1988): 492–525. Theologians: Thomas Carlyle, *Past and Present* (1843) (Berkeley: University of California Press, 2005); Albino Barrera, *Modern Catholic Social Documents and Political Economy* (Washington, DC: Georgetown University Press, 2001).

6. Work as Personal Fulfillment

1. First quote: Chris Riemenschneider, "Kiss' Spaceman Is Now Grounded in Solo Life," *StarTribune* (Minneapolis, May 2, 2008), F5. Second quote: John Steinbeck, *In Dubious Battle* (1936) (New York: Penguin Books, 2006), 225. Third quote: Robert Anthony Bruno, *Justified by Work: Identity and the Meaning of Faith in Chicago's Working-Class Churches* (Columbus: Ohio State University Press, 2008), 169. Physical activity: L. Miles, "Physical Activity and Health," *Nutrition Bulletin* 32 (December 2007): 314–63.

2. Abraham H. Maslow, "A Theory of Human Motivation," *Psychological Review* 50 (July 1943): 370–96. Nick Turner, Julian Barling, and Anthea Zacharatos, "Positive Psychology at Work," in C. R. Snyder and Shane J. Lopez, eds., *Handbook of Positive Psychology* (New York: Oxford University Press, 2002): 715–30.

3. Michael J. Burke and Sloane M. Signal, "Workplace Safety: A Multilevel, Interdisciplinary Perspective," in Hui Liao, Joseph J. Martocchio, and Aparna Joshi, eds., *Research in Personnel and Human Resources Management, Volume 29* (Bingley, West Yorkshire, UK: Emerald, 2010): 1–47.

4. First quote: Second Vatican Council, *Gaudium et Spes* (1965), § 35. Second quote: Joan Campbell, *Joy in Work, German Work: The National Debate, 1800–1945* (Princeton, NJ: Princeton University Press, 1989), 8. Third quote: Matthew Fox, *The Reinvention of Work: A New Vision of Livelihood for Our Time* (New York: HarperCollins, 1994), 102. Fourth quote: Armand Larive, *After Sunday: A Theology of Work* (New York: Continuum, 2004), 112. Fifth quote: Juan Mascaró and Simon Brodbeck, *The Bhagavad Gita* (New York: Penguin Classics, 2003), 83. Sixth quote: William C. Placher, ed., *Callings: Twenty Centuries of Christian Wisdom on Vocation* (Grand Rapids, MI: Eerdmans, 2005), 10.

5. First quote, also *Arbietsfreude:* Campbell, *Joy in Work, German Work,* 12. Utopian writers: David Meakin, *Man and Work: Literature and Culture in Industrial Society* (London: Methuen, 1976). Henri de Man, *Joy in Work* (1927), trans. Eden Paul and Cedar Paul (New York: Henry Holt, 1929).

6. First quote: Richard Sennett, *The Craftsman* (New Haven, CT: Yale University Press, 2008), 20. Second quote: Edwin A. Locke, "The Nature and Causes of Job Satisfaction," in Marvin D. Dunnette, ed., *Handbook of Industrial and Organizational Psychology* (Chicago: Rand-McNally, 1976): 1297–349 at 1300. Job characteristics model: Richard J. Hackman and Greg. R. Oldham, *Work Redesign* (Reading, MA: Addison-Wesley, 1980). Generally found: Timothy A. Judge et al., "Job Satisfaction: A Cross-Cultural Review," in Neil Anderson et al., eds., *Handbook of Industrial, Work, and Organizational Psychology, Volume 2* (London: Sage, 2001): 25–52.

7. Can also bring joy: Stephanie L. Brown et al., "Providing Social Support May Be More Beneficial Than Receiving It: Results from a Prospective Study of Mortality," *Psychological Science* 14 (July 2003): 320–27; Nel Noddings, *Caring: A Feminine Approach to Ethics and Moral Education,* 2nd ed. (Berkeley: University of California Press, 2003). Volunteering: Stephan Meier and Alois Stutzer, "Is Volunteering Rewarding in Itself?" *Economica* 75 (February 2008): 39–59. Religious perspectives: Bruno, *Justified by Work.*

8. Cognitive ability: Malcolm James Ree, Thomas R. Carretta, and James R. Steindl, "Cognitive Ability," in Neil Anderson et al., eds., *Handbook of Industrial, Work, and Organizational Psychology, Volume 1* (London: Sage, 2001): 219–32. Predictor of job performance: Frank L. Schmidt and John E. Hunter, "The Validity and Utility of Selection Methods in Personnel Psychology: Practical and Theoretical Implications of 85 Years of Research Findings," *Psychological Bulletin* 124 (September 1998): 262–74. Other dimensions might predict: Leaetta M. Hough and Deniz S. Ones, "The Structure, Measurement, Validity, and Use of Personality Variables in Industrial, Work, and Organizational Psychology," in Neil Anderson et al., eds., *Handbook of Industrial, Work, and Organizational Psychology, Volume 1* (London: Sage, 2001): 233–67. Overall usefulness debated: Deniz S. Ones et al., "In Support of Personality Assessment in Organizational Settings," *Personnel Psychology* 60 (Winter 2007): 995–1027. Core self-evaluations: Joyce E. Bono and Timothy A. Judge, "Core Self-Evaluations: A Review of the Trait and Its Role in Job Satisfaction and Job Performance," *European Journal of Personality* 17 (March 2003): S5–S18. Personal integrity: Christopher M. Berry, Paul R. Sackett, and Shelly Wiemann, "A Review of Recent Developments in Integrity Test Research," *Personnel Psychology* 60 (Summer 2007): 271–301.

9. Adverse consequences: Christopher M. Berry, Melissa L. Gruys, and Paul R. Sackett, "Educational Attainment as a Proxy for Cognitive Ability in Selection: Effects on Levels of Cognitive Ability and Adverse Impact," *Journal of Applied Psychology* 91 (May 2006): 696–705. Weeding out union supporters: John Logan, "The Union Avoidance Industry in the United States," *British Journal of Industrial Relations* 44 (December 2006): 651–75.

10. ASA model: Benjamin Schneider, Harold W. Goldstein, and Brent D. Smith, "The ASA Framework: An Update," *Personnel Psychology* 48 (Winter 1995): 747–73. Person-organization fit: Amy L. Kristof, "Person-Organization Fit: An Integrative Review of Its Conceptualizations, Measurement, and Implications," *Personnel Psychology* 49 (Spring 1996): 1–49; Jeffrey R. Edwards et al., "The Phenomenology of

Fit: Linking the Person and Environment to the Subjective Experience of Person–Environment Fit," *Journal of Applied Psychology* 91 (July 2006): 802–27.

11. Most researched attitude, also difficult to measure: Judge et al., "Job Satisfaction." Organizational commitment: John P. Meyer and Natalie J. Allen, *Commitment in the Workplace: Theory, Research, and Application* (Thousand Oaks, CA: Sage, 1997). Envy: Michelle K. Duffy, Jason D. Shaw, and John M. Schaubroeck, "Envy in Organizational Life," in Richard Smith, ed., *Envy: Theory and Research* (New York: Oxford University Press, 2008): 167–89. Mood: Andrew Miner, Theresa M. Glomb, and Charles Hulin, "Experience Sampling Mood and Its Correlates at Work," *Journal of Occupational and Organizational Psychology* 78 (June 2005): 171–93.

12. Distributive v. procedural justice, also large empirical literature: Robert Folger and Russell Cropanzano, *Organizational Justice and Human Resource Management* (Thousand Oaks, CA: Sage, 1998); Jason A. Colquitt et al., "Justice at the Millennium: A Meta-Analytic Review of 25 Years of Organizational Justice Research," *Journal of Applied Psychology* 86 (June 2001): 425–45; Stephen W. Gilliland and David Chan, "Justice in Organizations: Theory, Methods, and Applications," in Neil Anderson et al., eds., *Handbook of Industrial, Work, and Organizational Psychology, Volume 2* (London: Sage, 2001): 143–65. J. Stacy Adams, "Inequity in Social Exchange," in Leonard Berkowitz, ed., *Advances in Experimental Social Psychology, Volume 2* (New York: Academic Press, 1965): 267–99. Procedural justice: John Thibaut and Laurens Walker, *Procedural Justice: A Psychological Analysis* (Hillsdale, NJ: Lawrence Erlbaum Associates, 1975).

13. Significance of intrinsic rewards: John J. Donovan, "Work Motivation," in Neil Anderson et al., eds., *Handbook of Industrial, Work, and Organizational Psychology, Volume 2* (London: Sage, 2001): 53–76. Maslow, "A Theory of Human Motivation." Frederick Herzberg, *Work and the Nature of Man* (Cleveland: World Publishing, 1966).

14. Concerns with fairness: Adams, "Inequity in Social Exchange." Hackman and Oldham, *Work Redesign.* Edward L. Deci and Richard M. Ryan, *Intrinsic Motivation and Self-Determination in Human Behavior* (New York: Plenum Press, 1985). Sociological perspective: Boas Shamir, "Meaning, Self and Motivation in Organizations," *Organization Studies* 12 (1991): 405–24. Basic needs easily filled: Michele J. Gelfand, Lisa M. Leslie, and Ryan Fehr, "To Prosper, Organizational Psychology Should Adopt a Global Perspective," *Journal of Organizational Behavior* 29 (May 2008): 493–517. Western cultures that value individual fulfillment: Hazel R. Markus and Shinobu Kitayama, "Culture and the Self: Implications for Cognition, Emotion, and Motivation," *Psychological Review* 98 (April 1991): 224–53.

15. Importance of improving performance: Joel Lefkowitz, "To Prosper, Organizational Psychology Should Expand the Values of Organizational Psychology to Match the Quality of Its Ethics," *Journal of Organizational Behavior* 29 (May 2008): 439–53; Michael J. Zickar and Robert E. Gibby, "Four Persistent Themes throughout the History of I-O Psychology in the United States," in Laura L. Koppes, ed., *Historical Perspectives in Industrial and Organizational Psychology* (Mahwah, NJ: Lawrence Erlbaum, 2007): 61–80.

16. Lucius Junius Moderatus Columella, *De Re Rustica,* trans. Harrison Boyd Ash (London: William Heinemann, 1941), 79, 89, and 93.

17. Household production: E. P. Thompson, *The Making of the English Working Class* (London: Gollancz, 1963); Sheilagh C. Ogilvie and Markus Cerman, eds.,

European Proto-Industrialization (Cambridge: Cambridge University Press, 1996). Fixed working hours, also quote: Sidney Pollard, *The Genesis of Modern Management: A Study of the Industrial Revolution in Great Britain* (Cambridge, MA: Harvard University Press, 1965), 193. Saint Monday: E. P. Thompson, "Time, Work-Discipline, and Industrial Capitalism," *Past and Present* 38 (December 1967): 56–97.

18. Quote, also systematizing the human element: Sanford M. Jacoby, *Employing Bureaucracy: Managers, Unions, and the Transformation of Work in American Industry, 1900–1945* (New York: Columbia University Press, 1985), 20. Modern accounting methods: Joseph A. Litterer, "Systematic Management: Design for Organizational Recoupling in American Manufacturing Firms," *Business History Review* 37 (Winter 1963): 369–91. Systematizing the human element: Bruce E. Kaufman, *Managing the Human Factor: The Early Years of Human Resource Management in American Industry* (Ithaca, NY: Cornell University Press, 2008).

19. Frederick Winslow Taylor, *The Principles of Scientific Management* (New York: Harper and Brothers, 1911). Optimal shovel load: Robert Kanigel, *The One Best Way: Frederick Winslow Taylor and the Enigma of Efficiency* (New York, Penguin, 1997). Sharp separation: Harry Braverman, *Labor and Monopoly Capital: The Degradation of Work in the Twentieth Century* (New York: Monthly Review Press, 1974).

20. Diverse initiatives: Kaufman, *Managing the Human Factor.* Notable companies: M. M. Niven, *Personnel Management, 1913–63* (London: Institute of Personnel Management, 1967); Eugene C. McCreary, "Social Welfare and Business: The Krupp Welfare Program, 1860–1914," *Business History Review* 42 (Spring 1968): 24–49; Jacoby, *Employing Bureaucracy.* Welfare capitalism: Sanford M. Jacoby, *Modern Manors: Welfare Capitalism Since the New Deal* (Princeton, NJ: Princeton University Press, 1997); Kaufman, *Managing the Human Factor*; Frank Koller, *Spark: How Old-Fashioned Values Drive a Twenty-First-Century Corporation* (New York: PublicAffairs, 2010).

21. Quote: Kaufman, *Managing the Human Factor,* 133. Also: Laura L. Koppes, ed., *Historical Perspectives in Industrial and Organizational Psychology* (Mahwah, NJ: Lawrence Erlbaum Associates, 2007). Redesign jobs: Walter Dill Scott, *Increasing Human Efficiency in Business: A Contribution to the Psychology of Business* (New York: Macmillan, 1911). Select the right employees: Hugo Münsterberg, *Psychology and Industrial Efficiency* (Boston: Houghton Mifflin, 1913). Redesign jobs and select the right employees: Morris. S. Viteles, *Industrial Psychology* (New York: Norton, 1932).

22. Follow-up experiments: Elton Mayo, *The Human Problems of an Industrial Civilization* (New York: Macmillan, 1933). Also, and quote: F. J. Roethlisberger and William J. Dickson, *Management and the Worker: An Account of a Research Program Conducted by the Western Electric Company, Hawthorne Works, Chicago* (Cambridge, MA: Harvard University Press, 1939), 604. Banner of human relations: Kyle Bruce, "Henry S. Dennison, Elton Mayo, and Human Relations Historiography," *Management and Organizational History* 1 (May 2006): 177–99.

23. Poor managerial practices, also scientific management: Bruce E. Kaufman, "The Quest for Cooperation and Unity of Interest in Industry," in Bruce E. Kaufman, Richard A. Beaumont, and Roy B. Helfgott, eds., *Industrial Relations to Human Resources and Beyond: The Evolving Process of Employee Relations Management* (Armonk, NY: M. E. Sharpe, 2003): 115–46. Reducing piece rates: Jacoby, *Employing Bureaucracy.* Quotes: Taylor, *The Principles of Scientific Management,* 9 and 10. Also: Kaufman, *Managing the Human Factor.*

24. First three quotes: Clarence J. Hicks, *My Life in Industrial Relations: Fifty Years in the Growth of a Profession* (New York: Harper and Brothers, 1941), 67, 65, and 77. Fourth quote: Mary Parker Follett, "Business as an Integrative Unity," in Henry C. Metcalf and L. Urwick, eds., *Dynamic Administration: The Collected Papers of Mary Parker Follett* (New York: Harper and Brothers, 1942): 71–94 at 83. Fifth quote: Douglas McGregor, *The Human Side of Enterprise* (New York: McGraw-Hill, 1960), 49, emphasis in original.

25. Unitarist emphasis: Nick Bacon, "Human Resource Management and Industrial Relations," in Peter Ackers and Adrian Wilkinson, eds., *Understanding Work and Employment: Industrial Relations in Transition* (Oxford: Oxford University Press, 2003): 71–88; Kaufman, "The Quest for Cooperation and Unity of Interest in Industry"; David Lewin, "IR and HR Perspectives on Workplace Conflict: What Can Each Learn from the Other?" *Human Resource Management Review* 11 (Winter 2001): 453–85. Quote: Jackie Crosby, "Meet the New Target Boss," *StarTribune* (Minneapolis, May 4, 2008): D1. Also: Koller, *Spark*.

26. Belief system: John W. Budd and Devasheesh Bhave, "The Employment Relationship," in Adrian Wilkinson et al., eds., *Sage Handbook of Human Resource Management* (London: Sage, 2010): 51–70. Recognize diverse forms of conflict: Carsten K. W. De Dreu and Michele J. Gelfand, "Conflict in the Workplace: Sources, Functions, and Dynamics across Multiple Levels of Analysis," in Carsten K. W. De Dreu and Michele J. Gelfand, eds., *The Psychology of Conflict and Conflict Management in Organizations* (New York: Lawrence Erlbaum Associates, 2008): 3–54. Ignores unions: Michael J. Zickar, "An Analysis of Industrial-Organizational Psychology's Indifference to Labor Unions in the United States," *Human Relations* 57 (February 2004): 145–67. A notable exception: Julian Barling, Clive Fullagar, and K. Kevin Kelloway, *The Union and Its Members: A Psychological Approach* (New York: Oxford University Press, 1992).

27. Mao Tse-tung, *On Contradiction* (1937) (New York: International Publishers, 1953). Mao Tse-tung, *On the Correct Handling of Contradictions among the People* (1957) (Beijing: Foreign Languages Press, 1966).

28. Strategic human resource management: David Lepak and Scott A. Snell, "Employment Subsystems and the 'HR Architecture,'" in Peter Boxall, John Purcell, and Patrick Wrights, eds., *The Oxford Handbook of Human Resource Management* (Oxford: Oxford University Press, 2007): 210–30. Extent implemented elsewhere: Howard F. Gospel, "Human Resources Management: A Historical Perspective," in Adrian Wilkinson et al., eds., *Sage Handbook of Human Resource Management* (London: Sage, 2010): 12–30; Chris Brewster and Henrik Holt Larsen, "The Northern European Dimension: A Distinctive Environment for HRM," in Chris Brewster and Henrik Holt Larsen, eds., *Human Resource Management in Northern Europe: Trends, Dilemmas, and Strategy* (Oxford: Blackwell, 2000): 24–38.

29. Adrian Wilkinson et al., eds., *Sage Handbook of Human Resource Management* (London: Sage, 2010).

30. Behaviorally based scholarship: Edward L. Deci, Richard Koestner, and Richard M. Ryan, "A Meta-Analytic Review of Experiments Examining the Effects of Extrinsic Rewards on Intrinsic Motivation," *Psychological Bulletin* 125 (November 1999): 627–68; Ernst Fehr and Armin Falk, "Psychological Foundations of Incentives," *European Economic Review* 46 (May 2002): 687–724. Practitioner literature:

Bob Nelson, *1001 Ways to Reward Employees,* 2nd ed. (New York: Workman, 2005). Influence of perceptions: Kristin L. Scott, Jason D. Shaw, and Michelle K. Duffy, "Merit Pay Raises and Organization-Based Self-Esteem," *Journal of Organizational Behavior* 29 (October 2008): 967–80. See differences as fair: Jason D. Shaw, Nina Gupta, and John E. Delery, "Pay Dispersion and Workforce Performance: Moderating Effects of Incentives and Interdependence," *Strategic Management Journal* 23 (June 2002): 491–512.

31. Budd and Bhave, "The Employment Relationship."

32. Quote: Kaufman, *Managing the Human Factor,* 278. Identifying troublemakers: Michael J. Zickar, "Using Personality Inventories to Identify Thugs and Agitators: Applied Psychology's Contribution to the War against Labor," *Journal of Vocational Behavior* 59 (August 2001): 149–64.

33. Disguised rhetoric: Sharon C. Bolton and Maeve Houlihan, "Beginning the Search for the H in HRM," in Sharon C. Bolton and Maeve Houlihan, eds., *Searching for the Human in Human Resource Management: Theory, Practice and Workplace Contexts* (Basingstoke, Hampshire, UK: Palgrave Macmillan, 2007): 1–17; Thomas Klikauer, *Communication and Management at Work* (Basingstoke, Hampshire, UK: Palgrave Macmillan, 2007); Karen Legge, *Human Resource Management: Rhetorics and Realities* (Basingstoke, Hampshire, UK: Macmillan Press, 1995). Mentoring: compare: Connie R. Wanberg, Elizabeth T. Welsh, and John Kammeyer-Mueller, "Protégé and Mentor Self-Disclosure: Levels and Outcomes within Formal Mentoring Dyads in a Corporate Context," *Journal of Vocational Behavior* 70 (April 2007): 398–412; Mark A. Covaleski et al., "The Calculated and the Avowed: Techniques of Discipline and Struggles over Identity in Big Six Public Accounting Firms," *Administrative Science Quarterly* 43 (June 1998): 293–327. First quote: Barbara Townley, "Foucault, Power/Knowledge, and Its Relevance for Human Resource Management," *Academy of Management Review* 18 (July 1993): 518–45 at 529. Poor state of work: Paul Thompson and David McHugh, *Work Organisations: A Critical Introduction,* 3rd ed. (Basingstoke, Hampshire, UK: Palgrave, 2002). De-skilling: Braverman, *Labor and Monopoly Capital.* Second quote: Alan Fox, *Beyond Contract: Work, Power and Trust Relations* (London: Faber and Faber, 1974), 250.

34. Degradation of work: Meakin, *Man and Work*; Campbell, *Joy in Work, German Work.* Separation of hands and the brain: Sennett, *The Craftsman.* Promotion of psychological well-being: Turner, Barling, and Zacharatos, "Positive Psychology at Work." Far from universal: Francis Green, *Demanding Work: The Paradox of Job Quality in the Affluent Economy* (Princeton, NJ: Princeton University Press, 2006); Francis Green, Katy Huxley, and Keith Whitfield, "The Employee Experience of Work," in Adrian Wilkinson et al., eds., *Sage Handbook of Human Resource Management* (London: Sage, 2010): 377–92. Failure to provide intrinsic rewards: David A. Spencer, *The Political Economy of Work* (London: Routledge, 2009).

7. Work as a Social Relation

1. Quote: Frederick J. Teggart, "The Argument of Hesiod's *Works and Days,*" *Journal of the History of Ideas* 8 (January 1947): 45–77 at 68–69. Death from overwork: Paul A. Herbig and Frederick A. Palumbo, "*Karoshi:* Salaryman Sudden Death Syndrome," *Journal of Managerial Psychology* 9 (1994): 11–16. Jamestown: Edmund S.

Morgan, "The Labor Problem at Jamestown, 1607–18," *American Historical Review* 76 (June 1971): 595–611.

2. Diane Watson, "Individuals and Institutions: The Case of Work and Employment," in Margaret Wetherell, ed., *Identities, Groups, and Social Issues* (London: Sage, 1996): 239–82 at 247.

3. Mark Granovetter, "Economic Action and Social Structure: The Problem of Embeddedness," *American Journal of Sociology* 91 (November 1985): 481–510.

4. Rebecca F. Taylor, "Rethinking Voluntary Work," in Lynne Pettinger et al., eds., *A New Sociology of Work?* (Malden, MA: Blackwell, 2005): 119–35.

5. Peter M. Blau, *Exchange and Power in Social Life* (New York: Wiley, 1964). Russell Cropanzano and Marie S. Mitchell, "Social Exchange Theory: An Interdisciplinary Review," *Journal of Management* 31 (December 2005): 874–900. Lynn M. Shore et al., "Social and Economic Exchange: Construct Development and Validation," *Journal of Applied Social Psychology* 36 (April 2006): 837–67.

6. Psychological contract: Denise M. Rousseau, *Psychological Contracts in Organizations: Understanding Written and Unwritten Agreements* (Thousand Oaks, CA: Sage, 1995); Niall Cullinane and Tony Dundon, "The Psychological Contract: A Critical Review," *International Journal of Management Reviews* 8 (June 2006): 113–29. Bonds are more complex: Shore et al., "Social and Economic Exchange." Alphabet soup: Kathryn M. Sherony and Stephen G. Green, "Coworker Exchange: Relationships between Coworkers, Leader–Member Exchange, and Work Attitudes," *Journal of Applied Psychology* 87 (June 2002): 542–48.

7. Dennis W. Organ, Philip M. Podsakoff, and Scott B. MacKenzie, *Organizational Citizenship Behavior: Its Nature, Antecedents, and Consequences* (Thousand Oaks, CA: Sage, 2006). Sandy J. Wayne, Lynn M. Shore, and Robert C. Liden, "Perceived Organizational Support and Leader-Member Exchange: A Social Exchange Perspective," *Academy of Management Journal* 40 (February 1997): 82–111.

8. Quote: Daniel J. Brass et al., "Taking Stock of Networks and Organizations: A Multilevel Perspective," *Academy of Management Journal* 47 (December 2004): 795–817 at 795. Also: Stephen P. Borgatti and Pacey C. Foster, "The Network Paradigm in Organizational Research: A Review and Typology," *Journal of Management* 29 (December 2003): 991–1013; Granovetter, "Economic Action and Social Structure."

9. Social capital: Alejandro Portes, "Social Capital: Its Origins and Applications in Modern Sociology," *Annual Review of Sociology* 24 (1998): 1–24; Robert D. Putnam, *Bowling Alone: The Collapse and Revival of American Community* (New York: Simon & Schuster, 2000); Nan Lin, "Inequality in Social Capital," *Contemporary Sociology* 29 (November 2000): 785–95. Guanxi: Thomas Gold, Doug Guthrie, and David L. Wank, "An Introduction to the Study of *Guanxi*," in Thomas Gold, Doug Guthrie, and David L. Wank, eds., *Social Connections in China: Institutions, Culture, and the Changing Nature of Guanxi* (Cambridge: Cambridge University Press, 2002): 3–20. With respect to work: Joel M. Podolny and James N. Baron, "Resources and Relationships: Social Networks and Mobility in the Workplace," *American Sociological Review* 62 (October 1997): 673–93; Gail M. McGuire, "Gender, Race, Ethnicity, and Networks: The Factors Affecting the Status of Employees' Network Members," *Work and Occupations* 27 (November 2000): 500–23; Yanjie Bian, "Institutional Holes and Job Mobility Processes: *Guanxi* Mechanisms in China's Emergent Labor Markets," in

Thomas Gold, Doug Guthrie, and David L. Wank, eds., *Social Connections in China: Institutions, Culture, and the Changing Nature of* Guanxi (Cambridge: Cambridge University Press, 2002): 117–36; Heather Haveman and Mukti Khaire, "Organizational Sociology and the Analysis of Work," in Marek Korczynski, Randy Hodson, and Paul Edwards, eds., *Social Theory at Work* (Oxford: Oxford University Press, 2006): 272–98. Structural holes: Ronald S. Burt, *Structural Holes: The Social Structure of Competition* (Cambridge, MA: Harvard University Press, 1992); Ronald S. Burt, "The Contingent Value of Social Capital," *Administrative Science Quarterly* 42 (June 1997): 339–65. Normative control: Debra Osnowitz, "Occupational Networking as Normative Control: Collegial Exchange among Contract Professionals," *Work and Occupations* 33 (February 2006): 12–41.

10. Émile Durkheim, *The Rules of Sociological Method* (1895), trans. W. D. Halls (New York: Free Press, 1982). Max Weber, *Economy and Society: An Outline of Interpretive Sociology* (1922), trans. Guenther Roth and Claus Wittich (New York: Bedminster Press, 1968). Christine Horne, "Sociological Perspectives on the Emergence of Social Norms," in Michael Hechter and Karl-Dieter Opp, eds., *Social Norms* (New York: Russell Sage Foundation, 2001): 3–34. Victor Nee and Paul Ingram, "Embeddedness and Beyond: Institutions, Exchange, and Social Structure," in Mary C. Brinton and Victor Nee, eds., *The New Institutionalism in Sociology* (New York: Russell Sage Foundation, 1998): 19–45.

11. Phyllis Moen, "Beyond the Career Mystique: 'Time In,' 'Time Out,' and 'Second Acts,'" *Sociological Forum* 20 (June 2005): 189–208 at 190.

12. Geert Hofstede, *Culture's Consequences: Comparing Values, Behaviors, Institutions, and Organizations across Nations,* 2nd ed. (Thousand Oaks, CA: Sage, 2001). Psychologists: Michele J. Gelfand, Miriam Erez, and Zeynep Aycan, "Cross-Cultural Organizational Behavior," *Annual Review of Psychology* 58 (2007): 479–514.

13. First quote: Frederick Winslow Taylor, *The Principles of Scientific Management* (New York: Harper and Brothers, 1911), 22. Hawthorne experiments, and second quote: F. J. Roethlisberger and William J. Dickson, *Management and the Worker: An Account of a Research Program Conducted by the Western Electric Company, Hawthorne Works, Chicago* (Cambridge, MA: Harvard University Press, 1939), 517. Other studies example: Donald Roy, "Quota Restriction and Goldbricking in a Machine Shop," *American Journal of Sociology* 57 (March 1952): 427–42.

14. Social systems: Talcott Parsons, "Suggestions for a Sociological Approach to the Theory of Organizations," *Administrative Science Quarterly* 1 (June 1956): 63–85. Major research topic: Cheri Ostroff, Angelo J. Kinicki, and Melinda M. Tamkins, "Organizational Culture and Climate," in Walter C. Borman, Daniel R. Ilgen, and Richard J. Klimoski, eds., *Handbook of Psychology, Volume 12: I/O Psychology* (New York: Wiley, 2003): 565–94. Quote: James Lincoln and Didier Guillot, "A Durkheimian View of Organizational Culture," in Marek Korczynski, Randy Hodson, and Paul Edwards, eds., *Social Theory at Work* (Oxford: Oxford University Press, 2006): 88–120 at 110. Also: Michele J. Gelfand, Lisa M. Leslie, and Ryan Fehr, "To Prosper, Organizational Psychology Should Adopt a Global Perspective," *Journal of Organizational Behavior* 29 (May 2008): 493–517. Hierarchical social relations: Tim Hallett, "Symbolic Power and Organizational Culture," *Sociological Theory* 21 (June 2003): 128–49.

15. Stephen R. Barley and Gideon Kunda, "Design and Devotion: Surges of Rational and Normative Ideologies of Control in Managerial Discourse," *Administrative Science Quarterly* 37 (September 1992): 363–99 at 364.

16. Viewed as legitimate: Tom R. Tyler, "Psychological Perspectives on Legitimacy and Legitimation," *Annual Review of Psychology* 57 (2006): 375–400. Importance of workplace norms, and quote: Randy Hodson, "Organizational Anomie and Worker Consent," *Work and Occupations* 26 (August 1999): 292–323 at 294.

17. Violations: Sandra L. Robinson and Denise M. Rousseau, "Violating the Psychological Contract: Not the Exception but the Norm," *Journal of Organizational Behavior* 15 (May 1994): 245–59. Legitimacy for the social order: Cullinane and Dundon, "The Psychological Contract."

18. Intentionally create employee values and norms: Gideon Kunda, *Engineering Culture: Control and Commitment in a High-Tech Corporation* (Philadelphia: Temple University Press, 1992); Irena Grugulis, Tony Dundon, and Adrian Wilkinson, "Cultural Control and the 'Culture Manager': Employment Practices in a Consultancy," *Work, Employment and Society* 14 (March 2000): 97–116; Thomas Klikauer, *Communication and Management at Work* (Basingstoke, Hampshire, UK: Palgrave Macmillan, 2007). Self-disciplining: Mark A. Covaleski et al., "The Calculated and the Avowed: Techniques of Discipline and Struggles over Identity in Big Six Public Accounting Firms," *Administrative Science Quarterly* 43 (June 1998): 293–327; David Knights and Hugh Willmott, "Power and Subjectivity at Work: From Degradation to Subjugation in Social Relations," *Sociology* 23 (November 1989): 535–58.

19. Win-win situations: Dave Ulrich and Wendy Ulrich, *The Why of Work: How Great Leaders Build Abundant Organizations That Win* (New York: McGraw-Hill, 2010). Sophisticated campaigns: Kunda, *Engineering Culture;* Hugh Willmott, "Strength Is Ignorance; Slavery Is Freedom: Managing Culture in Modern Organizations," *Journal of Management Studies* 30 (July 1993): 515–52; Paul du Gay, *Consumption and Identity at Work* (London: Sage, 1996); Grugulis, Dundon, and Wilkinson, "Cultural Control and the 'Culture Manager'"; Mats Alvesson and Hugh Willmott, "Identity Regulation as Organizational Control: Producing the Appropriate Individual," *Journal of Management Studies* 39 (July 2002): 619–44. Organizational ideology: Lincoln and Guillot, "A Durkheimian View of Organizational Culture." Organizational ideology and communication: Klikauer, *Communication and Management at Work.*

20. Competition within multinationals: Miguel Martinez Lucio and Syd Weston, "New Management Practices in a Multinational Corporation: The Restructuring of Worker Representation and Rights?" *Industrial Relations Journal* 25 (June 1994): 110–21. European Works Councils: Andrew R. Timming, "European Works Councils and the Dark Side of Managing Worker Voice," *Human Resource Management Journal* 17 (July 2007): 248–64.

21. Reification: Hanna Fenichel Pitkin, "Rethinking Reification," *Theory and Society* 16 (March 1987): 263–93; Peter L. Berger and Thomas Luckmann, *The Social Construction of Reality: A Treatise in the Sociology of Knowledge* (Garden City, NY: Doubleday, 1966). Neoliberal market paradigm: Cullinane and Dundon, "The Psychological Contract: A Critical Review." Japan: Aviad E. Raz, *Emotions at Work: Normative Control, Organizations, and Culture in Japan and America* (Cambridge, MA: Harvard University Press, 2002).

22. David Grant and John Shields, "Identifying the Subject: Worker Identity as Discursively Constructed Terrain," in Mark Hearn and Grant Michelson, eds., *Rethinking Work: Time, Space, and Discourse* (Cambridge: Cambridge University Press, 2006): 285–307. Klikauer, *Communication and Management at Work*.

23. First quote: Herbert Applebaum, "Theoretical Introduction," in Herbert Applebaum, ed., *Work in Non-Market and Transitional Societies* (Albany: State University of New York Press, 1984): 1–44 at 2. Not a thing separate from society: Georg Lukács, *History and Class Consciousness: Studies in Marxist Dialectics,* trans. Rodney Livingstone (Cambridge, MA: MIT Press, 1971). Second quote: Karl Marx, *Capital: A Critique of Political Economy* (1867), trans. Samuel Moore and Edward Aveling (New York: Modern Library, 1936), 188. Third quote: Erik Olin Wright, "Foundations of a Neo-Marxist Class Analysis," in Erik Olin Wright, ed., *Approaches to Class Analysis* (Cambridge: Cambridge University Press, 2005): 4–30 at 10.

24. Marx, *Capital*.

25. Capitalist employment relationship: Richard Hyman, "Marxist Thought and the Analysis of Work," in Marek Korczynski, Randy Hodson, and Paul Edwards, eds., *Social Theory at Work* (Oxford: Oxford University Press, 2006): 26–55. Quotes: Marx, *Capital,* 363 and 708.

26. Marxist perspective defines classes: Richard Scase, *Class* (Minneapolis: University of Minnesota Press, 1992); Wright, "Foundations of a Neo-Marxist Class Analysis"; Hyman, "Marxist Thought and the Analysis of Work." Lens of capitalist reproduction: Michael Burawoy and Erik Olin Wright, "Sociological Marxism," in Jonathan H. Turner, ed., *Handbook of Sociological Theory* (New York: Plenum, 2002): 459–86. Job training programs: Gordon Lafer, *The Job Training Charade* (Ithaca, NY: Cornell University Press, 2002). Male-breadwinner social norm: Evelyn Nakano Glenn, *Unequal Freedom: How Race and Gender Shaped American Citizenship and Labor* (Cambridge, MA: Harvard University Press, 2002).

27. Richard C. Edwards, *Contested Terrain: The Transformation of the Workplace in the Twentieth Century* (New York: Basic Books, 1979), 12, emphasis in original.

28. Labor process theory: Paul Thompson, *The Nature of Work: An Introduction to Debates on the Labour Process,* 2nd ed. (London: Macmillan, 1989); Paul Thompson and Kirsty Newsome, "Labor Process Theory, Work, and the Employment Relation," in Bruce E. Kaufman, ed., *Theoretical Perspectives on Work and the Employment Relationship* (Champaign, IL: Industrial Relations Research Association, 2004): 133–62. Criticizing mainstream economics: Samuel Bowles and Herbert Gintis, "Contested Exchange: New Microfoundations for the Political Economy of Capitalism," *Politics and Society* 18 (June 1990): 165–222. Space for conflicts: Edwards, *Contested Terrain*; P. K. Edwards, *Conflict at Work: A Materialist Analysis of Workplace Relations* (Oxford: Basil Blackwell, 1986); Paul Thompson and Chris Smith, eds., *Working Life: Renewing Labour Process Analysis* (Basingstoke, Hampshire, UK: Palgrave Macmillan, 2010); Quote: Frank Dobbin, "Economic Sociology," in Clifton D. Bryant and Dennis L. Peck, eds., *21st Century Sociology: A Reference Handbook* (Thousand Oaks, CA: Sage, 2007): 319–30 at 321. Contested terrain: Edwards, *Contested Terrain*.

29. Quote, and manufacturing division of labor: Harry Braverman, *Labor and Monopoly Capital: The Degradation of Work in the Twentieth Century* (New York: Monthly Review Press, 1974), 90. Manufacturing division of labor: Karl Marx, *Eco-*

nomic and Philosophic Manuscripts of 1844 (1844), trans. Martin Milligan (Amherst, NY: Prometheus Books, 1988).

30. Literal implementation: Barley and Kunda, "Design and Devotion"; Edwards, *Contested Terrain*. Quote: Braverman, *Labor and Monopoly Capital,* 87. Robin Leidner, *Fast Food, Fast Talk: Service Work and the Routinization of Everyday Life* (Berkeley: University of California Press, 1993).

31. Quote: Edwards, *Contested Terrain*, 131. Intentionally designed: Tom Keenoy and Peter Anthony, "HRM: Metaphor, Meaning, and Morality," in Paul Blyton and Peter Turnbull, eds., *Reassessing Human Resource Management* (London: Sage, 1992): 233–55; Barbara Townley, "Foucault, Power/Knowledge, and Its Relevance for Human Resource Management," *Academy of Management Review* 18 (July 1993): 518–45; Paul Thompson and David McHugh, *Work Organisations: A Critical Introduction,* 3rd ed. (Basingstoke, Hampshire, UK: Palgrave, 2002).

32. Concertive control: James R. Barker, "Tightening the Iron Cage: Concertive Control in Self-Managing Teams," *Administrative Science Quarterly* 38 (September 1993): 408–37. Quote: Karen Legge, "Putting the Missing H into HRM: The Case of the Flexible Organization," in Sharon C. Bolton and Maeve Houlihan, eds., *Searching for the Human in Human Resource Management: Theory, Practice and Workplace Contexts* (Basingstoke, Hampshire, UK: Palgrave Macmillan, 2007): 115–36 at 127.

33. Self-managed teams: Barker, "Tightening the Iron Cage"; Laurie Graham, *On the Line at Subaru-Isuzu: The Japanese Model and the American Worker* (Ithaca, NY: Cornell University Press, 1995); Raz, *Emotions at Work*. Weakening support for unions: John Godard, "A Critical Assessment of the High-Performance Paradigm," *British Journal of Industrial Relations* 42 (June 2004): 349–78; Guillermo J. Grenier, *Inhuman Relations: Quality Circles and Anti-Unionism in American Industry* (Philadelphia: Temple University Press, 1988). Dark side of flexibility: Thompson and Newsome, "Labor Process Theory, Work, and the Employment Relation."

34. Marxist/materialist perspectives: Thompson, *The Nature of Work*. Worker noncompliance: Stephen Ackroyd and Paul Thompson, *Organizational Misbehavior* (London: Sage, 1999). Foucauldian labor process theory: Knights and Willmott, "Power and Subjectivity at Work"; Tim Newton, "Theorizing Subjectivity in Organizations: The Failure of Foucauldian Studies?" *Organization Studies* 19 (May 1998): 415–47. Emerging work: Abigail Marks and Paul Thompson, "Beyond the Blank Slate: Identities and Interests at Work," in Paul Thompson and Chris Smith, eds., *Working Life: Renewing Labour Process Analysis* (Basingstoke, Hampshire, UK: Palgrave Macmillan, 2010): 316–38.

35. Characterized by worker consent: Michael Burawoy, *Manufacturing Consent: Changes in the Labor Process under Monopoly Capitalism* (Chicago: University of Chicago Press, 1979); Knights and Willmott, "Power and Subjectivity at Work." Dialectic of control and accommodation: Thompson and Newsome, "Labor Process Theory, Work, and the Employment Relation."

36. Quote: Al Rainnie, Susan McGrath-Champ, and Andrew Herod, "Making Space for Geography in Labour Process Theory," in Paul Thompson and Chris Smith, eds., *Working Life: Renewing Labour Process Analysis* (Basingstoke, Hampshire, UK: Palgrave Macmillan, 2010): 297–315 at 312. China: Ngai Pun and Chris Smith, "Putting Transnational Labour Process in its Place: The Dormitory Labour Regime in Post-Socialist China," *Work, Employment and Society* 21 (March 2007): 27–45.

37. Friedrich Nietzsche, *Daybreak: Thoughts on the Prejudices of Morality* (1881), trans. R. J. Hollingdale (Cambridge: Cambridge University Press, 1982), 174. Gulag: Paul R. Gregory and Valery Lazarev, eds., *The Economics of Forced Labor: The Soviet Gulag* (Stanford, CA: Hoover Institution Press, 2003). Nazi forced labor: Michael Thad Allen, *The Business of Genocide: The SS, Slave Labor, and the Concentration Camps* (Chapel Hill: University of North Carolina Press, 2002); Wolf Gruner, *Jewish Forced Labor under the Nazis: Economic Needs and Racial Aims, 1938–1944*, trans. Kathleen M. Dell'Orto (Cambridge: Cambridge University Press, 2006). *Laogai:* Philip F. Williams and Yenna Wu, *The Great Wall of Confinement: The Chinese Prison Camp through Contemporary Fiction and Reportage* (Berkeley: University of California Press, 2004). American convict labor: Alex Lichtenstein, *Twice the Work of Free Labor: The Political Economy of Convict Labor in the New South* (London: Verso, 1996).

38. Recoding occupational information: Margo A. Conk, "Accuracy, Efficiency, and Bias: The Interpretation of Women's Work in the U.S. Census of Occupations, 1890–1940," *Historical Methods* 14 (Spring 1981): 65–72.

39. Quote: Jim Sidanius and Felicia Pratto, *Social Dominance: An Intergroup Theory of Social Hierarchy and Oppression* (New York: Cambridge University Press, 1999), 31. Meritocracies: Stephen J. McNamee and Robert K. Miller Jr., *The Meritocracy Myth* (Lanham, MD: Rowman & Littlefield, 2004).

40. Granovetter, "Economic Action and Social Structure." Human agency: William H. Sewell Jr., "A Theory of Structure: Duality, Agency, and Transformation," *American Journal of Sociology* 98 (July 1992): 1–29.

41. Job crafters: Amy Wrzesniewski and Jane E. Dutton, "Crafting a Job: Revisioning Employees as Active Crafters of Their Work," *Academy of Management Review* 26 (April 2001): 179–201. Renegotiate workplace norms: Randy Hodson, *Dignity at Work* (Cambridge: Cambridge University Press, 2001). Appropriate time, work, resources, and identity: Ackroyd and Thompson, *Organizational Misbehavior.* Mobilize: John Kelly, *Rethinking Industrial Relations: Mobilization, Collectivism and Long Waves* (London: Routledge, 1998); Dan Clawson, *The Next Upsurge: Labor and the New Social Movements* (Ithaca, NY: Cornell University Press, 2003).

42. Argentina: Maurizio Atzeni and Pablo Ghigliani, "Labour Process and Decision-Making in Factories under Workers' Self-Management: Empirical Evidence from Argentina," *Work, Employment and Society* 21 (December 2007): 653–71. Quote: Karl Marx, *The Eighteenth Brumaire of Louis Bonaparte* (1869), trans. C. P. Dutt (New York: International Publishers, 1963), 15. Structure-agency duality: Sewell, "A Theory of Structure"; Derek Layder, *Understanding Social Theory,* 2nd ed. (London: Sage, 2006).

8. Work as Caring for Others

1. Tim Barringer, *Men at Work: Art and Labour in Victorian Britain* (New Haven, CT: Yale University Press, 2005). Robert J. Saunders, "'American Gothic' and the Division of Labor," *Art Education* 40 (May 1987): 6–11.

2. Domestic work invisible: Jeanne Boydston, *Home and Work: Housework, Wages, and the Ideology of Labor in the Early Republic* (New York: Oxford University Press, 1990). Instinctual activities: Maria Mies, *Patriarchy and Accumulation on a World Scale: Women in the International Division of Labour* (London: Zed Books, 1986). China: Ste-

van Harrell, "The Changing Meanings of Work in China," in Barbara Entwisle and Gail E. Henderson, eds., *Re-Drawing Boundaries: Work, Households, and Gender in China* (Berkeley: University of California Press, 2000): 67–76. Ester Boserup, *Woman's Role in Economic Development* (London: Allen & Unwin, 1970).

3. Indeed work: Ann Oakley, *The Sociology of Housework* (London: Robertson, 1974); Marjorie L. DeVault, *Feeding the Family: The Social Organization of Caring as Gendered Work* (Chicago: University of Chicago Press, 1991). First quote: Carol T. Baines, Patricia M. Evans, and Sheila M. Neysmith, "Women's Caring: Work Expanding, State Contracting," in Carol T. Baines, Patricia M. Evans, and Sheila M. Neysmith, eds., *Women's Caring: Feminist Perspective on Social Welfare* (Toronto: Oxford University Press, 1998): 3–22 at 3. Second quote: Hilary Graham, "Caring: A Labour of Love," in Janet Finch and Dulcie Groves, eds., *A Labour of Love: Women, Work, and Caring* (London: Routledge and Kegan Paul, 1983): 13–30 at 30.

4. George P. Murdock and Caterina Provost, "Factors in the Division of Labor by Sex: A Cross-Cultural Analysis," *Ethnology* 12 (April 1973): 203–25. China: Susan Mann, "Work and Household in Chinese Culture: Historical Perspectives," in Barbara Entwisle and Gail E. Henderson, eds., *Re-Drawing Boundaries: Work, Households, and Gender in China* (Berkeley: University of California Press, 2000): 15–32. Quotes: Jenny B. White, *Money Makes Us Relatives: Women's Labor in Urban Turkey* (Austin: University of Texas Press, 1994), 7 and 38.

5. Drucilla K. Barker and Susan F. Feiner, *Liberating Economics: Feminist Perspectives on Families, Work, and Globalization* (Ann Arbor: University of Michigan Press, 2004), 21.

6. Social norm that triumphed: Evelyn Nakano Glenn, *Unequal Freedom: How Race and Gender Shaped American Citizenship and Labor* (Cambridge, MA: Harvard University Press, 2002); Barker and Feiner, *Liberating Economics*. Unproductive housewives: Nancy Folbre, "The Unproductive Housewife: Her Evolution in Nineteenth-Century Economic Thought," *Signs* 16 (Spring 1991): 463–84.

7. Intentional displays: Jane E. Simonsen, *Making Home Work: Domesticity and Native American Assimilation in the American West, 1860–1919* (Chapel Hill: University of North Carolina Press, 2006). Labor leaders: Boydston, *Home and Work*. Woman's responsibility: Alice Kessler-Harris, *Out to Work: A History of Wage-Earning Women in the United States* (New York: Oxford University Press, 2003).

8. Quote: Pat Armstrong and Hugh Armstrong, "Public and Private: Implications for Care Work," in Lynne Pettinger et al., eds., *A New Sociology of Work?* (Malden, MA: Blackwell, 2005): 169–87 at 175. Even children: Gloria Morris Nemerowicz, *Children's Perceptions of Gender and Work Roles* (New York: Praeger, 1979); Becky Francis, *Power Plays: Primary School Children's Constructions of Gender, Power and Adult Work* (Stoke-on-Trent, Staffordshire, UK: Trentham Books, 1998). Men do more domestic caring: Shannon N. Davis and Theodore N. Greenstein, "Cross-National Variations in the Division of Household Labor," *Journal of Marriage and Family* 66 (December 2004): 1260–71. Second shift: Arlie Russell Hochschild, *The Second Shift: Working Parents and the Revolution at Home* (New York: Viking, 1989).

9. Barker and Feiner, *Liberating Economics*.

10. Labor of love: Graham, "Caring: A Labour of Love." Quote: Katharine Silbaugh, "Turning Labor into Love: Housework and the Law," *Northwestern University Law Review* 91 (Fall 1996): 1–86 at 4.

11. Charlotte Perkins Gilman, *Women and Economics: A Study of the Economic Relation between Men and Women as a Factor in Social Evolution* (Boston: Small, Mayard and Co., 1898), 13 and 20.

12. More similar than different: R. W. Connell, *Gender* (Cambridge: Polity, 2002). Murdock and Provost, "Factors in the Division of Labor by Sex." China: Shanshan Du, "'Husband and Wife Do It Together': Sex/Gender Allocation of Labor among the Qhawqhat Lahu of Lancang, Southwest China," *American Anthropologist* 102 (September 2000): 520–37. Clerical office work: Margery W. Davies, *Woman's Place Is at the Typewriter: Office Work and Office Workers, 1870–1930* (Philadelphia: Temple University Press, 1984).

13. Socially constructed: Barbara Laslett and Johanna Brenner, "Gender and Social Reproduction: Historical Perspectives," *Annual Review of Sociology* 15 (1989): 381–404; Teresa Amott and Julie Matthaei, *Race, Gender, and Work: A Multicultural Economic History of Women in the United States,* rev. ed. (Boston: South End Press, 1996); Irene Browne and Joya Misra, "The Intersection of Gender and Race in the Labor Market," *Annual Review of Sociology* 29 (2003): 487–513. First and third quotes: Connell, *Gender,* 10. Second quote: Joan Wallach Scott, *Gender and the Politics of History,* rev. ed. (New York: Columbia University Press, 1999), 2.

14. Several streams: Stevi Jackson, "Feminist Social Theory," in Stevi Jackson and Jackie Jones, eds., *Contemporary Feminist Theories* (New York: New York University Press, 1998): 12–33; Heidi Gottfried, "Feminist Theories of Work," in Marek Korczynski, Randy Hodson, and Paul Edwards, eds., *Social Theory at Work* (Oxford: Oxford University Press, 2006): 121–54. Quote: Sylvia Walby, *Theorizing Patriarchy* (Oxford: Basil Blackwell, 1990), 20. Institutionalized heterosexuality: Adrienne Rich, "Compulsory Heterosexuality and Lesbian Existence," *Signs* 5 (Summer 1980): 631–60. Vulnerabilities: Shulamith Firestone, *The Dialectic of Sex: The Case for Feminist Revolution* (New York: Morrow, 1970). Physical coercion: Mies, *Patriarchy and Accumulation on a World Scale.* Common result: Christine Delphy, *Close to Home: A Materialist Analysis of Women's Oppression,* trans. Diana Leonard (Amherst: University of Massachusetts Press, 1984). Women serving capital: Eli Zaretsky, *Capitalism, the Family, and Personal Life* (New York: Harper & Row, 1976). Gender discrimination: Deborah Figart, "Gender as More Than a Dummy Variable: Feminist Approaches to Discrimination," *Review of Social Economy* 55 (March 1997): 1–32.

15. Dual systems theory: Heidi I. Hartmann, "The Unhappy Marriage of Marxism and Feminism: Towards a More Progressive Union," *Capital and Class* 8 (Summer 1979): 1–33; Walby, *Theorizing Patriarchy.* Diversity of experiences: Michèle Barrett, "Words and Things: Materialism and Method in Contemporary Feminist Analysis," in Michèle Barrett and Anne Phillips, eds., *Destabilizing Theory: Contemporary Feminist Debates* (Stanford, CA: Stanford University Press, 1992): 201–19.

16. Vary by race, ethnicity, and class: Amott and Matthaei, *Race, Gender, and Work*; Baines, Evans, and Neysmith, "Women's Caring"; Li Zhang, "The Interplay of Gender, Space, and Work in China's Floating Population," in Barbara Entwisle and Gail E. Henderson, eds., *Re-Drawing Boundaries: Work, Households, and Gender in China* (Berkeley: University of California Press, 2000): 171–96; Ethgender: James A. Geschwender, "Ethgender, Women's Waged Labor, and Economic Mobility," *Social Problems* 39 (February 1992): 1–16. Children's work efforts: Deborah Levison, "Children as Economic Agents," *Feminist Economics* 6 (March 2000): 125–34.

17. DeVault, *Feeding the Family*, 232.

18. First and second quotes: Carol Gilligan, *In a Different Voice: Psychological Theory and Women's Development* (Cambridge, MA: Harvard University Press, 1982), 79 and 98. Third quote: Virginia Held, *The Ethics of Care: Personal, Political, and Global* (Oxford: Oxford University Press, 2006), 10.

19. Other Western ethical theories: John W. Budd and James G. Scoville, "Moral Philosophy, Business Ethics, and the Employment Relationship," in John W. Budd and James G. Scoville, eds., *The Ethics of Human Resources and Industrial Relations* (Champaign, IL: Labor and Employment Relations Association, 2005): 1–21. Kantian ethics: Norman E. Bowie, *Business Ethics: A Kantian Perspective* (Malden, MA: Blackwell, 1999). Rawlsian ethics: John Rawls, *A Theory of Justice* (Cambridge, MA: Harvard University Press, 1971).

20. Privileges virtue: Robert C. Solomon, *Ethics and Excellence: Cooperation and Integrity in Business* (New York: Oxford University Press, 1992). Ethics of care, and quote: Held, *The Ethics of Care*, 19.

21. Carol Wolkowitz, *Bodies at Work* (London: Sage, 2006).

22. First quote, and ambivalent ways: Wolkowitz, *Bodies at Work*, 147. Also: Debra Gimlin, "What Is 'Body Work'? A Review of the Literature," *Sociology Compass* 1 (September 2007): 353–70. Second quote: Julia Twigg, "Carework as a Form of Bodywork," *Ageing and Society* 20 (July 2000): 389–411 at 408.

23. Victorian Age paintings: Barringer, *Men at Work*. Photographic exhibits: Ferdinand Protzman, *Work: The World in Photographs* (Washington, DC: National Geographic Society, 2006). Bring everyday aspects to life: Tim Strangleman, "Representations of Labour: Visual Sociology and Work," *Sociology Compass* 2 (September 2008): 1491–505. Masculine ideals: Melissa Dabakis, *Visualizing Labor in American Sculpture: Monuments, Manliness, and the Work Ethic, 1880–1935* (Cambridge: Cambridge University Press, 1999); Edward Slavishak, *Bodies of Work: Civic Display and Labor in Industrial Pittsburgh* (Durham, NC: Duke University Press, 2008). Chinese emperor: Mann, "Work and Household in Chinese Culture."

24. Joan Acker, "Hierarchies, Jobs, Bodies: A Theory of Gendered Organizations," *Gender and Society* 4 (June 1990): 139–58 at 149 and 151.

25. Disguises true nature: Patricia Yancey Martin and David L. Collinson, "Gender and Sexuality in Organizations," in Myra Marx Ferree, Judith Lorber, and Beth B. Hess, eds., *Revisioning Gender* (Thousand Oaks, CA: Sage, 1999): 285–309. First quote: Rosabeth Moss Kanter, *Men and Women of the Corporation* (New York: Basic Books, 1977), 22. Sexual harassment: Christopher Uggen and Amy Blackstone, "Sexual Harassment as a Gendered Expression of Power," *American Sociological Review* 69 (February 2004): 64–92. Second quote: Acker, "Hierarchies, Jobs, Bodies," 149–50. Ideal employee: Joan Williams, *Unbending Gender: Why Family and Work Conflict and What to Do about It* (New York: Oxford University Press, 2000). Feminization of jobs: Teri L. Caraway, *Assembling Women: The Feminization of Global Manufacturing* (Ithaca, NY: Cornell University Press, 2007).

26. Physical appearance: Gimlin, "What Is 'Body Work'?" Selling attractiveness: Wolkowitz, *Bodies at Work*.

27. One drop rule: Christine B. Hickman, "The Devil and the One Drop Rule: Racial Categories, African Americans, and the U.S. Census," *Michigan Law Review* 95 (March 1997): 1161–265. Socially constructed: Amott and Matthaei, *Race, Gender,*

and Work; Charles Hirschman, "The Origins and Demise of the Concept of Race," *Population and Development Review* 30 (September 2004): 385–415.

28. Product of norms and power: Amott and Matthaei, *Race, Gender, and Work;* Browne and Misra, "The Intersection of Gender and Race in the Labor Market"; Harriet Bradley and Geraldine Healy, *Ethnicity and Gender at Work: Inequalities, Careers and Employment Relations* (Basingstoke, Hampshire, UK: Palgrave Macmillan, 2008). Undocumented workers: Carolina Bank Muñoz, *Transnational Tortillas: Race, Gender, and Shop Floor Politics in the United States and Mexico* (Ithaca, NY: Cornell University Press, 2008).

29. Richard Anker, *Gender and Jobs: Sex Segregation and Occupations in the World* (Geneva: International Labour Office, 1998), 262–63 and 3.

30. International Labour Office, "Equality at Work: Tackling the Challenge," International Labour Conference, 96th Session 2007, Report I (B) (Geneva, 2007). Glass ceiling: David J. Maume Jr., "Is the Glass Ceiling a Unique Form of Inequality? Evidence from a Random-Effects Model of Managerial Attainment," *Work and Occupations* 31 (May 2004): 250–74.

31. First quote: International Labour Office, "Equality at Work," 20. Gender pay gap: Morley Gunderson, "Viewpoint: Male-Female Wage Differentials: How Can That Be?" *Canadian Journal of Economics* 39 (February 2006): 1–21. Cult of domesticity: Boydston, *Home and Work.* Second quote: Harrell, "The Changing Meanings of Work in China," 73.

32. United States: Barbara F. Reskin and Irene Padavic, "Sex, Race, and Ethnic Inequality in United States Workplaces," in Janet Saltzman Chafetz, ed., *Handbook of the Sociology of Gender* (New York: Kluwer, 1999): 343–74. Britain: Jonathan Wadsworth, "The Labour Market Performance of Ethnic Minorities in the Recovery," in Richard Dickens, Paul Gregg, and Jonathan Wadsworth, eds., *The Labour Market under New Labour: The State of Working Britain* (Basingstoke, Hampshire, UK: Palgrave Macmillan, 2003): 116–33. Field experiments: Roger Zegers de Beijl, *Documenting Discrimination against Migrant Workers in the Labour Market: A Comparative Study of Four European Countries* (Geneva: International Labour Office, 2000). Quote: Anthony F. Heath, "Crossnational Patterns and Processes of Ethnic Disadvantage," in Anthony F. Heath and Sin Yi Cheung, eds., *Unequal Chances: Ethnic Minorities in Western Labour Markets* (Oxford: Oxford University Press, 2007): 639–95 at 670.

33. Language difficulties: Halleh Ghorashi and Maria van Tilburg, "'When Is My Dutch Good Enough?' Experiences of Refugee Women with Dutch Labour Organizations," *Journal of International Migration and Integration* 7 (Winter 2006): 51–70. Britain: John Carter, *Ethnicity, Exclusion and the Workplace* (Basingstoke, Hampshire, UK: Palgrave Macmillan, 2003). Indonesia: Caraway, *Assembling Women.* Korean multinational: Jo Kim, "'They Are More Like Us': The Salience of Ethnicity in the Global Workplace of Korean Transnational Corporations," *Ethnic and Racial Studies* 27 (January 2004): 69–94. China: Blaine Kaltman, *Under the Heel of the Dragon: Islam, Racism, Crime, and the Uighur in China* (Athens: Ohio University Press, 2007).

34. Similarly sized networks: Gail M. McGuire, "Gender, Race, Ethnicity, and Networks: The Factors Affecting the Status of Employees' Network Members," *Work and Occupations* 27 (November 2000): 500–23. Real effects: Mark S. Granovetter, *Getting a Job: A Study of Contacts and Careers,* 2nd ed. (Chicago: University of Chicago Press, 1995); Deirdre A. Royster, *Race and the Invisible Hand: How White*

Networks Exclude Black Men from Blue-Collar Jobs (Berkeley: University of California Press, 2003). China and Singapore: Yanjie Bian and Soon Ang, "*Guanxi* Networks and Job Mobility in China and Singapore," *Social Forces* 75 (March 1997): 981–1005.

35. Perfectly competitive markets: Gary S. Becker, *The Economics of Discrimination* (Chicago: University of Chicago Press, 1957). Statistical discrimination: Dennis J. Aigner and Glen G. Cain, "Statistical Theories of Discrimination in Labor Markets," *Industrial and Labor Relations Review* 30 (January 1977): 175–87. Rooted in ignorance: Robert M. Guion, *Assessment, Measurement, and Prediction for Personnel Decisions* (Mahwah, NJ: Lawrence Erlbaum Associates, 1998). Market failure: Deborah M. Figart and Ellen Mutari, "Wage Discrimination in Context: Enlarging the Field of View," in Dell P. Champlin and Janet T. Knoedler, eds., *The Institutionalist Tradition in Labor Economics* (Armonk, NY: M. E. Sharpe, 2004): 179–89.

36. Not as social justice: Nancy MacLean, *Freedom Is Not Enough: The Opening of the American Workplace* (Cambridge, MA: Harvard University Press, 2006). Contemporary human resource management: Jeanette N. Cleveland, Margaret Stockdale, and Kevin R. Murphy, *Women and Men in Organizations* (Mahwah, NJ: Lawrence Erlbaum Associates, 2000); Peter Herriot and Carole Pemberton, *Competitive Advantage through Diversity: Organizational Learning from Difference* (London: Sage, 1995). Undermined by informal practices: Carter, *Ethnicity, Exclusion and the Workplace*.

37. Integration: Cynthia Estlund, *Working Together: How Workplace Bonds Strengthen a Diverse Democracy* (Oxford: Oxford University Press, 2003). Break down barriers: Stephen A. Woodbury, "Power in the Labor Market: Institutionalist Approaches to Labor Problems," *Journal of Economic Issues* 21 (December 1987): 1781–807.

38. Embedded in societal institutions: Samuel Bowles and Herbert Gintis, *Schooling in Capitalist America: Educational Reform and the Contradictions of Economic Life* (New York: Basic Books, 1976); Yossi Shavit and Hans-Peter Blossfeld, eds., *Persistent Inequalities: A Comparative Study of Educational Attainment in Thirteen Countries* (Boulder, CO: Westview Press, 1993). Genuine equality: Williams, *Unbending Gender*; MacLean, *Freedom Is Not Enough*; Manning Marable, Immanuel Ness, and Joseph Wilson, eds., *Race and Labor Matters in the New U.S. Economy* (Lanham, MD: Rowman & Littlefield, 2006). New sources of mobilization: Michael J. Piore and Sean Safford, "Changing Regimes of Workplace Governance, Shifting Axes of Social Mobilization, and the Challenge to Industrial Relations Theory," *Industrial Relations* 45 (July 2006): 299–325.

39. Relatively low paid: Paula England, Michelle Budig, and Nancy Folbre, "Wages of Virtue: The Relative Pay of Care Work," *Social Problems* 49 (November 2002): 455–73. Gendered discourse: Caraway, *Assembling Women*.

40. Blurred boundaries: Joan Acker, *Class Questions: Feminist Answers* (Lanham, MD: Rowman & Littlefield, 2006). Marginalize and devalue: Mies, *Patriarchy and Accumulation on a World Scale*. Interconnected nature: Miriam A. Glucksmann, "Why 'Work'? Gender and the 'Total Social Organization of Labour,'" *Gender, Work, and Organization* 2 (April 1995): 63–75. Work-family balance: Rosemary Crompton, Suzan Lewis, and Clare Lyonette, eds., *Women, Men, Work and Family in Europe* (Basingstoke, Hampshire, UK: Palgrave Macmillan, 2007); Amy Marcus-Newhall, Diane F. Halpern, and Sherylle J. Tan, eds., *The Changing Realities of Work and Family* (Malden, MA: Wiley-Blackwell, 2008).

41. Glucksmann, "Why 'Work'?" Miriam A. Glucksmann, "Shifting Boundaries and Interconnections: Extending the 'Total Social Organization of Labour,'" in Lynne Pettinger et al., eds., *A New Sociology of Work?* (Malden, MA: Blackwell, 2005): 19–36. Julie A. Nelson, "The Study of Choice or the Study of Provisioning? Gender and the Definition of Economics," in Marianne A. Ferber and Julie A. Nelson, eds., *Beyond Economic Man: Feminist Theory and Economics* (Chicago: University of Chicago Press, 1993): 23–36.

9. Work as Identity

1. Gary Sernovitz, *The Contrarians* (New York: Henry Holt, 2002), 118–19.

2. Work centrality: Moshe Sharabi and Itzhak Harpaz, "Changes in Work Centrality and Other Life Areas in Israel: A Longitudinal Study," *Journal of Human Values* 13 (December 2007): 95–106. Quote: MOW International Research Team, *The Meaning of Working* (London: Academic Press, 1987), 91. Lottery winners: Richard D. Arvey, Itzhak Harpaz, and Hui Liao, "Work Centrality and Post-Award Work Behavior of Lottery Winners," *Journal of Psychology: Interdisciplinary and Applied* 138 (September 2004): 404–20.

3. Defined in many ways: Roy F. Baumeister, "Identity, Self-Concept, and Self-Esteem: The Self Lost and Found," in Robert Hogan, John Johnson, and Stephen Briggs, eds., *Handbook of Personality Psychology* (San Diego, CA: Academic Press, 1997): 681–710; Timothy J. Owens, "Self and Identity," in John Delamater, ed., *Handbook of Social Psychology* (New York: Springer, 2003): 205–32; Peggy A. Thoits and Lauren K. Virshup, "Me's and We's: Forms and Functions of Social Identities," in Richard D. Ashmore and Lee Jussim, eds., *Self and Identity: Fundamental Issues* (New York: Oxford University Press, 1997): 106–33. Quote: Peter L. Berger, "Some General Observations on the Problem of Work," in Peter L. Berger, ed., *The Human Shape of Work* (New York: Macmillan, 1961): 211–41 at 215, emphasis in original. Intertwined dimensions: Roy F. Baumeister, *Identity: Cultural Change and the Struggle for Self* (New York: Oxford University Press, 1986).

4. Unique sense of self: Baumeister, *Identity*. Quote: Lee Braude, *Work and Workers: A Sociological Analysis,* 2nd ed. (Malabar, FL: Krieger, 1983), 159.

5. Marie Jahoda, *Employment and Unemployment: A Social-Psychological Analysis* (Cambridge: Cambridge University Press, 1982), 83.

6. To help understand: Owens, "Self and Identity." Personal identity dimension: John C. Turner and Rina S. Onorato, "Social Identity, Personality, and the Self-Concept: A Self-Categorization Perspective," in Tom R. Tyler, Roderick Moreland Kramer, and Oliver P. John, eds., *The Psychology of the Social Self* (Mahwah, NJ: Lawrence Erlbaum Associates, 1999): 11–46. Personality receives a lot of attention: Robert Hogan, John Johnson, and Stephen Briggs, eds., *Handbook of Personality Psychology* (San Diego, CA: Academic Press, 1997).

7. First quote: Henri Tajfel, "Social Categorization, Social Identity, and Social Comparison," in Henri Tajfel, ed., *Differentiation between Social Groups* (London: Academic Press, 1978): 61–76 at 63, emphasis omitted. Second quote: John C. Turner et al., "Self and Collective: Cognition and Social Context," *Personality and Social Psychology Bulletin* 20 (October 1994): 454–63 at 454.

8. Michael A. Hogg, "Social Identity Theory," in Peter James Burke, ed., *Contemporary Social Psychological Theories* (Stanford, CA: Stanford University Press, 2006): 111–36.

9. Through social interactions: Charles H. Cooley, *Human Nature and the Social Order* (New York: Scribner's, 1902); George H. Mead, *Mind, Self, and Society* (Chicago: University of Chicago Press, 1934). First quote: George J. McCall and J. L. Simmons, *Identities and Interactions* (New York: Free Press, 1966), 67. Negotiated through performances: Erving Goffman, *The Presentation of Self in Everyday Life* (Garden City, NY: Doubleday, 1959); Sheldon Stryker, "Identity Salience and Role Performance: The Relevance of Symbolic Interaction Theory for Family Research," *Journal of Marriage and the Family* 30 (November 1968): 558–64. Second quote: Thoits and Virshup, "Me's and We's," 121.

10. Result of ongoing processes: Thoits and Virshup, "Me's and We's." Identity is important for work: Robin Leidner, "Identity and Work," in Marek Korczynski, Randy Hodson, and Paul Edwards, eds., *Social Theory at Work* (Oxford: Oxford University Press, 2006): 424–63.

11. Intergroup and intragroup action: Turner and Onorato, "Social Identity, Personality, and the Self-Concept." Richer method: S. Alexander Haslam, *Psychology in Organizations: The Social Identity Approach* (London: Sage, 2001).

12. Social identity theory: Tajfel, "Social Categorization, Social Identity, and Social Comparison"; Hogg, "Social Identity Theory." Quote: Turner and Onorato, "Social Identity, Personality, and the Self-Concept," 18.

13. Undermine diversity initiatives: Sherry K. Schneider and Gregory B. Northcraft, "Three Social Dilemmas of Workforce Diversity in Organizations: A Social Identity Perspective," *Human Relations* 52 (November 1999): 1445–67. Theory of intergroup conflict: Carsten K. W. De Dreu and Michele J. Gelfand, "Conflict in the Workplace: Sources, Functions, and Dynamics across Multiple Levels of Analysis," in Carsten K. W. De Dreu and Michele J. Gelfand, eds., *The Psychology of Conflict and Conflict Management in Organizations* (New York: Lawrence Erlbaum Associates, 2008): 3–54. Speaking Spanish: Mindy E. Bergman, Kristen M. Watrous-Rodriguez, and Katherine M. Chalkley, "Identity and Language: Contributions to and Consequences of Speaking Spanish in the Workplace," *Hispanic Journal of Behavioral Sciences* 30 (February 2008): 40–68. Corporate mergers: Deborah J. Terry and Catherine E. Amiot, "Social Identification Processes, Conflict, and Fairness Concerns in Intergroup Mergers," in Carsten K. W. De Dreu and Michele J. Gelfand, eds., *The Psychology of Conflict and Conflict Management in Organizations* (New York: Lawrence Erlbaum Associates, 2008): 385–411.

14. Self-categorization theory: Turner et al., "Self and Collective." Depersonalizing group members: Hogg, "Social Identity Theory." Singular collective entity: Turner and Onorato, "Social Identity, Personality, and the Self-Concept." Understanding work and organizations: Michael A. Hogg and Deborah J. Terry, "Social Identity and Self-Categorization Processes in Organizational Contexts," *Academy of Management Review* 25 (January 2000): 121–40; Haslam, *Psychology in Organizations.*

15. High degree of shared perceptions, and quote: Haslam, *Psychology in Organizations,* 271, emphasis in original.

16. S. Alexander Haslam, Tom Postmes, and Naomi Ellemers, "More Than a Metaphor: Organizational Identity Makes Organizational Life Possible," *British Journal of Management* 14 (December 2003): 357–69.

17. Through interactions with others: McCall and Simmons, *Identities and Interactions*; Stryker, "Identity Salience and Role Performance"; Thoits and Virshup, "Me's and We's." First quote: Bill Martin and Judy Wajcman, "Markets, Contingency

and Preferences: Contemporary Managers' Narrative Identities," *Sociological Review* 52 (May 2004): 240–64 at 241, emphases omitted. Second quote: Edward M. Schortman and Patricia A. Urban, "Modeling the Roles of Craft Production in Ancient Political Economies," *Journal of Archaeological Research* 12 (June 2004): 185–226 at 201. Constantly presenting ourselves: Goffman, *The Presentation of Self in Everyday Life*. Renegotiating how society sees us: McCall and Simmons, *Identities and Interactions*.

18. First quote: Everett C. Hughes, *The Sociological Eye: Selected Papers* (Chicago: Aldine Atherton, 1971), 338. Second quote: Howard S. Becker, *Outsiders: Studies in the Sociology of Deviance* (New York: Free Press, 1963), 111.

19. First quote: Hughes, *The Sociological Eye,* 339–40. Second quote: quoted in Richard Hyman and Ian Brough, *Social Values and Industrial Relations: A Study of Fairness and Equality* (Oxford: Basil Blackwell, 1975), 55. Difficulty deriving desired meaning: Marcia Ghidina, "Social Relations and the Definition of Work: Identity Management in a Low-Status Occupation," *Qualitative Sociology* 15 (March 1992): 73–85. Rely on alternative social roles: Erving Goffman, *Encounters: Two Studies in the Sociology of Interaction* (Indianapolis, IN: Bobbs-Merrill, 1961).

20. Occupational prestige: Donald J. Treiman, *Occupational Prestige in Comparative Perspective* (New York: Academic Press, 1977); Xueguang Zhou, "The Institutional Logic of Occupational Prestige Ranking: Reconceptualization and Reanalyses," *American Journal of Sociology* 111 (July 2005): 90–140. Quote: Tak Wing Chan and John H. Goldthorpe, "Is There a Status Order in Contemporary British Society? Evidence from the Occupational Structure of Friendship," *European Sociological Review* 20 (December 2004): 383–401 at 385. Determinant of lifestyle: Benjamin D. Zablocki and Rosabeth Moss Kanter, "The Differentiation of Life-Styles," *Annual Review of Sociology* 2 (1976): 269–98.

21. Quote: Phyllis Moen, "Beyond the Career Mystique:'Time In,''Time Out,' and 'Second Acts,'" *Sociological Forum* 20 (June 2005): 189–208 at 190. Also: Stephen R. Barley, "Careers, Identities, and Institutions: The Legacy of the Chicago School of Sociology," in Michael B. Arthur, Douglas T. Hall, and Barbara S. Lawrence, eds., *Handbook of Career Theory* (New York: Cambridge University Press, 1989): 41–65. William H. Whyte, *The Organization Man* (New York: Doubleday, 1956). Boundaryless careers: Michael B. Arthur and Denise M. Rousseau, eds., *The Boundaryless Career: A New Employment Principle for a New Organizational Era* (New York: Oxford University Press, 1996). Free-agents: Daniel H. Pink, *Free Agent Nation: How America's New Independent Workers Are Transforming the Way We Live* (New York: Warner Books, 2001). Finding meaning in tumultuous world: Richard Sennett, *The Corrosion of Character: The Personal Consequences of Work in the New Capitalism* (New York: Norton, 1998).

22. Not to overstate: Paul Edwards and Judy Wajcman, *The Politics of Working Life* (Oxford: Oxford University Press, 2005). Quote: Martin and Wajcman, "Markets, Contingency and Preferences," 240. Blurring of organizational boundaries: Mick Marchington et al., eds., *Fragmenting Work: Blurring Organizational Boundaries and Disordering Hierarchies* (Oxford: Oxford University Press, 2005).

23. Services for adolescents: Committee on Children with Disabilities, "The Role of the Pediatrician in Transitioning Children and Adolescents with Developmental Disabilities and Chronic Illnesses from School to Work or College," *Pediatrics*

106 (October 2000): 854–56. Substance abusers: Rebecca Bausch, Genevieve Weber, and Eileen Wolkstein, "Work as a Critical Component of Recovery," unpublished paper, RRTC on Drugs and Disability, Wright State University (2000). Offenders in correctional facilities: Jeffrey A. Bouffard, Doris Layton MacKenzie, and Laura J. Hickman, "Effectiveness of Vocational Education and Employment Programs for Adult Offenders: A Methodology-Based Analysis of the Literature," *Journal of Offender Rehabilitation* 31 (2000): 1–41. Entitled to income support: Stuart White, "Liberal Equality, Exploitation, and the Case for an Unconditional Basic Income," *Political Studies* 45 (June 1997): 312–26; Catriona McKinnon, "Basic Income, Self-Respect and Reciprocity," *Journal of Applied Philosophy* 20 (October 2003): 143–58. Replacement of welfare: Joel F. Handler, *Social Citizenship and Workfare in the United States and Western Europe: The Paradox of Inclusion* (Cambridge: Cambridge University Press, 2004).

24. First quote: Erik Olin Wright, "Foundations of a Neo-Marxist Class Analysis," in Erik Olin Wright, ed., *Approaches to Class Analysis* (Cambridge: Cambridge University Press, 2005): 4–30 at 22 and 25, emphases omitted. Class relations cause inequality: Richard Scase, *Class* (Minneapolis: University of Minnesota Press, 1992). Max Weber, *Economy and Society: An Outline of Interpretive Sociology* (1922), trans. Guenther Roth and Claus Wittich (New York: Bedminster Press, 1968), 302. Divide up classes: David Grusky, "Foundations of a Neo-Durkheimian Class Analysis," in Erik Olin Wright, ed., *Approaches to Class Analysis* (Cambridge: Cambridge University Press, 2005): 51–81; Elliot B. Weininger, "Foundations of Pierre Bourdieu's Class Analysis," in Erik Olin Wright, ed., *Approaches to Class Analysis* (Cambridge: Cambridge University Press, 2005): 82–118.

25. Neo-Weberian class analysis: Frank Parkin, *Marxism and Class Theory: A Bourgeois Critique* (London: Tavistock, 1979); Richard Breen, "Foundations of a Neo-Weberian Class Analysis," in Erik Olin Wright, ed., *Approaches to Class Analysis* (Cambridge: Cambridge University Press, 2005): 31–50.

26. Quote: E. P. Thompson, *The Making of the English Working Class* (London: Gollancz, 1963), 9–10. False consciousness: Georg Lukács, *History and Class Consciousness: Studies in Marxist Dialectics,* trans. Rodney Livingstone (Cambridge, MA: MIT Press, 1971); Antonio Gramsci, *Selections from the Prison Notebooks of Antonio Gramsci,* trans. Quintin Hoare and Geoffrey Nowell-Smith (New York: International Publishers, 1971); John T. Jost, "Negative Illusions: Conceptual Clarification and Psychological Evidence Concerning False Consciousness," *Political Psychology* 16 (June 1995): 397–424.

27. Empirical evidence: Joseph Gerteis and Mike Savage, "The Salience of Class in Britain and America: A Comparative Analysis," *British Journal of Sociology* 49 (June 1998): 252–74. Force someone: Scase, *Class*; Grusky, "Foundations of a Neo-Durkheimian Class Analysis"; Paula Surridge, "Class Belonging: A Quantitative Exploration of Identity and Consciousness," *British Journal of Sociology* 58 (June 2007): 207–26. Quote: Michael Emmison and Mark Western, "Social Class and Social Identity: A Comment on Marshall et al.," *Sociology* 24 (May 1990): 241–53 at 241. European Works Council: Andrew R. Timming and Ulke Veersma, "Living Apart Together? A Chorus of Multiple Identities," in Michael Whittall, Herman Knudsen, and Fred Huijgen, eds., *Towards a European Labour Identity: The Case of the European Works Council* (London: Routledge, 2007): 41–54.

28. Class is significantly related to: Stefan Svallfors, *The Moral Economy of Class: Class and Attitudes in Comparative Perspective* (Stanford, CA: Stanford University Press, 2006). Globalization and other issues: Stanley Aronowitz, *How Class Works: Power and Social Movement* (New Haven, CT: Yale University Press, 2003); Michael Zweig, ed., *What's Class Got to Do with It? American Society in the Twenty-First Century* (Ithaca, NY: Cornell University Press, 2004). Reflecting antagonistic, socially rooted interests: Wright, "Foundations of a Neo-Marxist Class Analysis."

29. Hannah Arendt, *The Human Condition* (Chicago: University of Chicago Press, 1958).

30. First quote: Sean Sayers, "The Concept of Labor: Marx and His Critics," *Science and Society* 71 (October 2007): 431–54 at 434. Second quote: quoted in Shlomo Avineri, "Labor, Alienation, and Social Classes in Hegel's *Realphilosophie*," *Philosophy and Public Affairs* 1 (Autumn 1971): 96–119 at 102.

31. First and second quotes: Richard Wolin, *Heidegger's Children: Hannah Arendt, Karl Löwith, Hans Jonas, and Herbert Marcuse* (Princeton, NJ: Princeton University Press, 2001), 197 and 196. Third quote: Sigmund Freud, *Civilization and Its Discontents,* trans. Joan Riviere (London: Hogarth Press, 1930), 34.

32. Most famously advanced by Marx: Arendt, *The Human Condition*; Herbert Applebaum, *The Concept of Work: Ancient, Medieval, and Modern* (Albany: State University of New York Press, 1992); Sean Sayers, "Creative Activity and Alienation in Hegel and Marx," *Historical Materialism* 11 (2003): 107–28; Sayers, "The Concept of Labor: Marx and His Critics." First and second quotes: Karl Marx, *Economic and Philosophic Manuscripts of 1844* (1844), trans. Martin Milligan (Amherst, NY: Prometheus Books, 1988), 76–77. Third quote: Kai Erikson, "On Work and Alienation," in Kai Erikson and Steven Peter Vallas, eds., *The Nature of Work: Sociological Perspectives* (New Haven, CT: Yale University Press, 1990): 19–35 at 20.

33. Human resource management as rhetoric: Tom Keenoy and Peter Anthony, "HRM: Metaphor, Meaning, and Morality," in Paul Blyton and Peter Turnbull, eds., *Reassessing Human Resource Management* (London: Sage, 1992): 233–55. Only partial solutions: Alan Fox, *Beyond Contract: Work, Power and Trust Relations* (London: Faber and Faber, 1974).

34. Quote: Pope John Paul II, *Laborem Exercens* (1981), preface. Provides the foundation: Dominique Peccoud, ed., *Philosophical and Spiritual Perspectives on Decent Work* (Geneva: International Labour Office, 2004). Randy Hodson, *Dignity at Work* (Cambridge: Cambridge University Press, 2001). John W. Budd, *Employment with a Human Face: Balancing Efficiency, Equity, and Voice* (Ithaca, NY: Cornell University Press, 2004). Harry Braverman, *Labor and Monopoly Capital: The Degradation of Work in the Twentieth Century* (New York: Monthly Review Press, 1974). Francis Green, *Demanding Work: The Paradox of Job Quality in the Affluent Economy* (Princeton, NJ: Princeton University Press, 2006).

35. Postmodernism: Wayne Gabardi, *Negotiating Postmodernism* (Minneapolis: University of Minnesota Press, 2001). Michel Foucault, *The Archaeology of Knowledge,* trans. A.M. Sheridan-Smith (New York: Pantheon, 1972). Meaning comes from discourse: Sara Mills, *Discourse,* 2nd ed. (London: Routledge, 2004). Fluid and fragile: Paul du Gay, *Consumption and Identity at Work* (London: Sage, 1996); Bethan Benwell and Elizabeth Stokoe, *Discourse and Identity* (Edinburgh: Edinburgh University Press, 2006).

36. Manage these understandings, also not problematic: Dave Ulrich and Wendy Ulrich, *The Why of Work: How Great Leaders Build Abundant Organizations That Win* (New York: McGraw-Hill, 2010). Quote, also normative control: Mats Alvesson and Hugh Willmott, "Identity Regulation as Organizational Control: Producing the Appropriate Individual," *Journal of Management Studies* 39 (July 2002): 619–44 at 622. Form of normative control: David Knights and Hugh Willmott, "Power and Subjectivity at Work: From Degradation to Subjugation in Social Relations," *Sociology* 23 (November 1989): 535–58; du Gay, *Consumption and Identity at Work*.

37. Always involves power: Cynthia Hardy and Nelson Phillips, "Discourse and Power," in David Grant et al., eds., *The Sage Handbook of Organizational Discourse* (London: Sage, 2004): 299–316. First quote: Michel Foucault, "The Subject and Power," in Paul Rabinow and Nikolas Rose, eds., *The Essential Foucault: Selections from Essential Works of Foucault, 1954–1984* (New York: New Press, 2003): 126–44 at 138. Identifying an employee as a manager: Alvesson and Willmott, "Identity Regulation as Organizational Control." Second quote: Knights and Willmott, "Power and Subjectivity at Work," 550. Self-disciplining: Michel Foucault, *Discipline and Punish: The Birth of the Prison,* trans. Alan Sheridan (New York: Pantheon, 1977). Intentionally shaping identities: Tim Newton, "Theorizing Subjectivity in Organizations: The Failure of Foucauldian Studies?" *Organization Studies* 19 (May 1998): 415–47.

38. Mexican tortilla factory, also mixing documented and undocumented workers: Carolina Bank Muñoz, *Transnational Tortillas: Race, Gender, and Shop Floor Politics in the United States and Mexico* (Ithaca, NY: Cornell University Press, 2008). College strikebreakers: Stephen H. Norwood, *Strikebreaking and Intimidation: Mercenaries and Masculinity in Twentieth-Century America of the Labor Movement* (Chapel Hill: University of North Carolina Press, 2002). Hiring African American workers into predominantly white occupations: Susan Eleanor Hirsch, *After the Strike: A Century of Labor Struggle at Pullman* (Urbana: University of Illinois Press, 2003).

39. Nancy MacLean, *Freedom Is Not Enough: The Opening of the American Workplace* (Cambridge, MA: Harvard University Press, 2006).

40. Marx, *Economic and Philosophic Manuscripts of 1844.* Georg Simmel, *The Philosophy of Money* (1907), trans. Tom Bottomore and David Frisby (London: Routledge and Kegan Paul, 1978). Émile Durkheim, *The Division of Labor in Society* (1893), trans. George Simpson (New York: Macmillan, 1933). Weber, *Economy and Society.* Arendt, *The Human Condition.* Quote: Berger, "Some General Observations on the Problem of Work," 215. Renewed interest: Martin and Wajcman, "Markets, Contingency and Preferences."

41. Who they really are: Susan Harter, "The Personal Self in Social Context: Barriers to Authenticity," in Richard D. Ashmore and Lee J. Jussim, eds., *Self and Identity: Fundamental Issues* (New York: Oxford University Press, 1997): 81–105. Manage the impressions: Goffman, *The Presentation of Self in Everyday Life.* Quotes: Arlie Russell Hochschild, *The Managed Heart: Commercialization of Human Feeling* (Berkeley: University of California Press, 1983), 7 and 127.

42. Emotional dissonance: Joyce E. Bono and Meredith A. Vey, "Toward Understanding Emotional Management at Work: A Quantitative Review of Emotional Labor Research," in Charmine E. J. Härtel, W. J. Zerbe, and Neal M. Ashkanasy, eds., *Emotions in Organizational Behavior* (London: Routledge, 2005): 213–34; Theresa M. Glomb and Michael J. Tews, "Emotional Labor: A Conceptualization and

Scale Development," *Journal of Vocational Behavior* 64 (February 2004): 1–23. Goffman, *The Presentation of Self in Everyday Life.* Reminiscent of Marx's alienation: Hochschild, *The Managed Heart*; Blake E. Ashforth and Ronald H. Humphrey, "Emotional Labor in Service Roles: The Influence of Identity," *Academy of Management Review* 18 (January 1993): 88–115. Women might suffer more: Hochschild, *The Managed Heart*; Jennifer L. Pierce, *Gender Trials: Emotional Lives in Contemporary Law Firms* (Berkeley: University of California Press, 1995). Empirical research on inauthenticity: Rebecca J. Erickson and Christian Ritter, "Emotional Labor, Burnout, and Inauthenticity: Does Gender Matter?" *Social Psychology Quarterly* 64 (June 2001): 146–63. Can also be rewarding: Mary Godwyn, "Using Emotional Labor to Create and Maintain Relationships in Service Interactions," *Symbolic Interaction* 29 (November 2006): 487–506.

43. Uniforms and scripts: Robin Leidner, *Fast Food, Fast Talk: Service Work and the Routinization of Everyday Life* (Berkeley: University of California Press, 1993). Quote: Winifred Poster, "Who's on the Line? Indian Call Center Agents Pose as Americans for U.S.-Outsourced Firms," *Industrial Relations* 46 (April 2007): 271–304 at 295. Engender resistance: Sarah Jenkins and Rick Delbridge, "Disconnected Workplaces: Interests and Identities in the 'High Performance' Factory," in Sharon C. Bolton and Maeve Houlihan, eds., *Searching for the Human in Human Resource Management: Theory, Practice and Workplace Contexts* (Basingstoke, Hampshire, UK: Palgrave Macmillan, 2007): 195–218.

44. Assumption that the authentic self, also Asian cultures, also not a problematic issue: Aviad E. Raz, *Emotions at Work: Normative Control, Organizations, and Culture in Japan and America* (Cambridge, MA: Harvard University Press, 2002). Asian cultures: Hazel R. Markus and Shinobu Kitayama, "Culture and the Self: Implications for Cognition, Emotion, and Motivation," *Psychological Review* 98 (April 1991): 224–53.

45. David Grant and John Shields, "Identifying the Subject: Worker Identity as Discursively Constructed Terrain," in Mark Hearn and Grant Michelson, eds., *Rethinking Work: Time, Space, and Discourse* (Cambridge: Cambridge University Press, 2006): 285–307.

10. Work as Service

1. Biblical verse: Colossians 3:22–24. Glorifies lowliest work: Doug Sherman and William Hendricks, *Your Work Matters to God* (Colorado Springs, CO: NavPress, 1987).

2. Sherman and Hendricks, *Your Work Matters to God.* Armand Larive, *After Sunday: A Theology of Work* (New York: Continuum, 2004).

3. Biblical verses: 1 Timothy 5:8; Ephesians 4:28. Monastic rules, and quote: George Ovitt, *The Restoration of Perfection: Labor and Technology in Medieval Culture* (New Brunswick, NJ: Rutgers University Press, 1987), 105. Also: Birgit van den Hoven, *Work in Ancient and Medieval Thought: Ancient Philosophers, Medieval Monks and Theologians and Their Concept of Work, Occupations and Technology* (Amsterdam: J. C. Gieben, 1996).

4. Thomas Aquinas, *Summa Theologica, Volume 47: The Pastoral and Religious Lives (2a2æ. 183–189),* trans. Jordan Aumann (London: Blackfriars, 1973), 155–57.

5. First quote: quoted in William C. Placher, ed., *Callings: Twenty Centuries of Christian Wisdom on Vocation* (Grand Rapids, MI: Eerdmans, 2005), 211. Second quote

from "placed a thorn" through "God on earth": Adriano Tilgher, *Work: What It Has Meant to Men through the Ages,* trans. Dorothy Canfield Fisher (London: George Harrap, 1931), 48–50. Third quote: Henry Eyster Jacobs, ed., *Works of Martin Luther: With Introductions and Notes, Volume 1* (Philadelphia: A. J. Holman, 1915), 191. Fourth quote: Sherman and Hendricks, *Your Work Matters to God,* 87.

6. First quote: Miroslav Volf, *Work in the Spirit: Toward a Theology of Work* (New York: Oxford University Press, 1991), 98. Second quote: Pope John Paul II, *Laborem Exercens* (1981), § 25. Work in Judaism: David J. Schnall, *By the Sweat of Your Brow: Reflections on Work and the Workplace in Classic Jewish Thought* (New York: Yeshiva University Press, 2001). Third quote: François Garaï, "Work in the Jewish Tradition," in Dominique Peccoud, ed., *Philosophical and Spiritual Perspectives on Decent Work* (Geneva: International Labour Office, 2004): 111–17 at 111–12.

7. First quote: Michael J. Naughton, "Participation in the Organization: An Ethical Analysis from the Papal Social Tradition," *Journal of Business Ethics* 14 (November 1995): 923–35 at 928. Also: Sherman and Hendricks, *Your Work Matters to God*; Larive, *After Sunday.* Care deeply about the conditions: Volf, *Work in the Spirit*; Dominique Peccoud, ed., *Philosophical and Spiritual Perspectives on Decent Work* (Geneva: International Labour Office, 2004); Robert Anthony Bruno, *Justified by Work: Identity and the Meaning of Faith in Chicago's Working-Class Churches* (Columbus: Ohio State University Press, 2008). Free will: Samuel Gregg, *Challenging the Modern World: Karol Wojtyla / John Paul II and the Development of Catholic Social Teaching* (Lanham, MD: Lexington Books, 2002); Larive, *After Sunday.* Second quote: Edith H. Raidt, "Towards a Christian Spirituality of Work," Paper presented at the Work as Key to the Social Question Conference (John A. Ryan Center for Catholic Studies, University of St. Thomas, Rome / Vatican City, 2001), 5. Third quote: Matthew Fox, *The Reinvention of Work: A New Vision of Livelihood for Our Time* (New York: HarperCollins, 1994), 108. Not without its critics: Karl Barth, *Church Dogmatics, Volume 3, Part 4: The Doctrine of Creation* (London: T & T Clark International, 2004); Stanley Hauerwas, "Work as Co-Creation: A Critique of a Remarkably Bad Idea," in John W. Houck and Oliver F. Williams, eds., *Co-Creation and Capitalism: John Paul II's "Laborem Exercens"* (Washington, DC: University Press of America, 1983): 42–58.

8. Opinions differ: compare Khalil-ur-Rehman, *The Concept of Labour in Islam,* trans. K. Naziri (Karachi: Arif Publications, 1995); Darwish A. Yousef, "The Islamic Work Ethic as a Mediator of the Relationship between Locus of Control, Role Conflict, and Role Ambiguity—A Study in an Islamic Country Setting," *Journal of Managerial Psychology* 15 (2000): 283–98; Asef Bayat, "The Work Ethic in Islam: A Comparison with Protestantism," *The Islamic Quarterly* 36 (1992): 5–27. Quote: Khalil-ur-Rehman, *The Concept of Labour in Islam,* 15. Hindu theologians: Swami Agnivesh, "Decent Work: Perspectives of the Arya Samaj, a Hindu Reformist Movement," in Dominique Peccoud, ed., *Philosophical and Spiritual Perspectives on Decent Work* (Geneva: International Labour Office, 2004): 89–95; Gayatri Naraine, "Dignity, Self-Realization and the Spirit of Service: Principles and Practices of Decent Work," in Dominique Peccoud, ed., *Philosophical and Spiritual Perspectives on Decent Work* (Geneva: International Labour Office, 2004): 96–103.

9. Bruno, *Justified by Work,* 222, 230, and 171, emphasis omitted.

10. Medieval Christian thought, and second quote: Placher, *Callings,* 3. Biblical verse: 1 Corinthians 7:20. German word for occupation, and first quote: Max Weber,

Protestant Work Ethic and the Spirit of Capitalism (1904), trans. Talcott Parsons (London: Allen & Unwin, 1976), 81. Retained traditional beliefs: Herbert Applebaum, *The Concept of Work: Ancient, Medieval, and Modern* (Albany: State University of New York Press, 1992); Larive, *After Sunday.*

11. First quote: Placher, *Callings,* 237. Reveal one's destination, and second quote: Robert S. Michaelsen, "Changes in the Puritan Concept of Calling or Vocation," *New England Quarterly* 26 (September 1953): 315–36 at 334–35.

12. Weber, *Protestant Work Ethic and the Spirit of Capitalism,* 176–77. Extensively debated: Jacques Delacroix and François Nielsen, "The Beloved Myth: Protestantism and the Rise of Industrial Capitalism in Nineteenth-Century Europe," *Social Forces* 80 (December 2001): 509–53; Jere Cohen, *Protestantism and Capitalism: The Mechanisms of Influence* (New York: Aldine de Gruyter, 2002). Importance of work ethics and values: Paul Bernstein, *American Work Values: Their Origin and Development* (Albany: State University of New York Press, 1997); Geert Hofstede, *Culture's Consequences: Comparing Values, Behaviors, Institutions, and Organizations across Nations,* 2nd ed. (Thousand Oaks, CA: Sage, 2001); Michael J. Miller, David J. Woehr, and Natasha Hudspeth, "The Meaning and Measurement of Work Ethic: Construction and Initial Validation of a Multidimensional Inventory," *Journal of Vocational Behavior* 60 (June 2002): 451–89.

13. Sherman and Hendricks, *Your Work Matters to God.* Larive, *After Sunday.*

14. First quote: Gary L. Chamberlain, "The Evolution of Business as a Christian Calling," *Review of Business* 25 (Winter 2004): 27–36 at 31. Second quote: Second Vatican Council, *Lumen Gentium* (1964), § 41. Third quote: Volf, *Work in the Spirit,* 124.

15. First quote: Larive, *After Sunday,* 150. Second quote: Coleman Barks, trans., *The Soul of Rumi: A New Collection of Ecstatic Poems* (New York: HarperCollins, 2001), 103. Try to guard against: Barbara Brown Zikmund, "Christian Vocation—In Context," *Theology Today* 36 (October 1979): 328–37; Volf, *Work in the Spirit.* Third quote: Jacques Ellul, "Work and Calling," trans. James S. Albritton, in James Y. Holloway and Will D. Campbell, eds., *Callings!* (New York: Paulist Press, 1974): 18–44 at 19. Diversity of perspectives: Placher, *Callings.*

16. Wei-Ming Tu, "Confucius and Confucianism," in Walter H. Slote and Gregory A. DeVos, eds., *Confucianism and the Family* (Albany: State University of New York Press, 1998): 3–36. Xinzhong Yao, *An Introduction to Confucianism* (Cambridge: Cambridge University Press, 2000).

17. Emphasizes social harmony: Wei-Bin Zhang, *Confucianism and Modernization: Industrialization and Democratization of the Confucian Regions* (New York: St. Martin's Press, 1999). First quote, also model of good government: Jennifer Oldstone-Moore, *Confucianism: Origins, Beliefs, Practices, Holy Texts, Sacred Places* (New York: Oxford University Press, 2002), 55. Second quote: Michael Harris Bond and Kwang-Kuo Hwang, "The Social Psychology of Chinese People," in Michael Harris Bond, ed., *The Psychology of the Chinese People* (New York: Oxford University Press, 1986): 213–66 at 215. Third quote: David K. Jordan, "Filial Piety in Taiwanese Popular Thought," in Walter H. Slote and Gregory A. DeVos, eds., *Confucianism and the Family* (Albany: State University of New York Press, 1998): 267–83 at 268.

18. Household-based for centuries: Susan Mann, "Work and Household in Chinese Culture: Historical Perspectives," in Barbara Entwisle and Gail E. Henderson, eds., *Re-Drawing Boundaries: Work, Households, and Gender in China* (Berkeley: Uni-

versity of California Press, 2000): 15–32; Stevan Harrell, "The Changing Meanings of Work in China," in Barbara Entwisle and Gail E. Henderson, eds., *Re-Drawing Boundaries: Work, Households, and Gender in China* (Berkeley: University of California Press, 2000): 67–76. Failure of collective agriculture: Mann, "Work and Household in Chinese Culture." First quote: Stevan Harrell, "Why Do the Chinese Work So Hard? Reflections on an Entrepreneurial Ethic," *Modern China* 11 (April 1985): 203–26 at 217. Second quote: Dorinne K. Kondo, *Crafting Selves: Power, Gender, and Discourses of Identity in a Japanese Workplace* (Chicago: University of Chicago Press, 1990), 131.

19. First quote: Min Chen, *Asian Management Systems: Chinese, Japanese and Korean Styles of Business,* 2nd ed. (London: Thomson Learning, 2004), 158. Second quote: Andrew Eungi Kim and Gil-sung Park, "Nationalism, Confucianism, Work Ethic and Industrialization in South Korea," *Journal of Contemporary Asia* 33 (2003): 37–49 at 44.

20. Underlie economic success: Peter L. Berger, "An East Asian Development Model?" in Peter L. Berger and Hsin-Huang Michael Hsiao, eds., *In Search of an East Asian Developmental Model* (New Brunswick, NJ: Transaction Publishers, 1988): 3–11; Zhang, *Confucianism and Modernization.* Hindered economic development: Max Weber, *Confucianism and Taoism: The Religion of China* (1915), trans. Hans H. Gerth (New York: Free Press, 1951). Manipulatively serve own agendas: Keedon Kwan, "Economic Development in East Asia and a Critique of the Post-Confucian Thesis," *Theory and Society* 36 (March 2007): 55–83.

21. John H. Moore, *The Cheyenne* (Cambridge, MA: Blackwell, 1996), 159 and 262.

22. Shared within the band: Peter Bogucki, *The Origins of Human Society* (Malden, MA: Blackwell, 1999). First quote: Robert J. Steinfeld, *The Invention of Free Labor: The Employment Relation in English and American Law and Culture, 1350–1870* (Chapel Hill: University of North Carolina Press, 1991), 60. Second quote: quoted in Andrew Delbanco, ed., *Writing New England: An Anthology from the Puritans to the Present* (Cambridge, MA: Harvard University Press, 2001), 10. It takes work: Jane Parry, "Care in the Community? Gender and the Reconfiguration of Community Work in a Post-Mining Neighborhood," in Lynne Pettinger et al., eds., *A New Sociology of Work?* (Malden, MA: Blackwell, 2005): 149–66.

23. Be seen as work: Rebecca F. Taylor, "Rethinking Voluntary Work," in Lynne Pettinger et al., eds., *A New Sociology of Work?* (Malden, MA: Blackwell, 2005): 119–35; Mark Snyder and Allen M. Omoto, "Volunteerism: Social Issues Perspectives and Social Policy Implications," *Social Issues and Policy Review* 2 (December 2008): 1–36. Quote: Michael Sherraden, "Service and the Human Enterprise," unpublished paper, Center for Social Development, Washington University (2001), 5. Mandatory civic service: Justin Davis Smith, "Civic Service in Western Europe," *Nonprofit and Voluntary Sector Quarterly* 33 (December 2004 supplement): 64S–78S. Other forms of community building: Parry, "Care in the Community?"; Taylor, "Rethinking Voluntary Work."

24. First quote: James A. Morone, *The Democratic Wish: Popular Participation and the Limits of American Government,* 2nd ed. (New Haven, CT: Yale University Press, 1998), 16. Second quote: James L. Perry and Ann Marie Thomson, *Civic Service: What Difference Does It Make?* (Armonk, NY: M. E. Sharpe, 2004), 4. Local participation:

Parry, "Care in the Community?" Repaying one's debt to society: William F. Buckley Jr., *Gratitude: Reflections on What We Owe to Our Country* (New York: Random House, 1990). Third quote: Tim Ingold, *The Appropriation of Nature: Essays on Human Ecology and Social Relations* (Iowa City: University of Iowa Press, 1987), 227. Rewards provided to the volunteer: John Wilson and Marc Musick, "The Effects of Volunteering on the Volunteer," *Law and Contemporary Problems* 62 (Autumn 1999): 141–68; Stephan Meier and Alois Stutzer, "Is Volunteering Rewarding in Itself?" *Economica* 75 (February 2008): 39–59.

25. First quote: Edgar S. Furniss, *The Position of the Laborer in a System of Nationalism: A Study in the Labor Theories of the Later English Mercantilists* (Boston: Houghton Mifflin, 1920), 200. Also: David A. Spencer, *The Political Economy of Work* (London: Routledge, 2009). Second quote: Arthur P. McEvoy, "Freedom of Contract, Labor, and the Administrative State," in Harry N. Schneiber, ed., *The State and Freedom of Contract* (Stanford, CA: Stanford University Press, 1998): 198–235 at 202. Third quote: Kim and Park, "Nationalism, Confucianism, Work Ethic and Industrialization in South Korea," 41.

26. Second quote: V. I. Lenin, *Collected Works, Vol. 30: September 1919–April 1920*, trans. George Hanna (Moscow: Progress Publishers, 1965), 517. Also: Anna Feldman Leibovich, *The Russian Concept of Work: Suffering, Drama, and Tradition in Pre- and Post-Revolutionary Russia* (Westport, CT: Praeger, 1995). Third quote: Michael Thad Allen, *The Business of Genocide: The SS, Slave Labor, and the Concentration Camps* (Chapel Hill: University of North Carolina Press, 2002), 221. Also: Joan Campbell, *Joy in Work, German Work: The National Debate, 1800–1945* (Princeton, NJ: Princeton University Press, 1989).

27. Roy F. Baumeister, *Identity: Cultural Change and the Struggle for Self* (New York: Oxford University Press, 1986).

28. First and second quotes: Stephen A. Marglin, *The Dismal Science: How Thinking Like an Economist Undermines Community* (Cambridge, MA: Harvard University Press, 2008), 96 and 17–18. Third quote: Volf, *Work in the Spirit*, 129.

29. Naraine, "Dignity, Self-Realization and the Spirit of Service," 100.

Conclusion: Work Matters

1. Ferdinand Protzman, *Work: The World in Photographs* (Washington, DC: National Geographic Society, 2006).

2. Occupational devotion: Robert A. Stebbins, *Between Work and Leisure: The Common Ground of Two Separate Worlds* (New Brunswick, NJ: Transaction Publishers, 2004). Psychological well-being: Hans De Witte, "Job Insecurity and Psychological Well-Being: Review of the Literature and Exploration of Some Unresolved Issues," *European Journal of Work and Organizational Psychology* 8 (June 1999): 155–77; Melvin W. Kohn, "Unresolved Issues in the Relationship between Work and Personality," in Kai Erikson and Steven Peter Vallas, eds., *The Nature of Work: Sociological Perspectives* (New Haven, CT: Yale University Press, 1990): 36–68. Quote, also right to decent work: Kenneth L. Karst, "The Coming Crisis of Work in Constitutional Perspective," *Cornell Law Review* 82 (March 1997): 523–70 at 534. Unemployment and mental health: Marie Jahoda, *Employment and Unemployment: A Social-Psychological Analysis* (Cambridge: Cambridge University Press, 1982); Peter Warr, *Work, Unem-*

ployment, and Mental Health (Oxford: Clarendon Press, 1987); but compare: Arthur P. Brief et al., "Inferring the Meaning of Work from the Effect of Unemployment," *Journal of Applied Social Psychology* 25 (April 1995): 693–711. Right to decent work: William P. Quigley, "The Right to Work and Earn a Living Wage: A Proposed Constitutional Amendment," *New York City Law Review* 2 (Summer 1998): 139–82. New values for employment law: Marion Crain, "Work Matters," *Kansas Journal of Law and Public Policy* 19 (Spring 2010): 365–82. Layoffs as last resort: Frank Koller, *Spark: How Old-Fashioned Values Drive a Twenty-First-Century Corporation* (New York: PublicAffairs, 2010).

3. Quote: Stevan Harrell, "The Changing Meanings of Work in China," in Barbara Entwisle and Gail E. Henderson, eds., *Re-Drawing Boundaries: Work, Households, and Gender in China* (Berkeley: University of California Press, 2000): 67–76 at 67.

4. Quote: Russell Muirhead, *Just Work* (Cambridge, MA: Harvard University Press, 2004), 58. Strive for a balance: Stephen F. Befort and John W. Budd, *Invisible Hands, Invisible Objectives: Bringing Workplace Law and Public Policy into Focus* (Stanford, CA: Stanford University Press, 2009); John W. Budd, *Employment with a Human Face: Balancing Efficiency, Equity, and Voice* (Ithaca, NY: Cornell University Press, 2004).

5. Ellen Dannin, *Taking Back the Workers' Law: How to Fight the Assault on Labor Rights* (Ithaca, NY: Cornell University Press, 2006).

6. Beliefs about wage reductions: Truman F. Bewley, "Why Not Cut Pay?" *European Economic Review* 42 (May 1998): 459–90. Crowd out intrinsic motivators: Edward L. Deci, Richard Koestner, and Richard M. Ryan, "A Meta-Analytic Review of Experiments Examining the Effects of Extrinsic Rewards on Intrinsic Motivation," *Psychological Bulletin* 125 (November 1999): 627–68; Ernst Fehr and Armin Falk, "Psychological Foundations of Incentives," *European Economic Review* 46 (May 2002): 687–724. Create the behavior it was intended to counteract: Sumantra Ghoshal, "Bad Management Theories Are Destroying Good Management Practices," *Academy of Management Learning and Education* 4 (March 2005): 75–91.

7. Guy Standing, *Work after Globalization: Building Occupational Citizenship* (Cheltenham, Gloucestershire, UK: Edward Elgar, 2009).

8. Technological progress: Joel Mokyr, *The Lever of Riches: Technological Creativity and Economic Progress* (New York: Oxford University Press, 1990). Tolerant of diverse lifestyles: Richard Florida, *The Rise of the Creative Class: And How It's Transforming Work, Leisure, Community and Everyday Life* (New York: Basic Books, 2002). Volunteers excluded: Tara Kpere-Daibo, "Unpaid and Unprotected: Protecting Our Nation's Volunteers through Title VII," *University of Arkansas at Little Rock Law Review* 32 (Fall 2009): 135–54.

9. Peter Ackers, "Reframing Employment Relations: The Case for Neo-Pluralism," *Industrial Relations Journal* 33 (March 2002): 2–19 at 15.

10. Vinay Gidwani, "The Cultural Logic of Work: Explaining Labour Deployment and Piece Rate Contracts in Matar Taluka, Gujarat—Parts 1 and 2," *Journal of Development Studies* 38 (December 2001): 57–108 at 60.

INDEX

Adams, J. Stacy, 94
Africa: concepts of work in, 55; European colonization of, 8, 30, 37; women and work in, 127, 137
African Americans, 136, 138, 139, 158
agency, worker, 121, 122, 124–25
agricultural households, 86, 96
alienation, 29, 53–55, 73, 155, 158–60
America, colonial, 7, 175. *See also* United States
anthropology, 5, 12, 108, 128
apprenticeship, 6, 33, 39
Aquinas, Thomas, 25, 164
Arendt, Hannah, 29, 158
Argentina, 125
Aristotle, 22–23, 24, 123, 133
artisans, 4–6, 23, 96
Asian cultures: collective identity in, 160; Confucian values in, 170–72. *See also specific countries*
Attraction-Selection-Attrition model, 94
Australia, 19, 138
autonomy: in concepts of work, 87–88; human need for, 67, 145, 150; Industrial Revolution and loss of, 8, 38, 97; and job satisfaction, 92

bargaining: collective, 68–70, 72; power inequalities in, 65–66, 140
Bellamy, Edward, 10
Benedict, Saint, 20, 24, 164
Berger, Peter, 158–59
Bible, passages from, 20–21, 163–64, 167
body work, 134–36
Boserup, Ester, 127
Braverman, Harry, 119, 156
Britain: caring work in, 129; craft production in, 6; enclosure movement in, 55; labor unions in, 36; master-servant legal regime in, 33, 36; occupational stratification in, 138; penal colonies of, 19;

putting-out system in, 7; relative importance of life activities in, 144; utility-of-poverty doctrine in, 25; work as nationalistic duty in, 175
Buddhism, 21, 60
bureaucracy, 109, 151, 158

calling, work as, 164, 167–70
Calvin, John, 21, 24, 25, 162, 164, 167–68
Canada, 30, 129, 138
capitalism: alienation under, 29, 53–54, 73, 155, 158, 159; classes under, 118, 152; commodification of work under, 43–45, 46–47, 52–53; exchange value vs. use value under, 52; free/unfree work under, 37; industrial, 8–9, 43; interdependence under, 46; Locke's theories and, 32; Marx's critique of, 11–12, 52, 99, 116–17, 155; merchant, 6–7; and patriarchy, 116, 131–32; and Protestant work ethic, 168; as social relation, 116–18; and structure of work, 180; varieties of, 74
career: boundaryless, 151; idea of, 111; and status/identity, 150
caring for others, work as, 14*t,* 17, 126–42, 181; conceptual dualities associated with, 141–42; corporeal element of, 134; ethics of care and, 133; feminist perspectives on, 130, 131–33; importance of concept of, 141, 142; as labor of love, 130–32; marginalization of, 56–57, 75, 127, 139, 142, 152; and personal fulfillment, 92; as women's work, 17, 127, 129, 130–31, 141; work as service compared to, 163
Carlyle, Thomas, 106, 178
caste system, 23, 25
Catholicism: on laziness, 21; on work, 11, 91, 155–56, 169. *See also specific theologians*
Chekhov, Anton, 22

About the Author

John W. Budd is a professor at the University of Minnesota's Carlson School of Management, where he holds the Industrial Relations Land Grant Chair and is the director of the Center for Human Resources and Labor Studies. He is a graduate of Colgate University and earned a Ph.D. degree in economics from Princeton University. Professor Budd is the author of *Employment with a Human Face: Balancing Efficiency, Equity, and Voice* (Cornell University Press), *Labor Relations: Striking a Balance* (McGraw-Hill/Irwin), *Invisible Hands, Invisible Objectives: Bringing Workplace Law and Public Policy into Focus* (with Stephen Befort; Stanford University Press), and numerous journal articles. He has also been Director of Graduate Studies for the University of Minnesota's graduate programs in human resources and industrial relations.